MW01106874

Turning Point

Turning Point

The Arab World's Marginalization and International Security After 9/11

Dan Tschirgi

PRAEGER SECURITY INTERNATIONAL
Westport, Connecticut • London

Library of Congress Cataloging-in-Publication Data

Tschirgi, Dan.
Turning point : the Arab world's marginalization and international security after 9/11 / Dan Tschirgi.
p. cm.
Includes bibliographical references and index.
ISBN 978–0–275–99956–8 (alk. paper)
1. Security, international. 2. International relations and culture. 3. Terrorism.
4. September 11 Terrorist Attacks, 2001. I. Title.
JZ5595.5.T73 2007
355′. 0330174927–dc22 2007020590

British Library Cataloguing in Publication Data is available.

Library of Congress Catalog Card Number: 2007020590
ISBN-13: 978–0–275–99956–8
ISBN-10: 0–275–99956–4

First published in 2007

Praeger Security International, 88 Post Road West, Westport, CT 06881
An imprint of Greenwood Publishing Group, Inc.
www.praeger.com

Printed in the United States of America

The paper used in this book complies with the
Permanent Paper Standard issued by the National
Information Standards Organization (Z39.48–1984).

10 9 8 7 6 5 4 3 2 1

Contents

PREFACE

On September 11, 2001, Americans received a blow from which they have still not recovered, and with which they are still trying to cope. Like a boxer on the canvas after an unforeseen roundhouse punch, Americans on that terrible day were stunned, and from the fuzzy-minded shock into which they plunged there immediately arose one key question: "What happened?" The answer, of course, was painfully evident: the United States had been attacked and suffered significant loss of life. But even as the obvious crystallized into conscious awareness, the deeper essence of the colloquial "What Happened" remained terribly obscure in three major ways.

Yes, America had been attacked, but what did the attack signify, what did it mean?

There followed a second query that aimed at reassembling a suddenly shattered universe: Why did the attack occur? Only an answer to this could resolve the seeming disjunction between the morning hours of 9/11 and all that had gone before.

A third major question inevitably followed: What did the attack mean for the future, what were its implications for the country's future security? Only an answer to this could place 9/11 in a context that would link its morning hours with all that lay ahead.

America's leaders offered answers to these questions within hours of the 9/11 attack. Policy decisions, and a series of major actions flowing from them, came on the heels of the proffered answers. Some six years later, all Americans are living with the consequences. The passage of time and the consequences themselves have left many wondering if the initial answers were correct. This book partakes of those doubts and offers alternative answers to those that emanated from Washington on the evening of 9/11.

As an American, I shared my compatriots' horror and outrage over the 9/11 assault. As an academic whose work has primarily focused on the Middle East for over three decades, I was both saddened and intrigued by the fact that the attackers came from that region and were motivated by their view of political realities in the area. As an educator whose career has mainly been spent in "American-style" universities in developing countries, I was perhaps more cognizant than many Americans that what we unequivocally perceived as an "outrage" could be—and indeed was—seen by others in a much more ambivalent, and sometimes utterly contrary, light. Finally, as a long-term expatriate who has chosen for no ethnic reason to spend the bulk of his life in the Middle East, I was—and am—bothered by the possibility that 9/11 might reinforce simplistic convictions that we have all been plunged into a "clash of civilizations."

"Terrorism," as has been said so often already, is the enemy of the moment, and while I shall have much to say about "terrorism" that will disturb some readers, my chief point is this: the probability of victory over any enemy increases in direct proportion to the degree to which that same enemy is known. It is, therefore, not really important if in the process of knowing the enemy we must face some hard truths which challenge elements of our own self-image.

It is precisely in and through the process of confronting such "hard truths" that we can begin to know our enemy—and more importantly—what produced him, and, therefore, wherein lies the true threat we face. The search for security has a chance of proceeding usefully only if the threat to security is plainly understood.

What has just been said is not rocket-science; it is no more than common sense—that extremely valuable faculty that is unfortunately all too often shunted aside or disparaged in academic discourse. The following pages consciously try to return "common sense" to its rightful place as a useful contributor to clear thinking, while simultaneously relying heavily on the insights of a variety of scholars whose theoretical concerns are relevant to the tripartite problem at hand: what *is* the meaning of 9/11, why did it happen, and how can we best seek security in the wake of that event?

Given the amount of effort that scholars have devoted to the study of such things as political development, political violence, ideologies and globalization—not to mention the so-called Third World in general and the Middle East in particular—it would be more than strange to find that none of their theoretical speculations are pertinent to the questions dealt with here. Happily, of course, this is not the case. Yet, wherever elements of theoretical thought or models inform the discussion that unfolds below, every effort has been made to avoid jargon as much as possible. The issues under consideration are simply too important to risk the mystifications inherent in much of the professional vocabulary of contemporary scholarship. This, however, is a matter of style and presentation rather than of substance.

If there is a more serious villain blocking the way to the clear thinking that is required by the questions confronted in this book, the following pages identify it as that body of thought on the Middle East that can be labeled "Exceptionalist"—because it sees the region and its sociopolitical dynamics as somehow unique, and therefore having little in common with the rest of the world. Nothing could be more wrong, and no perspective could be potentially more harmful to the current search for international security.

Acknowledgments

In writing this book I had the active support of a great many people in various parts of the world. I acknowledge their contributions and offer my sincere thanks, while simultaneously absolving each of them from any responsibility for what follows.

First, I must thank my colleagues at the American University in Cairo, who encouraged me to explore many of the ideas set forth in this work in a series of graduate seminars I offered between 1996 and 2004. I also thank the graduate students who attended the seminars. Mr. Jeffrey Nedoroscik, Ms. Dina Younis, and Ms. Kim Shultz were particularly hardworking and productive.

On matters related to Nigeria, Mr. John Agbonifo provided invaluable support, keen insights, and wonderful introductions. My research in Port Harcourt benefited greatly from one such introduction to Mr. David M. Ugbe—an energetic young man who tirelessly worked to satisfy my curiosity about things of the Ogoni. Mr. Ledum Mitee, the Director of the Movement for the Survival of the Ogoni People (MOSOP), spent much time with me attempting to do the same. I am grateful for his efforts. The Dean of Graduate Studies at the University of Port Harcourt, Dr. Winston Bell-Gam, shepherded me through the arcane rituals of being a Visiting Academic and introduced me to many bright thinkers who grace the university with their presence, among them Drs. Mark Anikpo and Steve Ikodudu. Finally, Mr. Peter Jacobi, a German businessman and author who has resided in Nigeria for decades, shared his many insights into that fascinating country and its people in a Herculean effort to impart some of his knowledge.

In Chiapas, Manuel Burguete and the late Amado Avendaño bravely sought to explain the intricacies of the Zapatista conflict to me on multiple occasions. Sister Patricia Moysén, Gonzalo Ituarte, Raymundo Sánchez Barraza, and, finally, Bishop Felipe Arizmendi also strove on multiple occasions to explain the Church's role in that conflict. Colleagues in the Department of International Relations at the University of the Americas, Puebla, did their best to interpret for me the interwoven flows of Mexican and Chiapaneco politics and their impacts on the Zapatista conflict over time. I am grateful to Drs. Marco Almazán, Román López Villicaña, José Antonio Alonso, José Luis García, Augustín Aguilar, and Rafael Priesca.

Many people in Egypt also contributed to my efforts to fathom the struggle of the *Gam'a- al-Islamiyya*. I am particularly appreciative of the efforts along these lines made by Dr. Reem Saad, Dr. Nicholas Hopkins, and Dr. Maye Kassem.

I particularly appreciate the courtesy of the rural inhabitants of Ogoniland, the Chiapas Highlands, and Upper Egypt who took the time and effort to share their concerns with me.

Several persons read and commented on earlier versions of the manuscript. I am grateful to each of them. In Ottawa, Dr. Jose Havet, and in New York, Dr. Necla Tschirgi, as well as Mark and John Tschirgi, merit my thanks for their constructive criticisms. The same is true of my colleagues and friends at the Middle East Studies Center of the American University in Cairo, which offered me an opportunity to present my research at one of its regular seminars. I particularly thank Drs. Joel Beinin, Mark Sedgewick, and Nicholas Hopkins for that stimulating experience.

I also express my appreciation to the various publishers who kindly permitted me to include material adapted from my previous writings. Thus, parts of Chapter 1 draw from "Resolving the Palestinian Refugee Problem: Edward A. Norman's Unintended Contribution to Relevant Lessons in Perspectives, Values and Consequences," in Dietrich Jung (ed.), *The Middle East and Palestine: Global and Regional Conflict* (New York: Palgrave Macmillan, 2004), and from "Bringing Radical Change to the Arab World: The 'Democratizing' Legacy of George W. Bush," *UNISCI Discussion Papers* (12) (October 2006) [online at http://www.ucm.es/info/unisci/UNISCI-Review12.htm] (reprinted with permission). In the same vein, portions of Chapter 3 are adapted from the "Introduction," in *Development in the Age of Liberalization: Egypt and Mexico* (Cairo: The American University in Cairo Press, 1996) and from "Marginalized Violent Internal Conflict in the Age of Globalization," *Arab Studies Quarterly*, 21(3) (Summer 1999). Finally, portions of Chapter 6 are adapted from "The Middle East and Religious Fundamentalism as a Source of Identity-Based Conflict," in Mustafa Aydin and Kostas Ifantis (eds.), *International Security Today: Understanding Change and Debating Strategy* (Ankara: Center for Strategic Research, 2006), and from "The War on Terror: Marginalized Conflict as a Challenge to the International System," *Perceptions: Journal of International Affairs*, VII(3) (September–November 2002).

I am also deeply grateful to Praeger's amazingly effective editor, Ms. Hilary Claggett and her equally wonderful publishing team—they made the book's production almost easy.

Most of all, my deepest appreciation goes to my wife, Conchita, who participated from the start in this project. Despite the ominous subject matter, she helped make the experience enjoyable.

Introduction

The social history of the human race has revolved from the start around the search for security. It keeps doing so.

Confronted by the recognition of mortality and forced to face the inherent uncertainties and risks of life itself, our early ancestors eventually sought to broaden the realm of the predictable, the controllable, the regular, and the rhythmic. They tried, in short, to enhance their level of security. Taken in its fundamental sense, "security" refers to a state of mind, a "feeling," if you will, of comfort, of certainty that no imminent threat to that same feeling of comfort is on—or lurking just below—the horizon. However, since—as the modern saying goes—life has always been "what happens when you're planning something else," I suspect those earliest humans quickly learned that full security was unattainable; that the search for security is necessarily a multifaceted and ongoing process which can never be capped by definitive, enduring success. It was, perhaps, here that our ancestors first ran into the discomfiting lesson that life entails dealing with probabilities rather than with absolutes.

Whether or not this last point is accurate is largely immaterial. What is material and important is that somewhere along the course of human history, primordial *Homo sapiens* developed a strong response to the pervasive problem of insecurity: "society," that more or less organized human group whose members link their personal identities to the collective. This instrument—because of its necessarily multiple and multigenerational membership—was just as necessarily dynamic . . . a tool that could alter, modify, and adapt; an instrument that gave hope of effective flexibility in meeting the inevitably changing demands of the search for security. With the beginnings of the social group and its required element of organization, many problems, though not solved, were at least mitigated. Among these, of course, were such things as securing basic necessities of biological life: food, shelter, mates, and so forth. Important among the "so forth" must have been enhanced predictability, and therefore "security," in terms of relationships among immediate neighbors within the group itself. Then too, social—as opposed to simply individual—existence presumably also opened channels for reducing more intangible, but still pressing, sources of psychological insecurity: isolation, loneliness, existential *Angst.* Finally, and not least important, the social unit promised hope of protection against other social units whose own ambitions, actions, and existence threatened "security." On a planet where by definition resources are limited, it is important to ponder this last point: that the very existence of one social unit might be seen—and perhaps accurately so—as a threat to the security of another.

Most of the above is only a brief sketch drawn from what various thinkers from classic times until today have speculated as to the origins of human society. It all, of course, remains speculation, for the actual beginnings of society will forever remain blurred by the passage of time. This is part of the uncomfortable truth we inherit from our ancestors. If we are to be guided by evidence—whether derived from experience or rational thought—we are ultimately condemned to less than certainty. We remain mired in the probable. Still, the centrality that has traditionally been assigned to security concerns of one sort or another as the motive force behind the birth of social organization seems compelling. It is useful to keep this in mind while trying to fathom the nature and implications of our current search for security in the aftermath of the attacks of 9/11.

In many ways, the coordinated assaults on New York and Washington epitomized the nature of our contemporary world. Possibly the strongest aspect of this representational quality lies in two of the glaring paradoxes that were involved. Nineteen "modern" young men, several of whom were trained in highly technological professions, chose to commit murderous suicide for an extremely ancient reason: the belief that a deity would be pleased by such an act of human sacrifice. The weapons employed extend the paradoxical mixture. Fuel-filled modern jetliners wreaked the havoc that brought death to some 3,000 unsuspecting people, but the instruments that apparently helped the hijackers gain control of the airplanes—box cutters—were merely recent variants of that very ancient weapon, the knife.

This mixture of old and new, of ancient and modern, of the past and the most recent, lies at the heart of our contemporary existence on this planet. It's not really difficult to see, for it is all around us. The charming "Made in China" basket one picks up and pays for electronically with a credit card in a Miami Wal-Mart is probably produced by a peasant whose personal experiences have little in common with its American buyer. Nonetheless, the producer and buyer become intimately connected. For that same peasant-producer's welfare, and therefore his or her hopes and dreams, are now inextricably linked to the buying power and desires of consumers half a world away. By the same token, the enterprising elderly carpenter near Cairo's Khan al-Khalili, who has learned that an outdated Apple computer and a creaky Internet connection allow him to find, download, copy, and possibly sell an uncountable variety of designs for the interior moldings he and his assistant produce by hand, ties the fate of his dusty, miniscule enterprise to the dynamics of people and places he will probably never see.

It is part of what has become known as "Globalization," of which we hear much in discussions of "larger" issues. Will the movement of major manufacturing industries from the United States (and other major Western states) to Third World locales undermine our economies, our jobs? Will the influx of foreign capital into our U.S. economy (and those of other Western states) be beneficial or pernicious? Yet, it is at the micro-level—at the level where it can be seen to involve identifiable individuals around the world—that globalization perhaps exercises it most striking impacts. On this very personal plane, globalization loses its abstract quality and becomes starkly clear with all the curious paradoxes it entails. It is "Chapo" (a local Zapatista leader of whom more will be said below) standing calmly one night under huge trees that were unable to contain the rain pouring onto a highland valley in Chiapas—sincerely expounding his people's readiness for armed struggle, while dressed in blue jeans and a freshly ironed T-shirt emblazoned with the legend "Rodeo Drive." It is listening to an intense discussion of the certain vengeance ancestors will wreak upon descendants who fail to protect their graves in the torrid swamps of Nigeria's Ogoniland . . . against the background of a blaring AM radio broadcast of the Swedish pop group ABBA's *Voulez Vous*. It is conversing with a Western-educated young Egyptian whose thirst for the latest fashions of Rome or Paris is matched by the conviction that evil djinns are entities that must be guarded against.

This, in small part, is the world we now inhabit. It is a world of mix, of paradox, a world configured by different mind-sets, glorious (perhaps) in its diversity and threatening (certainly) in its potential for fatal clashes among its heterogeneously oriented inhabitants. The advance of technology—specifically, the technology of death, of mass destruction—forces the last consideration into a position of primacy.

Nearly four decades ago, Marshall McLuhan drew widespread attention to the tensions, promises, and perils of what he saw as an emerging "Global Village." "Globalization" is here taken to mean the process through which the combination of economics, politics, and technology unleashes forces that increasingly make the various societies of our world not only more interconnected but also susceptible to similar experiences, both good and bad. Because the goal of social analysis is to reach valid general propositions regarding human social behavior, globalization's unifying thrust holds out an unprecedented promise of meaningful comparisons among different societies. Such comparisons, the stairways to generalization, are vital if social analysis is to help us understand our experiences as social beings.

A cautionary note is in order. If the notion of globalization causes us to expect diverse communities around the world to face similar phenomena, it should also remind us that the phenomena themselves are apt to be colored differently in different contexts, molded by specific cultural and historical conditions. However, it can also be expected that the core dynamics of those phenomena, and the central issues and choices they raise for the societies concerned will be essentially similar.

Grasping the full significance of 9/11 and its implications for our current search for security requires an awareness that social behavior is a product of the intertwining of political, economic, and social conditions with the cognitive faculties of human beings. If this sounds complex, it both is and isn't really. It *is* somewhat complex in the sense that uncovering how these factors and their interconnections help produce patterns of social behavior requires time-consuming and painstaking effort. It *isn't* really all that complex in that at bottom the proposition only amounts to the assertion that social behavior is produced by the interplay between objective conditions forming the actors' contexts and the subjective makeup's of those same actors, their perceptions and psychologies.

The injection of this small dose of "complexity" into the discussion of the post-9/11 search for security may help relieve some of the almost unmitigated oversimplification that has marked nearly all of the discourse so far. "Is the 'War on Terrorism' Being Prosecuted Correctly?" "Is Islam the Enemy or Is It Not?" "Can Terrorism be Defeated?" "Is 'The West' to Blame for the Assault against It, or Is It Not?" These and others of their tenor are the questions being most widely debated even now, almost six years from the events of 9/11. For the most part, there may be nothing particularly wrong with the questions themselves, but the tendency to deal with them through reductionist lenses that seek only clear "yes" or "no" answers is not useful. On the contrary, it is harmful and dangerous. Facile approaches only reduce possibilities of understanding the threat raised by 9/11 and, of course, equally undermine possibilities of overcoming it.

This book tries to uncover the demands that have been placed on our world by security concerns after 9/11. To do so it seeks to identify the political, economic, social, and spiritual dimensions of the dynamics that have given rise to today's insecurity. Modern social thought, perhaps especially my own discipline, political science, has considerable difficulty in dealing with the "spiritual" as an analytical category. However, recognition of a spiritual dimension to the motives of social behavior need not necessarily rest on an attribution of objective reality to the spiritual itself. It is quite enough to acknowledge and give weight to the fact that the human psyche has since time immemorial expressed a longing for some transcendental reality in which the individual might find, or create, meaning for his or her existence. For the limited purpose of trying to understand social behavior, it is unimportant whether this simply stems from a curious quirk of human cerebral synaptic transmissions or signals some greater reality of which we are all part.

The premise of this work is that the Middle East's sociopolitical dynamics are not exceptional; that they are, in other words, essentially similar to those shaping patterns of social action in other regions of the globe. If this is so, it is to be expected that the attack of 9/11 would not constitute a totally unique event but rather have recognizable counterparts in the broader human experience. Even more to the point, to the extent that 9/11 found roots in the globalization of the modern world, one should expect to find evidence of analogous conflicts in regions that are geographically, culturally, and historically far removed from the Middle East.

Evidence along these lines exists and is found in a type—or, better said, a subtype—of conflict that in the past two or three decades has brewed, and erupted, in Third World locales that include both the Middle East and non-Middle Eastern regions. The hallmark of this sort of conflict is its initiation by groups who on the basis of all objective criteria should have virtually no hope at all of winning the fight they have started.

The generic category, of which the subtype is a part, has a very ancient history and is currently widely referred to in social science circles as "asymmetrical conflict"—a political conflict that is characterized by an overwhelming imbalance of power between the protagonists. The subtype of this sort of conflict most closely related to 9/11 is of much more recent origin, for it is tightly linked to processes and tensions that are central to our globalizing world. Within recent years, this subcategory—to which (for reasons explained below) I give the unfortunate label "Marginalized Violent Internal Conflict" (MVIC)—has been visible in various parts of the world, including Latin America, sub-Saharan Africa, and the Middle East. The very range of the phenomenon warns that something much broader than the Middle East is amiss in our world. That all of the MVIC precursors to 9/11 involved suicidal or possibly suicidal commitments by marginalized groups to struggle against a status quo they found intolerable underscores the dangers to security in a world where death increasingly seems to be no deterrent to militancy.

A major contention of this book is that an understanding of 9/11 and what it signifies is furthered by looking closely at certain resoundingly asymmetrical domestic conflicts that have recently wracked the so-called Third World. Thus, the following pages devote considerable attention to three such conflicts: Mexico's Zapatista Rebellion, the insurgency of Egypt's *Gama'a al-Islamiyya*, and Nigeria's Ogoni Uprising. The parallels between the development and evolution of these domestic conflicts and the struggle epitomized by 9/11 illuminate much—but certainly not all—of the nature and dynamics of today's threat to international security. Indeed, the darker, and even more menacing implications of 9/11 are, if anything, highlighted by the basic differences between that event and its more limited antecedents in the developing world.

The plan of the book is as follows. Part I reviews the impact of 9/11 on the United States, with particular emphasis on how dominant efforts to explain the attack mystified rather than clarified, even while they led to policies of questionable worth as means of securing the country's long-term security. Part II examines the conflicts in Mexico, Egypt, and Nigeria referred to above. Finally, Part III looks at the contemporary Middle East, and particularly the Arab World, in the hope of identifying the nature of today's threat to the United States and suggesting policy directions for meeting and defeating it.

Part I

The United States and 9/11

CHAPTER 1

THE MYSTIFICATION OF 9/11

The American reaction to 9/11 was paradoxical. The initial overwhelming unity of outrage that marked the American public and its leaders did not evaporate but was soon accompanied by acrimonious divisions, reflected in a strident discourse that produced much heat but shed little light on the chief questions of the day. The questions themselves were clear enough, and nobody doubted their importance. They were: (1) What did the attack mean; what did it signify? (2) Why did it happen? (3) What did the attack imply for the nation's security? These clear, and key, questions deserved thoughtful and clear answers. Such answers were not forthcoming. Instead, a series of immediate answers was provided. In their wake, the American "debate" over 9/11 failed to focus on fundamental questions and turned instead to issues regarding the strategy and tactics that should be employed to counter the threat embodied by 9/11. At best, the ensuing discussion helped clarify the pros and cons of some options; at worst, it degenerated into dangerous absurdities. What it utterly failed to do was to clarify the nature of the very threat under discussion and, therefore, also of what it implied for the search for international security.

President George Bush made the initial attempt to answer the key questions raised by 9/11. In remarks he delivered only hours after the attacks, Bush sought to reassure his countrymen that Washington had things under control. In the process of doing so, he provided clear, and all too easy, answers. These, however, were not immediately subjected to the careful close scrutiny they deserved. By the time various aspects of Bush's interpretation of 9/11 came under critical review, the president's understanding of the matter had become accepted wisdom for millions of Americans.

In his address to the nation on the evening of September 11, Bush offered these unequivocal answers:

> *What was the significance of the attack? [The essence of America was attacked].* "Today ... our way of life, our very freedom, came under attack."
>
> *Why did it happen? [Because we are good and the attackers are evil].* "America was targeted for attack because we're the brightest beacon for freedom and opportunity in the world.... Today ... our nation saw evil ..."
>
> *What did it mean for future security? [A long, hard, but eventually victorious struggle].* "... we stand together to win the war against terrorism.... America has stood down enemies before and we will do so this time."[1]

The circularity of Bush's position was disturbingly patent from the start: "it happened," went his essential response, "because we are good and they are bad; it means that we will fight until good prevails over bad." Clearly, there is no really satisfying answer here to the critical questions posed above. No one who thought about what the president said on September 11 could have doubted this—had time been taken to analyze the content of his message. But, of course, that did not happen. Nobody wanted that. On the night of September 11, Americans wanted and needed sure answers, certainties that would dispel—or at least stave off—the menacing confusion into which all had been thrown. Thus, the questions still remain, still demand more satisfying answers—that is, answers that will be more useful as guideposts for overcoming the threat that was made manifest on 9/11.

The vacuum into which the critical questions regarding 9/11 have fallen has allowed George Bush's early explanation to hold sway for a longer period than it merited. Perhaps the most telling example of the limited thrust of American attempts to explain to themselves the significance of 9/11 was the bulky final report of the bipartisan National Commission on Terrorist Attacks Upon the United States (popularly known as the "9/11 Commission"), which was released in the summer of 2004. Informative, well-balanced, often insightful, and very well written, the Report has been validly criticized for not even attempting to indicate how and why al-Qaeda's goals led it to attack the United States.[2] By default, the absence of such commentary forces the Report to imply that some darkly unfathomable motive led to the 9/11 attacks. This is hardly helpful to efforts to understand 9/11 and therefore guard against the threat it represented.

There was one relatively prompt and deep challenge to the Bush interpretation. Because of its source, it certainly qualifies as part of the "American discourse" on 9/11, although it was primarily voiced not in the United States, but in the United Kingdom. However, largely because its source had been a major embarrassment to the Democratic Party and was not a pleasing voice to the newly installed Republican Administration, the alternative interpretation seemed to fall on deaf ears. It was expressed three months after 9/11, when former president and Democratic Party standard-bearer Bill Clinton delivered the Richard Dimbleby Lecture in London. Clinton's vice president, Al Gore, had lost the 2000 election to Bush, after waging a campaign that marginalized his former boss. Clinton's remarks in London might have subsequently been taken by the Democrats as a foundation for probing the Bush administration's response to 9/11. They weren't. Although a preliminary version had been delivered at Yale in early October, the speech went largely unnoticed in the United States.[3]

Entitled "The Struggle for the Soul of the 21st Century," the ex-president's address offered a wide-ranging overview of the causes, meaning, and security implications of the 9/11 attack. After all the struggles of his presidency, he said, he had sensed in its closing days that world conditions were heralding "a larger battle brewing." He linked these conditions to the impact of scientific, technological, and economic changes whose combined force was furthering global interdependence to hitherto undreamed heights: "September 11," he said, "was the dark side of this new age of global interdependence."[4]

Much of the former president's analysis highlighted the bifurcation that global interdependence has produced among the inhabitants of this planet. Science, technology, and economics have yielded untold benefits for part of the world in living standards, quality of life, and life choices. Yet, those same benefits have been denied to massive numbers of human beings. Poverty, repression, illness, and hopelessness pervade the lives of the latter.

Clinton did not simply attribute terrorism to economic and social injustice. Instead he dwelled at length on a deeper, more sinister factor—a mind-set rooted in convictions of possessing absolute, exclusive truth. Terrorists, he said, "Like fanatics everywhere throughout history ... think they've got the truth, and if you share their truth, your life has value. And if you don't, you're a legitimate target ...."[5] Describing the alternative to this mind-set, Clinton pointed to the post-Enlightenment mentality:

> Now most of us believe that no-one has the absolute truth. Indeed, in our societies, the most religious among us sometimes feel that most strongly because as children of God, we are by definition, limited in this life. ... [We believe] that life is a journey toward truth, that we have something to learn from each other.[6]

For the ex-president, the basic and most important struggle highlighted by 9/11 was between these two perspectives: "The clash between these two views ... will define the shape and the soul of this new century."[7]

Turning to the problem of achieving security in the face of the terrorist threat, Clinton's speech stressed four requirements. The immediate need was to defeat those responsible for 9/11, "first, we have to win the fight we're in."[8] But, he went on to argue that security could not be achieved by this alone. It was, he indicated, necessary to think of a second stage—one going beyond the al-Qaeda assailants of 9/11:

> ... it's not enough to defeat the terrorist[s]. We have to make a world where there are far fewer terrorists, where there are far fewer potential terrorists and more partners.[9]

A third requirement had to do with the global economy. Clinton's address strongly suggested that long-term security in today's world would require a reordering of international priorities and practices. The key, he indicated, lay with the world's "wealthy nations," who had "a responsibility ... to spread the benefits and shrink the burdens" which divide the global community.[10] He referred not only to foreign aid, but also indicated that revised trade regulations would be in order: "the rich countries ought to open their markets to poor countries."[11] These steps would "cost money," he proclaimed; then added, "but I can tell you this, it's a lot cheaper than going to war."[12]

Finally, the ex-president cited a necessary step for pursing these prescriptions effectively: "All of us will have to develop a truly global consciousness."[13] He contrasted such an outlook with that of the terrorist enemy:

> Think about how we all organize our lives in little boxes—man, woman, British, American, Muslim, Christian, Jew ....
>
> ...
>
> We have to organize [like] that, but somewhere along the way, we finally come to understand that our life is more than all these boxes we're in. And that if we can't reach beyond that, we'll never have a fuller life. And the fanatics of the world, they love their boxes and they hate yours ... that's what this is all about.[14]

The Dimbleby Lecture outlined in simple, straightforward terms an understanding of 9/11 that differed strikingly from the White House's. Rather than being tied simply to evil impulses, terrorism was linked to motivating perspectives, and these were in turn tied to modern global conditions. The suggestion was that the terrorists' motive might be an understandable product of identifiable dynamics rather than merely an outgrowth of malignant inclinations. More importantly, by seeking such a causal explanation, Clinton raised the prospect that al-Qaeda's defeat would not in itself provide security. If certain conditions in this interdependent world had led to al-Qaeda, that group's eclipse could hardly guarantee that other terrorist movements would not sprout in its place. Moreover, by placing the post-9/11 threat in the context of "fanatics everywhere throughout history ... [who] think they've got the truth," Clinton clearly implied that the long-term terrorist threat was not necessarily limited to Islamic or other religious movements.

Clinton's speech raised many important questions, the main ones being these: if, as he suggested, 9/11 was a violent manifestation of global conditions that on the one hand produced poverty and massive misery and, on the other, absolutist transcendental visions capable of mobilizing people for violent action, what was the connection between these two factors? What was the link between socioeconomic conditions and transcendental cognitive outlooks that could lead a relatively small group of individuals to challenge the strongest military power on earth and what dynamic could explain the violent outcome? Can evidence be found to move answers to such questions beyond the realms of sheer speculation or the tautological conclusions of prefabricated ideological frameworks?

Clinton's characterization of 9/11 as signaling a battle based on the opposition of two mind-sets, or worldviews, recalls the division posited by political sociologists, such as David Apter, between "instrumental" and "consumatory" values as motive forces behind political actions.[15] The former, rests on the assumption that the human being's grasp of truth—including normative truth—is necessarily less than certain, while the latter assumes that absolute, or transcendental truth is attainable. The mind-set Clinton described as what "most of us believe" hearkens back to the foundations of the American Republic, which was conceived and born within the specific context of the Enlightenment, the intellectual environment that sprang from faith in the twin pillars of individual human reason and the progress that joint human effort could achieve through science. The amazing strength of this faith in both the individual and the power of the combined efforts of multiple individuals in the scientific enterprise is best revealed by the Enlightenment's ability to incorporate, rather than be destroyed by, the eighteenth-century philosopher David Hume's proof that science can at best provide only probabilistic, rather than absolute, knowledge. The "modern post-enlightenment" mind proved able to absorb this limitation on the human ability to achieve certainty and transpose the lesson to the sociopolitical realm. In the final analysis, this is what in time allowed the progressive emergence of political organization based on tolerance, secularism—the separation of church and state—and the rough and ready pragmatism that is the hallmark of modern democracies.

The London speech's reminder of the epistemological base upon which the American political system was created came at an appropriate moment, for groups in conflict are always tempted to adopt "fundamentalist" positions that are taken to be transcendental and absolute. In a very real sense, all actors in violent political confrontations are driven toward a reliance on pristine, basic values from which nuances, ambiguities, and doubts are stripped. The reason for this—as old as politics itself—is the premium that must be placed on group-cohesion and group-will if victory is to be attained. In short, enemies "must know that they are facing people who have made a basic choice and will not waiver."[16] Thus, in conflict situations foundational elements of group identity tend to surge to the fore, while potentially divisive or discordant threads in the desired tapestry of group unity are discarded, ignored, suppressed, or placed in abeyance. Clinton's unfortunately ignored views would have been a healthy addition to the discourse of a nation that had suddenly found itself at war.

BACKGROUND: THE NEOCONSERVATIVES IN POSITION

Whatever judgment history ultimately renders on George W. Bush's presidency, the impact of what has become known as neoconservatism will figure largely in the evaluation. Neither a coherent philosophy nor an analytical academic "theory," neoconservatism nonetheless became a significant phenomenon in U.S. policymaking by the end of the twentieth century. Its origins trace back at least to the late 1960s, the period following Israel's sweeping victory in the 1967 War. The initiators and primary spokesmen of neoconservatism, which might most accurately be termed a political "orientation," were mainly disillusioned liberal Jewish intellectuals in the U.S. northeast who turned sharply away from what they saw as the liberals' undue optimism regarding human nature and excessive naiveté regarding practical politics. Although numerically insignificant, the "neocons" had some significant assets. First, their most important spokespersons enjoyed positions of influence in the media and in public affairs. Second, in addition to the force of ideological orientation, neocons were bound by personal, professional, and familial ties. These lent the incipient movement considerable potential force from its onset.

Following the 1967 Arab-Israeli War, U.S.-Soviet rivalry over the Middle East provided neoconservatives with their first major operational cause and an opportunity to pursue it in government service. When the Soviet Union, claiming to be concerned over Israeli efforts to colonize the Arab lands seized in 1967, acted to restrict Jewish emigration from the USSR, Democratic Senator Henry (Scoop) Jackson moved to mobilize penalties against Moscow. The budding neoconservative movement flocked to Jackson's banner. Neocons took Moscow's ensuing retreat and modification of its emigration policy as confirmation that hardball politics paid off.

Under Ronald Reagan's presidency, neoconservatives—many of whom had by then formally joined the Republican Party—won appointments to important positions, particularly in the Defense Department. The trend was maintained when George Bush Senior followed Reagan to the White House. Among neoconservatives from the 1980s who were destined to reappear in influential government roles in the new millennium figured Richard Perle, Douglas Feith, Paul Wolfowitz, Lewis Libby, John Bolton, and Elliott Abrams.

Bill Clinton's election in 1992 meant that the rest of the decade was a political wilderness for the neocons and marked a hiatus in the growth of their input into policymaking. In retrospect it is obvious that this did not undermine the neocon outlook's gathering political strength. Not invited to assume positions of immediate influence during Clinton's two terms in office, neoconservatives put the years to good use expanding their organizational base, and refining their policy goals and the arguments used to support them. Many worked with and through Washington-based think tanks to disseminate the neoconservative message. The American Enterprise Institute, the Jewish Institute for National Security Affairs, and the Institute for Advanced Strategic and Political Studies were major venues for such endeavors.[17]

As an "orientation" or "outlook," rather than a comprehensively articulated philosophy or fully developed academic theory, neoconservatism retained the inchoate quality of an ideological position-in-the-making. Thus, it could accommodate a range of views that were not always completely in harmony and which, indeed, were sometimes marked by sharp differences.[18] Nonetheless, neoconservative proponents shared key tenets that effectively gave them a common political direction. Three convictions formed the core of the neoconservative outlook: (1) that the United States is morally superior to other countries and is the vanguard of historical political development; (2) that power should and must be unapologetically exercised on behalf of moral and historical necessity; and (3) that Israel and the United States share common values and goals, and that unstinting support of Israel must therefore be a pillar of American foreign policy.

The neoconservative worldview gained widespread attention in March, 1992, some ten months before Clinton took office, when a draft document prepared for then Secretary of Defense Richard Cheney was leaked to the *New York Times*. The document had been written under the supervision of the Pentagon's Under Secretary for Policy, Paul Wolfowitz. Its contents immediately produced a firestorm of criticism, both domestic and foreign. The furor arose because the draft paper, labeled the "Defense Planning Guidance" for the 1992–1994 period, suggested a formalized basis upon which "guidance" from the President and Secretary of Defense would be offered to the military for setting budgetary priorities.[19] The Wolfowitz draft called for Washington to cap its victory over the Soviet Union in the Cold War by gearing foreign policy to the overriding goal of ensuring that the United States would remain the world's only superpower. In both tone and content, the argumentation advanced in support of this position caused widespread offense and alarm. Referring less than diplomatically to the possibility that future political challenges might emanate from such countries as Germany and Japan, the document's unrelieved unilateralist bent and emphasis on U.S. military might seemed to rest on contempt for close allies and unbridled arrogance vis-à-vis the rest of the world.

The controversy over Wolfowitz's draft forced a change. The push for a more moderate version of "Defense Planning Guidance," generally credited to Secretary of Defense Richard Cheney and Chairman of the Chiefs of Staff Colin Powell, prevailed. The final version lacked the earlier draft's offensiveness and sharp edges. While hinting at a preference for unilateral directions, the final draft also seemed to support multi-lateral approaches to international problems. Over the next eight years, neconservatives presented their message in various ways. By the end of the decade, it had become part of the daily American political discourse.

The goal of preventing Bill Clinton from winning a second term in 1996 led to unprecedented levels of neoconservative proselytizing. In 1995 prominent right-wing spokesmen William Kristol and Robert Kagan founded *The Weekly Standard*, a Washington-based political magazine that quickly became the most relentless and prominent purveyor of neoconservative views. The publication was funded and owned by Rupert Murdoch, the famed politically conservative international mass media tycoon, who had acquired U.S. citizenship a decade earlier.

Between them, Kristol and Kagan manifested many of the most striking qualities that would mark neoconservative luminaries in the coming decade. Both were highly intelligent, articulate political observers, both had records of government service in the Reagan Administration (in addition to other posts, Kristol had been Chief of Staff to Vice President Dan Quayle; Kagan had been Secretary of State George Shultz's principal speechwriter). Thus, Kagan and Kristol were intimately familiar with Washington's intricate political environment. Both were also products of Ivy-League educations, and both had ties to East Coast intellectual circles. In Kristol's case, these last constituted a primordial bond to the very origins of the neoconservative orientation. His father, Irving Kristol, is widely known as the "godfather" of neoconservatism, a sobriquet reflecting his own intellectual journey from a Trotskyist position in the 1940s to a Right-Wing Conservative stance by the late 1960s. In August 2003 the elder Kristol would use the pages of his son's magazine to reflect upon the meaning of the neoconservative label and conclude that the orientation's essential purpose in today's world is "to convert the Republican party and American conservatism in general, against their respective wills, into a new kind of conservative politics suitable to governing a modern democracy." Irving Kristol clearly indicated the "new kind of conservative politics" he wanted to promote. It was the politics of power. "Suddenly," he noted, referring to the 1990s after the Soviet Union's collapse:

> ... the United States emerged as uniquely powerful. ... With power come responsibilities, whether sought or not, whether welcome or not. And it is a fact that if you have the kind of power we now have, either you will find opportunities to use it, or the world will discover them for you.[20]

The elder Kristol wanted the United States to determine where, when, and how its own power would be used. Kristol's view that the United States, as the world's dominant power, had "ideological" interests—which meant an obligation "to defend, if possible, a democratic nation under attack from non-democratic forces"—produced the only specific policy recommendation in his article: the United States should defend Israel.

In the summer of 1996, just as the struggle over Clinton's second term approached its climax, the younger Kristol and Kagan coauthored a major article, a clarion call urging conservatives to commit themselves to the new kind of politics Irving Kristol would later describe. Kristol and Kagan did not choose their own magazine as the vehicle for this piece, presumably because *The Weekly Standard*, then barely a year old, was still a struggling, fledgling publication. In any event, the work, entitled "Toward a Neo-Reaganite Foreign Policy," appeared in *Foreign Affairs*, then as now the most prestigious vehicle in the United States for discussions of international affairs.

In strong and succinct terms, the authors outlined their version of "a conservative view of the world and America's proper role in it."[21] The state of the world, they argued, was simply that the United States enjoyed a position of unchallengeable power. American conservatives had lapsed into confusion over the significance of this and, in consequence, were tending to coalesce around a "lukewarm consensus about America's reduced role in a post-Cold War world ..."[22] This, they warned, would prevent conservatives from governing the country. What was needed was something to attract and indeed inspire the voting public—"a more elevated vision of America's international role."[23]

Kristol and Kagan's definition of the proper U.S. role was straightforward: "Benevolent global hegemony."

> Having defeated the "evil empire," the United States enjoys strategic and ideological predominance. The first objective of U.S. foreign policy should be to preserve and enhance that predominance by strengthening America's security, supporting its friends, advancing its interests, and standing up for its principles around the world.[24]

This, of course, was no more than a reiteration of the main thrust of Paul Wolfowitz's 1992 draft Defense Planning Guidance. No doubt mindful that only four years had passed since a public outcry caused that draft to be discarded in favor of a much watered-down version, Kristol and Kagan stressed that there was a need to educate "the citizenry to the responsibilities of global hegemony . . . ."[25]

Among the primary lessons to be imparted was the view that "American hegemony is the only reliable defense against a breakdown of peace and international order." Once this were understood, it would be clear to all that "the appropriate goal of American foreign policy ... is to preserve that hegemony as far into the future as possible." That strategic goal, they maintained, required a "foreign policy of military supremacy and moral confidence."[26]

The *Foreign Affairs* article was above all a cry to American conservatives, one seeking to rally conservative opinion to an activist ideological stance. It therefore sought to link conservatives' concern over the role of moral values within American society to the role Kristol and Kagan hoped to see those values play in U.S. foreign policy. The messianic implications of such an approach to international affairs could not be hidden, nor did the authors attempt to disguise them:

> The remoralizing of America at home ultimately requires the remoralization of American foreign policy. For both follow from Americans' belief that the principles of the Declaration of Independence are not merely the choices of a particular culture but are universal, enduring, "self-evident" truths. That has been, after all, the main point of the conservatives' war against a relativistic multiculturalism. For conservatives to preach the importance of upholding the core elements of the Western tradition at home, but to profess indifference to the fate of American principles abroad, is an inconsistency that cannot help but gnaw at the heart of conservatism.[27]

Kristol and Kagan concluded by chastising conservatives who did not favor an activist foreign policy aimed at securing American benevolent global hegemony. These were accused of pursuing a "pinched nationalism." In contrast, Kristol and Kagan claimed to promote "a true 'conservatism of the heart.'" The prose used to describe this brand of conservatism (or Neoconservatism) is notable for its romantic, virtually rhapsodic, character as well as for its careful employment of words written by George F. Kennan half a century ago. As an ideological statement of purpose, Kristol and Kagan produced an article which leaves no doubt that neoconservative moral confidence is ultimately rooted in a conviction of divine or historically sanctioned mission:

> A true "conservatism of the heart" ought to emphasize both personal and national responsibility, relish the opportunity for national engagement, embrace the possibility of national greatness, and restore a sense of the heroic, which has been sorely lacking in American foreign policy—and American conservatism in recent years. George Kennan was right 50 years ago in his famous "X" article: the American people ought to feel a "certain gratitude to a Providence, which by providing [them] with this implacable challenge, has made their entire security as a nation dependent on pulling themselves together and accepting the responsibilities of moral and political leadership that history plainly intended them to bear." This is as true today—if less obviously so—as it was [when Kennan wrote] at the beginning of the Cold War.[28]

In 1997 Kristol and Kagan cofounded the Project for the New American Century (PNAC). Based in Washington, DC, the new organization was devoted to furthering the neoconservative outlook. According to its "Statement of Principles," this boiled down to promoting "the propositions that American leadership is good both for Americans and for the world; that such leadership requires military strength, diplomatic energy and commitment to moral principle; and that too few political leaders today are making the case for global leadership."[29]

From the outset, the PNAC received politically significant support. Its founding document was signed by a host of high-profile personalities from the national political scene, among whom figured Elliot Abrams (former Assistant Secretary of State for Human Rights), William Bennett (former Secretary of Education), Jeb Bush (son of ex-president George Bush), Dick Cheney (former Secretary of Defense), Fred C. Ikle (former Undersecretary of Defense), I. Lewis Libby (former holder of senior positions in the State Department and the Pentagon), Dan Quayle (former Vice President), Donald Rumsfeld (former Secretary of Defense and White House Chief of Staff), and Paul Wolfowitz (former Under Secretary of Defense).

Within a few short years, many of these individuals would hold high office under the presidency of George W. Bush. Abrams would become the National Security Council's Director for Near East and North African Affairs. Cheney would become Vice President, and Libby would become Cheney's Chief of Staff. Rumsfeld would become Secretary of Defense, and Wolfowitz would be his number two man.

In retrospect it is obvious that the 1990s provided neoconservatives with an opportunity to consolidate their message as well as their political efforts. Their first challenge was to sway the Republican Party into neoconservative channels, the second was to gain support from the country as a whole. George W. Bush's selection as the Republican presidential candidate in 2000 capped the neocons' winning confrontation with the first challenge. However, Bush's questionable electoral victory and subsequent serious domestic differences over his administration's prosecution of the War on Terror long frustrated the neoconservatives' search for national approbation. Indeed, it is no exaggeration to contend that Bush's campaign for a second term was essentially a search for overall approval of his first-term performance.

The highlights of that performance were linked to the War on Terror, and therefore to the Arab and Islamic Worlds. Given that the neoconservative orientation had been shaped from its inception at least partly by events in the Middle East, it was only natural that the ascendant neoconservatism of the late 1990s and early 2000s had clear positions regarding the region.

NEOCONSERVATISM AND THE MIDDLE EAST

Neoconservative discussion of the Middle East has mainly focused on three topics: Israel, Iraq, and the overall context of Arab-Muslim culture. The neoconservative position on Israel has been straightforward, consistent, and strong: Israel must be supported. Norman Podhoretz, acknowledged as one of the neoconservatives' "founding fathers," set the tone very early on as editor in chief of *Commentary*, the publication of the American Jewish Committee. Once a mainstay of liberal political positions, *Commentary* followed its editor's increasing shift to the right after the late 1960s—becoming what has long been accurately described as "a neoconservative journal."[30] Podhoretz, *Commentary*, and neoconservatives in general proved to be not simply supportive of Israel but especially committed to the Israeli political spectrum's right wing. Thus, American neoconservatives quickly and steadfastly aligned themselves with Israel's Gahal, subsequently known as Likud, party—the direct descendent of Vladimir Jabotinsky's Revisionist Zionist movement. The significance of this should not be minimized, and is worth a small digression into recent history.

By the early 1930s, Jabotinsky, a Russian Zionist activist, had become thoroughly alienated from the strategy that the World Zionist Organization, under the leadership of its president, Chaim Weizmann, was following in its effort to build up and develop the Jewish community in Palestine. That effort was the necessary avenue toward creating in Palestine a "national home for the Jewish people," an objective approved by the British government in 1917 and incorporated into the mandate for Palestine that London received from the League of Nations following World War I.

Jabotinsky's quarrel with Weizmann stemmed from the latter's commitment to a policy of "gradualism." A lifelong anglophile, as well as a thoroughgoing pragmatist, Weizmann saw "gradualism" as a way to seek a Jewish state by following the path of least resistance. "Gradualism" meant that the ultimate objective would not be stressed, indeed, would hardly be mentioned—thus averting problematical reactions from the Arabs as well as from the British mandatory administration. Jabotinsky saw this strategy not only as cowardly but also as promising only failure. For Jabotinsky,

Zionist success depended on an unabashed nationalism committed to realize its goal through violence if necessary—and taking particular pride in that commitment. Action, reflecting spiritual determination, defined a people; the opportunity to manifest national values through action—and by doing so win or confirm national identity—should be welcomed, not shunned. Jabotinsky was a product of his era. The same sort of romantic extreme nationalist thought led to similar political movements during the 1930s in Germany, Italy, Portugal, and Spain.

Significant friction inevitably developed between mainstream Zionists and their Revisionist challengers. World War II set the stage for tensions to become serious clashes. The most salient point of contention was over the policy to be adopted toward the British Government, which in an eleventh-hour attempt to shore up its position in the Middle East on the eve of the war, severely restricted development of the Jewish national home in Palestine.

Weizmann and his mainstream Zionists concluded that no enemy of Hitler, including the British, should be assailed by Jews during the coming war. The Revisionist Zionists, now under the leadership of another east European Zionist, Menachem Begin, took another position: armed struggle on behalf of a Jewish state should be continued during the war, whether against local Arabs or the British mandatory regime. The division between mainstream and Revisionist Zionists was now complete—and destined to play itself out in Israel's body politic through ideological rivalries, political tensions, and fratricidal bloodshed. Perhaps symbolically the most important clash came during Israel's war of independence, when—fearful of a Revisionist coup d'etat—the nascent Jewish State's Prime Minister, David Ben Gurion, ordered Israel's fledgling army into battle against Revisionist forces.

In short, mainstream Zionists, represented by the Labor Party leaders who would dominate Israeli politics for twenty years after the state's birth, were politically challenged—but, for a long while, not really threatened—by their Revisionist rivals. Thus, Menachem Begin long remained in the background of Israel's politics. His political enemies, Chaim Weizmann, David Ben Gurion, Abba Eban, Golda Meir, and all the rest of the Labor luminaries formed the international—and liberal—face of the Jewish state. That face began to dissolve in the aftermath of the June 1967 War.

Following various turns in domestic Israeli politics after 1967, it fell to a Labor Prime Minister, Yitzhak Rabin, to preside over the Oslo initiative, the first development in nearly fifty years that held promise of ending the Arab-Israeli conflict. In 1993, Israel and the Palestine Liberation Organization (PLO) signed a Declaration of Principles, a seminal agreement whereby the two sides acknowledged each others' legitimacy and pledged to settle outstanding differences politically. An Israeli who could not bear the thought of a territorial compromise with Palestinians assassinated Rabin in 1995.

The assassination's aftermath not only witnessed a growing divide in Israel between right and left political tendencies but also the rising dominance of the right-wing Likud view. In 1996, Likud leader Benjamin Netanyahu, became Israel's Prime Minister. Born in Tel-Aviv in 1949, Netanyahu was taken to the United States by his family at a young age. He acquired U.S. citizenship but retained his Israeli citizenship as well. After graduating from high school in the United States, he completed military service in the Israeli Army. He then received his higher education at MIT, after which he briefly entered the world of business. However, by the early 1980s Netanyahu had entered public life—an arena in which his rise would prove meteoric. In 1982, upon the request of the Israeli ambassador, Netanyahu was appointed Deputy Chief of Mission in the Israeli embassy in Washington. Two years later he became Israel's Ambassador to the United Nations, a post he retained for some four years. In 1988 he was elected to the Knesset and appointed Deputy Foreign Minister. In 1993, he became the Likud Party's Chairman. Three years later he was elected Prime Minister.

Benjamin Netanyahu's right-wing credentials were impeccable. His father, Binzion Netanyahu, a renowned historian and Revisionist Zionist theoretician, once served as Vladimir Jabotinsky's secretary.[31] Netanyahu himself unwaveringly saw things through Revisionist lenses as he surveyed the more recent twists of the struggle for Palestine. He thoroughly disliked the Oslo Peace Process, and was just as strongly opposed to the cornerstone upon which supporters of the Process hoped to achieve peace: a two-state solution that would provide for Israel's security while allowing Palestinians to have a state of their own. As prime minister, he faced the delicate—but not impossible—task of presiding over Israel's participation in the peace process, in which the Clinton administration had placed high hopes, without allowing the process to move toward the two-state solution it was designed to achieve.

Netanyahu's strong links to the United States had brought him into contact with the full spectrum of pro-Israeli Americans, but his closest ties were with the most politically conservative elements of this group, and it was from them that he received encouragement and support for his political ambitions.[32] Such neoconservative quarters shared Netanyahu's antipathy to the Oslo Peace Process and the prospect of Palestinian statehood. It was, therefore, not unduly surprising that he looked to American neocons for suggestions as to how the Oslo Peace Process could best be scuttled.

Because they profoundly disagreed with the Clinton administration's commitment to the Oslo Process, leading American neoconservatives were eager to counsel Israel's new anti-Oslo prime minister. An Israeli think tank, the Institute for Advanced Strategic and Political Studies (IASPS), promptly commissioned a high-powered group of neoconservative "Washington insiders" to recommend policy directions for the new Netanyahu government. The Institute, based in Jerusalem and Washington, adhered to such an extremely conservative political line that by 2001 its founder and president, Robert J. Loewenberg, was branding Israel's Likud leader Ariel Sharon "socialist Sharon."[33]

Richard Perle headed the consultancy group hired by IASPS. Perle, well known for favoring confrontational conservative international policies, had a multifaceted neoconservative career path. He spent several years on the staff of Senator Henry "Scoop" Jackson and then went on to hold a variety of official and quasi-official government positions. He was Assistant Secretary of Defense in the Reagan Administration and later served as a foreign policy advisor to George W. Bush during the latter's first presidential campaign. At the same time, Perle was a Senior Fellow of the American Enterprise Institute and associated with the PNAC. He became well known to the general public as a conservative publicist and talk show guest. He also became known—sometimes problematically—as an international investor. In addition to Perle and Loewenberg, three other members of the seven-person consultancy group were particularly prominent as hard-line activist supporters of Israel in the Washington area. These were Douglas Feith and David and Meyrav Wurmser.

Feith also upheld a family tradition of ultra-Rightist politics; his father, Dalek, had been a member of Betar, the brown-shirted youth movement of Vladimir Jabotinsky's Revisionist Zionism.[34] Feith himself entered into public service in the early 1980s, serving in the Reagan Administration—first as a Middle East expert on the National Security Council, and then in the Defense Department, working with Richard Perle—who was then Assistant Secretary of Defense. By 1984, Feith had risen to the level of Deputy Assistant Secretary of Defense for Negotiations Policy. In 1986, he left government service to launch his own law firm, to which he devoted himself for the next fifteen years. Feith would reenter government under the George W. Bush administration. Allegations of conflict of interest between his private and public roles would quickly surface.[35] From 1988 to 1984, David Wurmser worked as a Project Officer for the congressionally funded U.S. Institute for Peace. He later headed the Division of Research and Strategy in the same think tank that produced the 1996 study for Benjamin Netanyahu.[36] Still later, he became the Director of Middle East Studies at the American Enterprise Institute.

David Wurmser's wife, Meyrav, was an at least equally bright and energetic member of Washington's policy-relevant community. An Israeli national, she boasted an impressive record of achievement. A firm opponent of the Oslo peace accords, Ms. Wursmer worked as a columnist for the *Jerusalem Post* and was also a Senior Fellow at the right-wing think tank, the Hudson Institute.

The 1996 report produced by this group for the IASPS and Israel's new prime minister minced no words. The document's thrust was captured by its title: *A Clean Break: A New Strategy for Securing the Realm.* It argued that

Israel should decisively turn away from what was condemned as an impractical, dangerous, and politically immoral recent past—the entire trajectory toward a settlement along the lines of the Oslo Program.[37]

In keeping with this, the advice given to Israel's new prime minister argued that the Netanyahu government had an opportunity to establish Israel's policy "on an entirely new intellectual foundation." Most important was the flat advice that Israel should abandon any notion of "land for peace" and instead commit itself totally to "peace through strength."[38] In short, the Oslo Process should be discarded. By the same token, the report suggested that Syria's internal dynamics could be helpfully swayed by a policy of harsh confrontation. A regime change in Iraq, argued the report, would accomplish "an important Israeli strategic objective in its own right."[39]

Perle, Feith, and Wurmser acquired influential positions in the George W. Bush administration. Wurmser became Vice President Dick Cheney's Middle East Adviser. Perle was named Chairman of the Defense Policy Board. Composed of former high officials and policymakers, the DPB exists to offer independent advice to the Secretary of Defense. While its members serve without financial compensation, they have the satisfaction of being privy to inside information and having the ear of those in power. Perle would resign from the chairmanship in 2003 and severe all connections with the DPB a year later under the cloud of allegations of having improperly sought to promote his own business interests. Douglas Feith became the third-ranking civilian in the Defense Department, following Secretary of Defense Donald Rumsfeld and Deputy Secretary Paul Wolfowitz. Part of Feith's duties involved serving as the Pentagon's liaison with the DPB and, in consultation with the Secretary of Defense, naming that group's members. In August of 2005, Feith resigned from his Pentagon position, publicly citing a desire for more time with his family. Other sources indicated that Feith's professional demise had more to do with an espionage scandal involving one of his subordinates, Larry Franklin, who was then under investigation by the FBI for passing classified material to Israel. In January 2006, Franklin was convicted and sentenced to over twelve years in prison.[40]

Ever since the end of the 1990–1991 Gulf War, neoconservatives had been unanimous in condemning U.S. policy toward Iraq. In their view, Saddam Hussein should never have been allowed to remain in power following that conflict, and the quicker Washington overturned the dictator's regime, the better things would be. Initially, the main reason behind this outlook was the conviction that Saddam would be a potential danger to regional and world stability so long as he remained in office. In 1998, a group calling itself the Committee for Peace and Security in the Gulf published an open letter to President Clinton calling on the United States to launch "a determined program to change the regime in Baghdad."[41] The committee's membership was practically a roster of leading neoconservative spokesmen, thinkers, and personalities, many of whom would later assume important positions in the

George W. Bush administration. Among them were Richard Perle, William Kristol, Robert Kagan, Paul Wolfowitz, and Donald Rumsfeld.

However, as the neoconservatives' political vision became more clearly defined over the next several years, the basis of their insistence on the need for regime change in Baghdad shifted to a broader focus. Saddam's record and aggressive personality were not discarded as valid reasons, but they were superceded by the neocons' growing enthusiasm for a global U.S. benevolent hegemony. In short, regardless of what happened to Saddam Hussein, the geopolitical importance of the Middle East would require a permanent (or at least open-ended) U.S. military presence in the Persian Gulf. In itself, this consideration heightened the attraction of a pro-American regime change in Iraq. There is no doubt that such thoughts went into a major report issued by the PNAC on the eve of George W. Bush's election to the presidency. Entitled *Rebuilding America's Defenses: Strategy, Forces and Resources for a New Century*, the report maintained that "the need for a substantial American force presence in the Gulf transcends the issue of the regime of Saddam Hussein.[42] However, in referring to North Korea's Kim Jong Il and Iraq's Saddam Hussein, the report strongly criticized previous Pentagon planning efforts for having "given little or no consideration to the force requirement not only to defeat [those countries] but to remove these regimes from power and conduct post-combat stability operations."[43]

From the neoconservative perspective, then, Iraq was vitally important to the goal of U.S. global hegemony, a conclusion deriving directly from Iraq's regional significance. It is not difficult to make or perceive the case for Iraq's regional importance, and neoncons made at least parts of the case repeatedly—for example, in the 1996 paper prepared for Israeli Prime Minister Netanyahu. The long and short of it is simply this: a pro-American, or American-controlled, Iraq would: (a) eliminate Syria's strategic depth in its confrontation with Israel, thereby rendering Damascus much more likely to reach an accommodation with Israel on Jerusalem's terms; (b) provide a secure Western base for protecting all oilfields in the Arab/Persian Gulf, including those of Saudi Arabia, independently of any preferences local governments might have; and (c) stand as a strong bastion against radical tendencies emanating from Iran's Islamic Republic and, at the same time, possibly provide an important base of support for moderate factions seeking regime change in that country.

WHAT WAS MISSING FROM THE NEOCONSERVATIVE DISCOURSE ON IRAQ?

In itself, the above litany of geopolitical considerations would have provided substantial grounds for arguing the neoconservatives' demand for regime change in Baghdad. There was, however, almost certainly an additional consideration shaping many neocons' approach to Iraq, but one which—so far as I have found—was not publicly declared as a reason to remove Saddam Hussein from power. Yet, an awareness of the factor must have imposed itself on neocon strategic thinking about the Middle East by the mid-1990s for at least three reasons. First, the issue was repeatedly being brought up and widely disseminated by think tanks and academic forums whose activities would have been known to neoconservative organizations. Second, the issue related very much to Israel and its future—a subject of deep concern to leading neoconservative spokesmen. Finally, the issue not only related to Israel and its future but also linked Israel's future to a particular role Iraq might play in an effort to resolve the Palestine conflict. Given the intensity of neoconservatives' interest in Israel and in Iraq, it is inconceivable that they were unaware of suggestions that in the mid-1990s began to be made regarding Iraq's possible role in a definitive Palestine settlement. If neoconservatives refrained from participating in discussions of the point at that time, it was likely due to a belief that the moment was not yet ripe for any in-depth exploration of the issue. In any case, scenarios envisaging a major Iraqi contribution to a resolution of the Palestine conflict could only have reinforced the neoconservative desire to see Saddam Hussein's rule replaced by a friendly government in Baghdad.

The end of the 1990–1991 Gulf War, coinciding as it did with the approaching demise of the Soviet Union, reenergized the decades-old American search for Arab-Israeli peace. The administration of George Bush, Sr. moved quickly once the fighting stopped, engineering the Madrid Peace Conference and promoting the notion that a peaceful Middle East would be an essential part of a vibrant and productive "new world order." After 1992, the Clinton administration retained Washington's commitment to the pursuit of Mideast peace. However, it was the 1993 Oslo Accords, by which Israel and the Palestine Liberation Organization mutually recognized one another's legitimacy and pledged to work for a political solution, that persuaded Washington and much of the world that a negotiated settlement over Palestine might soon be within reach.

The Oslo Process provided for a Palestinian Authority, thus allowing Palestinian self-rule in parts of the occupied West Bank and Gaza. This was envisaged as an interim (five-year) arrangement. Final status issues were to be resolved through negotiations during that period. Such issues—which included the problems of Jerusalem's ultimate status, the fate of Israeli settlements in occupied Arab lands, the Palestinian refugee problem, and final security arrangements and borders—constituted the core elements of Israeli-Palestinian enmity. The Palestinian refugee issue was the most difficult of them all, not only tapping the deepest emotional wellsprings of both sides but also presenting the narrowest range of options for maneuvering toward any sort of agreement. To Palestinians, displacement and dispossession—the defining conditions of the refugees—resulted directly from the ruthless employment of Zionist force on behalf of Zionist cupidity. To Israelis, the

Palestinian refugee problem was the unfortunate outcome of shortsighted Arab policies that forced wars of survival upon the Jewish state, first at its birth in 1948 and then again in its robust youth, twenty years later. Palestinians professed to see only one solution—the right of all refugees to return to the homes or locations from which they had been expelled or fled. For Palestinians, or at least so claimed their spokesmen, this was the entire reason for which their campaign had been waged from the start: to cancel the injustice of losses suffered in the course of Israel's existence. The prospect of a massive influx of Arab refugees cut just as deeply in the Israeli psyche. Any such eventuality would clearly pose an unacceptable security threat . . . but, even worse, it would amount to a mortal demographic menace, undermining Israel's very purpose—that of being a *Jewish* State.

Because of its centrality to each side's belief system, the refugee issue was soon frozen within a terrible wrapping of silence that only occasionally was broken by the unthinking reiteration of the standard Palestinian or Israeli positions. In private, Palestinian thinkers or leaders would sometimes acknowledge—strictly off the record—that the demand for the full, unrestricted return of all refugees was neither realistic nor helpful to the peace process. In private, their Israeli counterparts would—also off the record—admit much the same with reference to Israel's established refusal to accept the return of more than a minimally symbolic number of refugees in the context of a peace settlement and its utter refusal to acknowledge—even symbolically—guilt for the problem's creation. There were very few exceptions to this general refusal to express dissenting views publicly.

It presented a bizarre scene to those who watched the Oslo Process unfold in the 1990s. While it was plain to all that the enduring silence would prevent even minimal efforts to begin bridging the gap between the Israeli and Palestinian positions, it was also clear that the silence had to be broken lest the entire Peace Process grind to a halt. The problem was to find some way to launch a more or less realistic discussion of how the refugees might be dealt with in the context of a peace settlement. Neither Arabs nor Israelis could do this. Nor could the United States. As a third party claiming to be a facilitator of the Peace Process, Washington was obviously not going to take the initiative on an issue that was guaranteed to alienate one or both of the protagonists.

It was in the mid-1990s that cracks in the silence began to appear—not through the agency of Palestinian, Israeli, or "third party" official channels but rather through activities of academic centers and private think tanks. Through this prism it was possible to get a sense of the direction of thinking on the Palestinian refugee issue.

Two clear examples of this were the 1996 book, *From Refugees to Citizens: Palestinians and the End of the Arab-Israeli Conflict*,[44] by Syracuse University Professor of Law Donna Arzt, and a 1998 concept paper produced by a nongovernmental Israeli-Palestinian team working under the umbrella of Harvard's Program on International Conflict Analysis and Resolution.[45] Significantly, two highly influential U.S. think tanks with close ties to policy-making circles were associated with Arzt's work. The New York-based Council on Foreign Relations published the book and the Washington-based Brookings Institution distributed it. Arzt had directed the Council on Foreign Relations project "The Arab-Israeli Conflict: Demographic and Humanitarian Issues." *From Refugees to Citizens*, she wrote, advanced for discussion "the basic components of a plan for permanent regional absorption of Palestinian refugees that is intended to result in a mutually agreeable division of responsibilities among all parties to the peace process." The heart of Arzt's proposal was, as she put it, "an adjustment in the demographic distribution of Palestinian refugees . . . ."[46]

Casting her plan in terms of a seven- to ten-year time frame, Arzt projected a total (refugee and nonrefugee) Palestinian population of some 8.2 million by the year 2005. She dismissed the standard Palestinian and Israeli stands on the refugee issue as non-starters, totally incompatible with any conceivable political settlement. "Get real" was her blunt advice to would-be Middle East peacemakers. What Arzt put forth as a preliminary idea, a basis for discussion, was a strategy designed to resolve the refugee problem within the existing context of Middle Eastern political reality. The essential truth of that reality was that neighboring Arab states did not want the refugees and that any Palestinian political entity created through a political settlement would have neither the space nor resources to absorb them, or at least not most of them.

Arzt was correct in her appraisal of the regional political scene. Israel was adamantly opposed to refugee return and Arab states were generally unwilling to allow permanent Palestinian resettlement within their borders. Thus, Egypt and Syria had severely restricted Palestinian residency since 1948 and showed all intentions of continuing to do so; Lebanon was strongly on record demanding that any Israeli-Palestinian settlement lead to a reduction in the size of Lebanon's Palestinian community. Jordan, the Arab state that had done most to facilitate refugee resettlement within its borders, argued that it had done its share and would accept no additional refugees.

Artz's suggested approach was predicated on the coordinated use of the full range of traditional options for resolving massive refugee situations. Thus, her plan envisaged repatriation, but only under stringent conditions: refugee repatriation to Israel would be allowed for only a miniscule, purely symbolic number of individuals. On the other hand, significant numbers of refugees would be repatriated to the territories of a Palestinian state. Compensation, both to individual refugees and to host countries willing to incorporate large numbers of refugees into their populations, would be used to promote resettlement as an option. Artz calculated that, if acted on immediately, the approach she advocated would lead to just over one-third (34.4 percent) of the world's Palestinians residing in the West Bank and Gaza by

2005. The other two-thirds would be found outside Palestine in accordance with Arzts's recommended demographic adjustments. As a result of these, the West Bank's Palestinian population would rise to twice its 1995 level. Israel, Syria, Lebanon, and Jordan would absorb small percentages of the remaining refugees, but Arzt reserved the most significant contributions in this regard for non-Middle Eastern states and what she termed "the sparsely populated Gulf countries such as Saudi Arabia, Iraq and Kuwait."[47] Each was to double the size of its 1995 Palestinian population. Thus, non-Middle Eastern states would allow the resettlement of some 10.8 percent of the world's 2005 Palestinian population, increasing their own Palestinian population to approximately 900,000. What Arzt conceived of as underpopulated Gulf countries—Saudi Arabia, Iraq, and Kuwait—were to more than match this contribution by taking in 11.6 percent of the world's Palestinians, thus raising their own combined Palestinian populations to some 965,000.

As noted above, Artz had a very sound grasp of the Palestinian factor in regional politics. She must have been fully aware of the bitter, widespread, and profound anti-Palestinian reaction that swept all levels of society in the Arab Gulf states—and particularly in Kuwait and Saudi Arabia—as a result of the 1990–1991 Gulf War. This, plus the fact that Iraq has a far more diversified economy than Kuwait or Saudi Arabia and is, therefore, potentially much more able than the latter to absorb a refugee population, forces one to conclude that despite her reference to the "Gulf countries," Artz actually saw Iraq as the primary venue for relocating the nearly one million Palestinian refugees to whom she referred.

In contrast to Arzt's work, the 1998 Harvard concept paper, *The Palestinian Refugee Problem and the Right of Return,* did not present a detailed plan for resolving the refugee problem.[48] In particular, it avoided Arzt's penchant for suggesting specific numbers of refugees to be demographically adjusted. The paper was the result of mock negotiations held over two years under Harvard's auspices by influential private Israeli and Palestinian citizens. The very valuable goal of the exercise was to introduce "insights and ideas . . . into the public debate and decision-making processes of the two communities."[49] Several important general principles emerged from the Harvard project. Chief among these, perhaps, was the Palestinian-Israeli group's agreement that neither of the traditional (or maximalist) positions on refugees was compatible with a settlement leading to enduring peace. In addition to this seminal point, the exercise produced general acceptance of a number of important insights, among which were that compensation, repatriation, and resettlement would have to be employed to resolve the refugee problem and that any political settlement would have to include the return to Israel proper of a restricted number of refugees; the return of a larger number of refugees to a Palestinian state; and the large-scale permanent absorption of refugees in host countries as well as in third-country resettlement venues.

Donna Arzt's book and the Harvard concept paper differed in a variety of ways but were strikingly parallel in their common insistence that repatriation, resettlement, and compensation be combined as tools for resolving the Palestinian refugee problem; that only limited numbers of Palestinians return to Israel, while the bulk of refugees resettle permanently in non-Israeli parts of Palestine and other parts of the Middle East and the world at large; that full resolution would require a period of several years; and, finally, that the international community must play an active role in any viable settlement. The parallels, of course, arose because each effort was grounded in the conviction that established official Israeli and Palestinian positions could not be part of any viable political settlement.

Unfortunately, the professed goal of both works—to spark a broad and free-flowing discussion of the refugee issue and how it might be dealt with in the peace process—was not really attained, or, at best, it was only partly reached. By the late 1990s, the Israeli and Palestinian ideological establishments had zeroed in on Arzt's book and the Harvard paper. The unimaginative, hackneyed outpouring of venom was predictable, and pathetic. Palestinian spokesmen, including Edward Said and his fellow Columbia University faculty member, Joseph Massad, not only denounced Artz's work and the Harvard paper, but went out of their way to excoriate any Palestinian thinker or leader whom they suspected of favoring a pragmatic, or realistic, approach to the refugee problem. Neither seemed concerned that their purely ideological stand might condemn millions of their fellow Palestinians to an open-ended existence as refugees.[50]

On the other hand, Israeli ideologues found their own grounds for condemning Arzt and the Harvard project. Right-wing political commentator Emanuel A. Winston, for example, railed against what he saw as the beginning of a clear plot to destroy the Jewish state by allowing some refugees to return to Israel proper and permitting masses of hostile Palestinian refugees to set up their own state on Israel's borders. Winston and his ilk in Israel were evidently not bothered by the possibility that their rejection of any concession on the refugee issue promised to condemn their fellow citizens to the uncertainties and tragedies of open-ended conflict.[51]

By the end of the 1990s, the Oslo Peace Process was in the grip of the terminal crisis that would finally bury it in 2000, when Ariel Sharon's provocative "visit" to the Al-Aqsa Mosque triggered the Second Intifadah. All thoughts of a Palestinian-Israeli political settlement were soon put on hold, if not cancelled altogether. History marched on and the "War on Terror" and its derivatives in Afghanistan and Iraq replaced the Palestine issue as the main focus of American and Western concern in the Middle East.

The thing about history is that it never stops "marching on." In other words, nothing on this earth—not even the seemingly unending violent confrontation between Palestinians and Israelis—is eternal. Someday, in some way, that conflict too will reach its end. If at that point the prospect still exists that the end may be attained politically, instead of militarily, the message of the Arzt and Harvard studies will still be important. Artz's admonition to "get real" will still be valid and relevant. Would-be Israeli and Palestinian peacemakers will still have to abandon their traditional positions and find common ground somewhere within the broad parameters indicated by Artz's book and Harvard's concept paper.

If the swift deterioration of the peace process in the late 1990s did not allow time for the development of a full and balanced debate over the Arzt Plan and the Harvard paper, the two works still managed to ensure that public awareness of possible connections among Iraq, the Palestinian refugee problem, and the Middle East peace process reached a new high. In 1998, Saddam Hussein suddenly granted Iraqi citizenship to resident Palestinians who had become refugees in 1949. The move was taken by some observers to signal Baghdad's readiness to receive large numbers of Palestinian refugees in exchange for an end to the economic and trade sanctions imposed on Iraq at the end of the 1991 Gulf War.[52]

By 1999, the world press was virtually riddled by ongoing, but unconfirmed, reports of Western and Israeli efforts to enlist Iraq as a partner in resolving the Palestinian refugee problem. While similar stories had appeared occasionally since the early 1990s, the sustained and widespread nature of the spate of rumors in 1999 and 2000 was notable.[53] Western and Arab press accounts claimed that Washington, working through the good offices of France and Morocco, was secretly offering to support an end to the international embargo against Iraq in return for that country's agreement to the permanent resettlement within its borders of some 400,000 Palestinian refugees.[54] The Israeli daily, *Maariv*, carried essentially the same report near the end of 1999. Citing "senior political sources" in Jerusalem, the paper also claimed that the Iraq scheme had been explicitly discussed by Israeli Prime Minister Ehud Barak and U.S. President Bill Clinton.[55] Similar stories, including widespread accounts of secret Israeli-Iraqi contacts, continued to appear throughout the spring of 2000.[56] During this same period, Laura Drake, a Washington-based academic and Middle East consultant, published an article in the *Washington Report on Middle East Affairs* in which she claimed to have confirmed "with some of the participants" earlier rumors of an unsuccessful 1997 attempt by a U.S. congressional staff delegation to convince the six Gulf Cooperation Council states to accept large-scale Palestinian refugee resettlement in their territories. Specifically, Drake claimed to have confirmed that New York congressman and member of the House International Relations Committee Benjamin Gilman sent a group of congressional staff, under the leadership of "Gilman's top pro-Israeli staffer," Deborah Bohdlanders, to hold security-related discussions with the Gulf State governments. Drake maintained that the staff delegation asked each of the GCC countries to "agree to receive 30,000 Palestinian refugees from Lebanon." The Gulf countries reportedly declined.[57]

These relatively widespread and vociferous discussions of Baghdad's possible role in helping to resolve the Palestinian refugee problem ensured that nobody with an interest in Middle East political currents in the late 1990s could have been unaware that Iraq theoretically offered a potential site for the relocation of massive numbers of Palestinian refugees. The idea itself was not at all new. It was, in fact, almost as old as the modern Zionist idea of seeking a Jewish national home in Palestine, which at Theodore Herzl's behest, was adopted by the World Zionist Congress in 1897. At least as early as 1918, some observers of the Zionist project, recognizing that it would inevitably require the displacement of most, if not all, Palestinian Arabs, pointed to Iraq as the most suitable site for the latter's relocation. The same idea surfaced again in the late 1930s, prompting a serious, though ultimately ineffective, campaign to interest London and Washington in the transferal of Palestinian Arabs to Iraq. In each case, the argument was the same: Iraq was underpopulated; Iraq's economic development would be boosted by additional population; Palestinians are culturally compatible with Iraqis; Palestinians, therefore, would be ideal additions to Iraq's population. It was a neat syllogism, perhaps, but one that utterly failed to take Palestinian preferences into account.[58]

On balance, the evidence appears to point conclusively to Iraq's anticipated assignment to receive massive numbers of Palestinian refugees as the primary unstated motive behind the Bush administration's decision to invade that country in March of 2003.[59]

THE NEOCONSERVATIVE VIEW OF THE SOURCE OF 9/11

The neoconservative outlook on Iraq derived from prevailing neocon views of the Arab World and broader Islamic culture as a whole. These were unabashedly negative. Even prior to 9/11, Arab-Islamic culture was taken to be chronically out of step with modern reality, and therefore dangerous—a loose atavistic cannon threatening to pour chaos into the pragmatic, reasonable contemporary world. Political correctness required that this sort of sweeping judgment usually be voiced only when protected by a veritable phalanx of qualifiers. Thus, "militant Islamists"—rather than "Muslims"—or "Arab extremists," rather than "Arabs," typically signified the relevant actors. Nonetheless, neoconservative discourse generally made plain neoconservative meaning. A typical example was a lengthy article published in 2004 by Norman Prodhoretz, the neoconservative luminary who in 2004 received the highest U.S. civilian honor, the Presidential Medal of Freedom. Quickly identifying "radical Islamism" as the "truly malignant force" that the West must confront and defeat in today's world, Podhoretz offered no suggestion as to why "radical Islamism" arose—leaving only the impression that something—some inherent seed or dynamic—within Islam itself inevitably gave rise to the malignant radical variant. Some thousands of words later, Podhoretz's discussion confirms that this impression was exactly what he sought to convey. Explaining the neoconservative hope that the remolding of Iraq by force would lead to positive political and cultural change in the Arab/Islamic worlds, Podehoretz wrote:

> As with democratization, so with the reform and modernization of Islam. In considering this . . . we found ourselves asking whether Islam could really go on for all eternity resisting the kind of reformation and modernization that had begun within Christianity and Judaism in the early modern period. Not that we were so naïve as to imagine that Islam could be reformed overnight, or from the outside. In its heyday, Islam was able to impose itself on large parts of the world by the sword; there was no chance today of an inverse instant transformation of Islam by the force of American arms.
>
> There was, however, a very good chance that a clearing of the ground, and a sowing of the seeds out of which new political, economic, and social conditions could grow, would gradually give rise to correlative religious pressures from within. Such pressures would take the form of an ultimately irresistible demand on theologians and clerics to find warrants in the Quran and *sharia* under which it would be possible to remain a good Muslim while enjoying the blessings of decent government, and even of political and economic liberty. In this way a course might finally be set toward the reform and modernization of the Islamic religion itself.[60]

In these few short sentences, Podhoretz managed to ignore the diversity of contemporary Muslim societies and approaches to Islam, postulating some single mythical Islamic entity in which political and economic liberties are totally absent while simultaneously implying that the millions of followers of Islam who are productive citizens in the United States, Canada, and Western Europe (where Prodhoretz would, presumably, locate "decent government") are something less than "good Muslims." This notable achievement was made possible by the profound ignorance that marked most of Podhoretz's references to things Middle Eastern.[61]

If the views of Podhoretz, who can lay no claim to Middle East expertise, partly reflected ignorance, they also clearly derived from a well-worn neoconservative outlook that has been given legitimacy by Bernard Lewis, a true authority on the Middle East and a man whose facile misrepresentations can hardly be attributed to unfamiliarity with the subject. Lewis has long and deservedly been one of the most internationally respected students of Middle Eastern history and culture. His interest in the region dates back to the 1920s, when he was required to learn a limited amount of Hebrew for his Bar Mitzvah. The experience so captivated him that he intensified his study of the language. By the time he entered university, Lewis had "read widely and deeply in Hebrew."[62] This led him to focus his higher education on Middle Eastern history and languages. After visiting the region in 1937, he joined the University of London as assistant lecturer in Islamic studies. In 1974, he moved to Princeton, where he remained until his retirement in 1986.

Lewis' contributions to Middle East Studies have been multiple and important. While his forte remains his work as a historian, he has also not infrequently dealt with current affairs. Here, his record must at best be judged as mixed. Although Lewis often offers valuable insights into contemporary regional events and dynamics, he has also tended to indulge in grossly oversimplified and distorted analyses that mystify and misinform rather than illuminate. By doing so, Lewis has mightily furthered the notion of Middle East "exceptionalism": the idea that the region—its people and its cultures—respond to unique and mysterious social dynamics that set them apart from all other peoples and cultures.

In 1990, Lewis published "The Roots of Muslim Rage," a widely circulated article (it appeared in a popular magazine, not an academic journal) in which he claimed that relations between the West and the Islamic World were entering a historic moment, one directly pitting the peoples of both sides against each other— "transcending the level of issues and policies and the governments that pursue them."[63] What was occurring, he said, was nothing less than "a clash of civilizations—the perhaps irrational but surely historic reaction of an ancient rival against our Judeo-Christian heritage, our secular present, and the worldwide expansion of both."[64]

Neoconservatives welcomed Lewis' thesis both because of its clear upholding of Western Judeo-Christian values over Islamic values and for its implicit support of the notion that military strength would ultimately determine the relationship between East and West. The argument was clear, sharp, and—to some—compelling.

But the limits on Lewis' role as an observer of the modern Middle East can be gleaned from his participation in the 1998 public letter to President Clinton calling for the United States to force a regime change in Iraq. The letter argued that Saddam was so "hated by his own people and the rank and file of his military" that "a broad based insurrection" would erupt in support of such a U.S. effort.[65]

An even better example of the almost embarrassingly off-the-mark arguments with which this distinguished scholar has sometimes sought to promote his exceptionalist views of the Middle East and Islam is found in the article referred to above, his popular 1990 "The Roots of Muslim Rage." After arguing that the struggle between the West and Islam "has now lasted for some fourteen centuries," and rehearsing some of the more recent tensions, including those precipitated by the rise of fundamentalist Islam under Ayatollah Khomeini in Iran, Lewis wrote:

> There is something in the religious culture of Islam which inspired, in even the humblest peasant or peddler, a dignity and a courtesy toward others never exceeded and rarely equaled in other civilizations. And yet, in moments of upheaval and disruption, when the deeper passions are stirred, this dignity and courtesy toward others can give way to an explosive mixture of rage and hatred which impels even the government of an ancient and civilized country—even the spokesman of a great spiritual and ethical religion—to espouse kidnapping and assassination . . . .[66]

The import of this paragraph—that the syndrome it describes is peculiar to a Muslim context—is unalloyed nonsense. The real mystery about the mysterious "something in the religious culture of Islam" that Lewis strives to conjure up is why he so artificially limited the issue to Islam.

It is a truism that while most if not all religions value and enjoin neighborly and considerate human interactions, "moments of upheaval and disruption" often cause even the most pious to violate these values and injunctions. No great erudition or powers of perception are required to see that all religions seem to suffer from this sad phenomenon. Thus, although early New England Puritans accorded extremely high value to the virtues of neighborliness and hospitality, their "moment of upheaval" in the late seventeenth century led to the infamous Salem Witch Trials. Mexican peasants' dignity and warm hospitality to strangers are legendary, but the social disruption of the Cristero Rebellion in the late 1920s produced horrendous atrocities, the culmination of which perhaps came in April 1927 when dozens of civilian train passengers were burned alive by order of the priest-warrior José Reyes Vera.

Parallels to such examples of what Protestant and Roman Catholic "religious cultures" can do are easily found in non-Christian religions. One of the main religious duties of Hinduism is to pay homage to others, which includes the extension of kindness to strangers. This, however, has not prevented the stirring of "deeper passions" and the ensuing spread in India of violence by Hindu fanatics in recent years. By the same token, despite Judaism's humanist message, Israel's political landscape has been badly stained by Jewish fanaticism in the last decade. Both Yigal Amir, who assassinated Prime Minister Yitzhak Rabin, and Baruch Goldstein, who murdered some twenty-nine unarmed Palestinians in Hebron, are seen by some sectors of the Israeli public as courageous defenders of religious principle.

Bernard Lewis did not err in pointing to the mysterious paradox that "religious culture" lies at the root of some of the loftiest and most noble as well as some of the vilest and most base forms of human behavior. He erred by implying that this somehow pertains exclusively or particularly to Islamic religious culture.

This was unfortunate, for his authoritative voice carried weight with those who decided the U.S. response to 9/11.

Chapter 2

Responding to 9/11: The Implications of Action and the Limits of Discourse

A major feature of the U.S. response to the September 2001 attacks was the glaring imbalance between the actions it entailed and the amount and extent of post-9/11 thought or deliberation that led to them. Washington's reaction was not only remarkably swift but also retained a strikingly consistent and purposeful direction. These qualities were apparent because the steps that formed the U.S. response were soon recognizable as a chain aiming at a clear goal, despite the nebulousness of the label under which they were taken. That label—the War on Terror—was imprecise and vague on nearly all counts, raising a host of questions while answering virtually none. Was, for example, the "war" to be a military conflict, such as World War II or Vietnam, or was it to be more of a social struggle for law enforcement, such as the "War on Drugs"? Or, on the other hand, did this new conflict resemble or have any similarity to the moral/economic campaign that had once been known as the "War on Poverty?"

If the type of conflict was unclear, so too was the precise identity of the opponent. This, of course, was partly due to the truth of the old adage that "one man's terrorist is another's freedom fighter." Who, or what, would define the enemy? Moreover, even were the enemy precisely marked, were there geographic or political boundaries to the War on Terror? Was the United States committed to fighting only those terrorist who threatened its own interests or the interests of its friends? Or was the country embarking on a comprehensive campaign against all forms of terrorism in all parts of the world?

Such issues did not become the focus of official deliberations in the immediate aftermath of 9/11. Speaking to the nation on the evening of September 11, 2001, only hours after the WTC towers collapsed in New York, George Bush simply pledged that the United States, together with all those wanting peace and security in the world, would win "the war against terrorism."[1]

REACTING TO 9/11

In part—but only in part—the president's speedy use of the "war-on-terror" label as a rallying cry was an understandable tactic to meet immediate needs. The events of the day had shocked and stunned the country. A foreign force had just successfully attacked the continental United States for the first time since the War of 1812. Dismay, outrage, and fear were rampant. Americans wanted and expected their government to show determined defiance in the face of the enemy. It was no time for Washington to show hesitation of confusion as to who was the enemy.

"Terrorism" admirably suited the immediate requirement. Whatever hairs one might care to split in arriving at a definition of "terrorism," the actions of the men who hijacked the four airplanes on 9/11 certainly qualified them as terrorists. Then too, "terrorism" was not only aptly descriptive of the attacks but also soundly opprobrious and—at least in an American context—appeared to draw a clear-cut distinction between the evil enemy and its intended victim.[2]

This should not be construed as arguing that expediency alone drove the administration's decision to raise the War-on-Terror banner. U.S. officials strongly suspected the perpetrators were linked to the al-Qaeda network from the moment the attacks occurred.[3] By noon, September 11, Senator Orrin Hatch was telling CNN that he'd received FBI and intelligence briefings indicating that Osama Bin Laden was behind the attacks.[4] By early afternoon, the administration was clearly convinced of al-Qaeda's guilt, and by 9:00 p.m., the president was indicating that the Taliban—Bin Laden's Afghani hosts—would bear the consequences.

To a degree, the swiftness of the response can be attributed to the government's long-standing awareness of al-Qaeda's determination to wage war on the United States. While the terrorist group had so far attacked only U.S. targets overseas, steps had been taken to warn its Taliban sponsors against countenancing an escalation of al-Qaeda activity. Speaking to a meeting of government leaders on the evening of 9/11, Deputy Secretary of State Richard Armitage said: "Look . . . we told the Taliban in no uncertain terms that if this happened, it's their ass. No difference between the Taliban and al-Qaeda now. They both go down."[5] President Bush confirmed the indicated policy shortly afterward in his first remarks to the American people since that morning's attacks: "We will make no distinction between the terrorists who committed these acts and those who harbor them."[6]

In a deeper and more operationally significant sense, the tenor and shape—the strategic coherence—of Washington's reaction to 9/11 stemmed from much more than the government's lengthy preoccupation with al-Qaeda and the Taliban. What would emerge as the Bush administration's guiding vision had been worked out over the course of nearly three decades—and particularly during the decade since the Soviet Union's demise—by many of the neoconservative individuals who dominated George W. Bush's foreign policy apparatus. At the highest levels, these included the so-called "Vulcans": Vice President Dick Cheney, Secretary of State Colin Powell, Secretary of Defense Donald Rumsfeld, Deputy Secretary of State Richard Armitage, Deputy Secretary of State Paul Wolfowitz and National Security Advisor Condoleeza Rice.

James Mann has shown that the "Vulcans," while sometimes differing both among themselves and with the loosely defined orientation that has become known as neoconservatism, had maintained professional trajectories that gave them a common belief in the supremacy of American values and in the notion that American power should strive to ensure the dominance of those values in the post-Cold War world. In this sense, notes Mann, the Vulcans "were influenced by their own history."[7]

This internationalist-conservative paradigm provided the framework, the certainty, and the impetus for the Bush administration's prompt, decisive, and consistent response to 9/11. It drew on positions and objectives developed long before 9/11. The attacks, in that sense, were a catalyst—an opportunity to act on a policy direction that had been gestating before al-Qaeda existed. Among key steps in this direction were actively seeking regime change in Iraq and—in keeping with the view represented by Bernard Lewis—promoting far-reaching cultural change in the Middle East.

This was not initially understood by Richard Clarke, who after holding high office in the first Bush administration was kept on as Clinton's National Coordinator for Security, Infrastructure Protection and Counterterrorism and then retained in that capacity by George W. Bush. As the administration's crisis manager on September 11, Clarke was fully aware of the trail of evidence that established al-Qaeda's culpability before the end of the day. He was, therefore, astonished and dismayed upon attending his first high-level meeting in the early morning hours of September 12:

> I expected to go back to a round of meetings examining what the next attacks could be, what our vulnerabilities were, what we could do about them in the short term. Instead, I walked into a series of discussions about Iraq. At first I was incredulous that we were talking about something other than getting al-Qaeda. Then I realized with almost a sharp physical pain that Rumsfeld and Wolfowitz were going

> to try to take advantage of this national tragedy to promote their agenda about Iraq. Since the beginning of the administration, indeed well before, they had been pressing for a war with Iraq. My friends in the Pentagon had been telling me that the word was we would be invading Iraq sometime in 2002.[8]

Clarke would soon learn what James Mann later encapsulated so well when he indicated that 9/11 galvanized the administration, bringing to the fore its own intellectual resources and perspectives as never before:

> The internal logic was simple: Terrorism had emerged as America's principal security threat; terrorism arose primarily in the Middle East; therefore, "shaping the future security environment" meant transforming the entire politics and social fabric of the Middle East.[9]

The syllogism was clear, direct and, in the eyes of those who promoted it, compelling. Despite the discomfort of some ranking officials—such as Clarke, who would later resign in protest over what he saw as the administration's flawed approach to the war on terror—this "internal logic" effectively and securely underpinned the reaction envisaged by the G. W. Bush administration's leading figures within hours of 9/11. The logic's binding power was striking, holding fast throughout Bush's first term and well into his second.

It was, then, with remarkably little consideration or discussion that the active American response began to unfold—literally within hours of the attacks. What little attention was given to basic questions related mainly to whether military action should be taken against Iraq or Afghanistan. As Richard Clarke quickly discovered, the Department of Defense, represented by Rumsfeld and Wolfowitz, was initially inclined to favor targeting Iraq. Clarke and Secretary of State Colin Powell argued that no evidence linked Saddam Hussein to 9/11. They wanted military action against al-Qaeda's Taliban hosts in Afghanistan. According to *Washington Post* reporter Bob Woodward, it required only three days for the administration to decide that Afghanistan would be the immediate target while Iraq would be put off for the time being.[10] By then, Undersecretary of Defense for Policy Douglas Feith and a team of mid-level Pentagon planners had already started working on ways of "toppling the Taliban," a step which to them "seemed the obvious first priority."[11]

Events moved rapidly between October 2001 and December 2003. The Bush administration fought a war in Afghanistan; revamped America's long-standing policy on nuclear weapons use; invaded, defeated, and occupied Iraq; and embarked on an ambitious policy reorientation toward the Middle East.

On October 8, 2001, the United States launched its war on Afghanistan's regime. The Taliban government was finished before the end of November. A new Afghan Transitional Government under Hamid Karzai assumed office in late December.

Within less than a year, the administration was pushing the full-blown drive toward war with Iraq that culminated in the outbreak of hostilities in March 2003. By May, Bush could declare the end of major combat operations in Iraq. Saddam's monstrous regime was no more and the dictator himself would be captured in December 2003.

The two wars—and the open-ended struggle to sustain the ongoing occupation of Iraq—went far beyond simply establishing that a major part of America's War on Terror would be devoted to destroying governments that actually aided and abetted terrorist enemies of the United States, as well as those that seemed likely to do so.

The core rationale for the Bush administration's projection of force into Afghanistan and Iraq actually emerged in piecemeal fashion. Not until close to the end of 2003 would it be articulated in a public presidential statement. In the run up to that clarifying event, the administration worked its way through an embarrassingly large number of rationalizations for its military involvement in Iraq. None really worked. Initial claims of a preemptive basis on grounds of Saddam's alleged development of weapons of mass destruction foundered when no evidence was forthcoming to support the position even once U.S. forces controlled Iraq. There followed suggestions of long-term preemption, based on the notions that Saddam Hussein's Iraq would have somehow, someday menaced American interests and that Saddam's elimination would advance humanitarian, democratic values in the Middle East.[12] What remained inflexibly constant in the Bush administration's approach to Iraq and the rest of the world was its clear sense of moral certainty. American values, as Washington understood them, provided guidelines that could not be doubted. "Moral truth," Bush assured West Point's 2002 graduating class, "is the same in every culture, in every time, and in every place."[13]

The fundamental operative logic behind the administration's war on Iraq was made officially explicit in November 2003—once the persuasive power of various earlier explanations proved wanting. It came wrapped in clear ideological ribbons that made all too many who heard it dismiss the words as mere political rhetoric, the insubstantial terms of cosmetic public relations. They weren't. The president meant them and his commitment to the overall strategy they represented—that of seeking fundamental sociocultural-political change in the Middle East—was deep. His declaration, delivered in a November 2003 speech to the National Endowment for Democracy, a bipartisan private organization dedicated to the furtherance of democratic values, placed Iraq squarely at the center of U.S. plans for the Middle East:

> The failure of Iraqi democracy would embolden terrorists around the world, increase dangers to the American people, and extinguish the hopes of millions in the region. Iraqi democracy will succeed—and that success will send forth the news, from Damascus to Tehran—that freedom can be the future of every nation. The establishment of a free Iraq at the heart of the Middle East will be a watershed event in the global democratic revolution.[14]

Michael Hirsh, the incisive journalist who serves as senior editor at *Newsweek*'s Washington bureau, succinctly described the progression of military incursions from Afghanistan to Iraq:

> ... as the administration grappled with the pathology of the Arab World, a larger neoconservative agenda began to assert itself: Now was the time to "kick over the apple cart" in the Mideast. Invading Iraq, transforming it into a democracy and US ally, would in one bold stroke marginalize Saudi Arabia and its oil, force Riyadh to open up and discard its virulent brand of Islamism, do the same to Iran, and make Israel stronger.[15]

Hirsh also provided a very plausible explanation of the administration's lengthy endeavor to sell a variety of unsatisfying explanations of its Iraq policy: "One reason the administration had so much trouble justifying the shift to Iraq is that it could not admit to such a quasi-imperialist strategic vision."[16] By late 2003, with the death toll from the effort to occupy and pacify Iraq rising daily, there was little option left but to begin unwrapping the "quasi-imperialist strategic vision." Many of Washington's critics would balk at the qualifying "quasi" in that statement, insisting that George Bush's policy had become unabashedly focused on promoting global American hegemony. Support for their position came both from the administration's earlier modifications of long-standing U.S. nuclear policies and its subsequent launching of the much publicized "New Middle East Initiative."

In early March 2002 the *Los Angeles Times* published an article entitled "Secret Plan Outlines the Unthinkable." The piece claimed that "a secret policy review" by the Bush administration had advanced "chilling new contingencies for nuclear war."[17] The sober truth behind the story almost bore out the sensationalist headline. The newspaper's account was based on a leaked classified document—the Nuclear Posture Review (NPR)—the administration had submitted to Congress in early January. In essence, the NPR announced a new direction in U.S. nuclear policy. The critical new element permeating the document was its determined treatment of nuclear weapons as resources whose use, at various levels and in a variety of circumstances, could and should be considered. As UCLA economist and political scientist Michael Intriligator—notes, the NPR treated nuclear weapons "like other weapons with no sharp distinction from non-nuclear weapons." Intriligator finds the NPR to be a major pillar of "a new doctrine, the Bush Doctrine," which ends the strategic security system of the Cold War, "thus representing a discontinuous sea change."[18]

In concrete terms, the NPR unified U.S. military policy by linking "offensive strike systems" (both nuclear and non-nuclear) with defensive components and a "revitalized defense infrastructure that will provide new capabilities in a timely fashion to meet emerging threats."[19] Shorn of Defense Department jargon, the message was that this new triangular concept (a new "triad" in NPR's text) would rely on non-nuclear weapons and a flexible approach to nuclear weapons use to deal with new threats, including those posed by post-9/11 terrorists. The NPR specifically cited seven countries that were objects of nuclear strike contingency plans. These included Iraq, Iran, North Korea, Russia, China, Libya, and Syria. Coupled with George Bush's pledge on the night of September 11 to "make no distinction between terrorists... and those who harbor them," the NPR not only announced a far-reaching change in nuclear doctrine but also sought to prevent further, and worse, terrorist attacks. A major consequence of the leaked document could only have been to encourage other countries—and particularly those listed as potential nuclear targets—to use their own resources to protect the United States from terrorists bent on using weapons of mass destruction.

However, over and above this, the new doctrine generated consternation around the world, for it gave unambiguous notice that Washington viewed its nuclear arsenal as a resource whose use was not out of the question and which, as an integral part of American military power, would form part of the foundation upon which U.S. international goals would be pursued. In short, the administration was announcing a new readiness to put U.S. power, including nuclear power, at the service of its international agenda.

DEMOCRATIZING THE MIDDLE EAST

By late 2003, the Bush administration declared that a central feature of its commitment to the war on terror was to promote fundamental social and political change in the Middle East. The vehicle for this was to be the Greater Middle East Initiative (GMEI), a step designed to bring democracy to a region extending from Morocco to Afghanistan and including the Arab countries, Afghanistan, Turkey, and Pakistan. This bold and ambitious aim was heralded by the president in November when he spoke before the National Endowment for Democracy, a congressionally funded private organization dedicated to the worldwide promotion of democratic institutions.

Shortly after 9/11, Bush had promised a "crusade" against terrorism. It was a poor choice of words that did not go down well in the Middle East, where the Crusades are still bitterly remembered as a series of Western Christian invasions of Muslim lands. Although the White House quickly dropped the offending term from its lexicon, Bush's 2003 speech announcing what he called a new "forward strategy of freedom in the Middle East" rang with the messianic certainty of a true crusader. Equating freedom with democracy, the president found a solid link between Divine approval and practical earthly benefits. "Liberty is both the plan of Heaven for humanity, and the best hope for progress here on earth," he proclaimed.[20] The United States would strive to further democracy in the Middle East partly for ideological reasons ("We believe that liberty is the design of nature ... the direction of history") and partly out of sheer self-interest:

> As long as the Middle East remains a place where freedom does not flourish, it will remain a place of stagnation, resentment and violence ready for export. And with the spread of weapons that can bring catastrophic harm to any country ... it would be reckless to accept the status quo.[21]

In Bush's view, the mission—and it was a crusade—was clear: "The advance of freedom is the calling of our time; it is the calling of our country." As a clarion call for national commitment to a proactive policy of democratization in the Middle East, the speech was one of the best—possibly the best—he delivered during his first term. It was concise and straightforward, simultaneously lofty and practical. It also provided a plausible explanation of why America's terrorist enemies sprang from the Middle East and, therefore, of why America's national security required fundamental changes in the region. The problem, argued Bush, was not rooted in any "failures of a culture or a religion," but rather in "the failures of political and economic doctrines."[22] The antidemocratic structural conditions that had, in consequence, long prevailed in the Middle East created a "freedom deficit," which in turn underlay the "stagnation and resentment" that the president blamed for producing "violence ready for export."

Much of Bush's argument resounded with validity to anyone having the least familiarity with the contemporary Middle East, and particularly with the Arab World. Certainly, most governments in the area could not be accused of being either responsible or responsive to the needs of their people. Certainly, various forms of authoritarianism predominated, and along with them a general climate in which the rule of law and concepts of human rights suffered grievously. Certain, too, those same governments presided over societies in which poverty was rampant, the gap between rich and poor stark and widening, and opportunities for decent education and health care were available only to the affluent. Moreover, it simply could not be denied that these and other ills had indeed helped produce a societal miasma of long-standing, widespread, and profound "stagnation and resentment."

Yet, there were at least two glaring shortcomings in Bush's diagnosis of the Mid-East's malaise. One was that he severely downplayed the key roles of the

United States and other developed nations in fomenting the very conditions he decried. True, he did note that "sixty years of Western nations excusing and accommodating the lack of freedom in the Middle East did nothing to make us safe—because in the long run, stability cannot be purchased at the expense of liberty."[23] The truth, however, is much sharper. For much longer than sixty years (indeed, since the Ottoman Empire's collapse in World War I), a combination of strategic and economic interests led the West not just to "excuse" and "accommodate" the region's authoritarian rulers but actually to sponsor their creation and actively work for their survival. This clientalistic pattern, while congenial to Western interests, inevitably linked the West to the limited, closed interests of local ruling elites—and just as inevitably placed the West in opposition to the broader interests of the area's downtrodden masses.

Failure to give due weight to the responsibility that non-Middle Eastern actors bear for the region's current ills necessarily leads to an exaggerated and unhelpful emphasis on the supposed internal dynamics of Middle East societies as the underlying force behind the area's sorry condition. If blame cannot be assigned to the region's dominant religion or culture—the argument runs—then surely it must lie in traits of "national character" or, at least, in national styles and patterns of leadership. In all cases, the shameful sociopolitical realities that marked the Middle East by the twenty-first century are seen as ultimately explicable by some factor, or combination of factors, peculiar to the peoples of the area. Clinging to such an outlook brands the Middle East and those who inhabit it as somehow unique, exceptions to the "normal" patterns of human social behavior. For some, this may be a comforting perspective from which to view terrorism in the post-9/11 world. It is not one that is likely to further an understanding of the phenomenon.

The second feature of Bush's 2003 speech that had to be questioned was the ease with which he singled out democracy as the remedy for the Middle East problem and the vehicle for global peace. Few could disagree with the president's assertion that "for too long, many people [in the Middle East] have been victims and subjects. They deserve to be active citizens." Fewer still would question his argument that repressive and unresponsive governments had produced vast reservoirs of bitterness and resentment. What was, however, questionable, was whether Bush's prescription—democracy—was as feasible as he seemed to believe. Noting that observers had often questioned "whether this country, or that people, or this group are 'ready' for democracy," Bush roundly rejected such doubts. Instead, he asserted, "it is the practice of democracy that makes a nation ready for democracy and every nation can start on this path."

Yet, Bush immediately cast doubt on his own optimism by insisting that while democratic governments "will reflect their own cultures," they will also exhibit common "essential principles." He outlined the latter by reciting a list of legal and institutional desiderata: "rule of law"; "healthy civic institutions"; "political parties"; "labor unions"; "independent newspapers"; "religious liberty"; and "... rights of women." Afghanistan and Iraq, Bush proudly proclaimed, were now nations "where these vital principles are being applied."

And there, of course, was the rub. The real question was, and remains, whether the institutional and legal characteristics of a democratic polity can be erected and sustained in any society or, on the other hand, are there certain sociocultural prerequisites for the successful establishment and survival of democratic systems such as Bush outlined?

It is possible to make a plausible argument that democratic institutions and processes must, if they are to be stable, rest on a framework of generally accepted values that are conducive to the trade-offs of power, limitations on governmental authority, and tolerance of opposing views upon which democratic systems depend. Put this way, political culture can be seen as the basis of democratic political systems, and it becomes necessary to ask whether all cultures can sustain that form of government.

Is the Arab World unsuitable for the development of democratic institutions? Bush strongly denied the claim that the Arabs or Islam are inherently unsupportive of democratic practices: "There is a notion that certain people can't self-govern; certain religions don't have the capacity of self-government.... And I refuse to accept that view."[24]

The president's position evaded the real question. The issue is not whether the Arabs or Islam per se are inimical to democratic development. It is whether democracy can flourish in societies where a predominant section of the population approaches politics on the basis of transcendental beliefs, whether these are linked to religious or secular absolute consummatory value-systems.

A few examples underscore the problem. It must be recalled that the United States itself experiences a constant tension between those approaching politics within consummatory, or transcendental, absolute frameworks and those who do so on the basis of secular, probabilistic frameworks. The heated controversies over abortion, stem cell research, and gay rights in the United States are only some of the more prominent examples that come to mind. So far, the probabilistic outlook has generally managed to prevail. Much the same holds true for other long-established Western democracies. On the other hand, the problems confronted by various countries whose democratic traditions are far more recent have repeatedly underscored the fragility of democratic government. The classic example, of course, is the fate of Germany's Weimar Republic—erected in 1919 on a constitutional foundation that made it (on paper) the most democratically liberal country of its day. After fourteen years of constant domestic challenge, German citizens succumbed to the secular consummatory message of National Socialism and brought Hitler to power. In more modern times, the challenges facing the democratic systems of Turkey, Israel, and India repeatedly remind us that the injection of absolutist ideologies threatens democratic processes.

The Bush administration's desire to press forward with a democratizing campaign focused on the Arab World was not diminished by the lack of local enthusiasm that greeted its Greater Middle East Initiative (GMEI). In early 2004, the administration forwarded a set of "guidelines for coordinating efforts by the United States and other members of the G-8 [the eight leading industrialized nations of the world] to promote political and economic reform in the 'Greater Middle East.'"[25] Washington hoped this would form the basis of a joint democratization project that could be announced at the G-8 Summit meeting scheduled to be held in June at Sea Island, a resort off the coast of Georgia.

While much of the draft guidelines simply called for a continuation of policies already followed by G-8 members, three points generated a furious reaction from Arab governments when the proposal was leaked in February. Taken together, the offending elements were seen by Arab regimes not only as the core of the GMEI but also as designed to establish direct links between G-8 countries and local populations in order to pressure Middle East governments into democratizing reforms. What specifically provoked official Arab ire were the suggestions that G-8 countries increase "direct funding to democracy, human rights, media, women's and other NGOs in the region"; that they should "encourage the region's governments to allow civil society organizations, including human rights and media NGOs to operate freely without restrictions"; and, finally, that G-8 members "fund an NGO that would bring together legal and media experts from the region to draft annual assessments of judicial reform efforts or media freedom in the region."[26]

Two leading students of democracy's prospects in the Middle East, Marina Ottaway and Thomas Carothers, point out that the GMEI's commitment to "transform the region politically, economically and socially" was intended as a "vital, visionary complement to the war on terror," and that the entire conceptual package was initially widely seen within the Bush administration as modeled on the Helsinki Process that had helped boost Eastern European liberal forces in the Soviet Union's waning years.[27] Launched in 1972, the drawn-out Helsinki negotiations culminated in the West's formal recognition of post-World War II international borders in Eastern Europe and of the Soviet Union's presence in the area. In return, the USSR agreed to the liberalization of flows of people and information in Warsaw Pact countries. The Helsinki Accords also provided for periodic public reviews of compliance. "Over the next fifteen years," note Ottaway and Carothers, "the Helsinki Accords turned into an important tool through which the United States and Western Europe pressured the Warsaw Pact countries to improve their human rights records and move slowly toward political reform."[28]

These same scholars underscore a basic flaw in hopes that the Helsinki model provided a paradigm for the GMEI. The former, they stress, was grounded in reciprocity: the Soviet Union won security guarantees in Eastern Europe while the West won the softer, but important, prize of freer access to the region, along with an acknowledgment in principle of the validity of key Western values.

In contrast, the GMEI offered no trade-off to existing Arab regimes. Nowhere was this more evident than in regard to their existing security concerns. These, of course, hinged on Israel and the Palestine problem, issues that the Bush administration was determined to keep separate from its campaign to alter the sociopolitical sinews of the Arab World. In short, the original GMEI did no more than offer the region's authoritarian governments the prospect of setting in motion dynamics that could lead to their own demise. The dilemma of seeking democratization under the auspices of such regimes remained exactly as described by the perceptive Egyptian political scientist, Mustapha al-Sayyid, more than a decade ago:

> Ruling groups that currently hold the reins of government are probably the most influential actors.... They are not likely to undertake any initiative that would obviously jeopardize their hold on power.[29]

Not surprisingly, then, Arab reaction was intensely negative when news of the Greater Middle East Initiative leaked in early 2004. Washington's closest Arab allies were in the forefront of the outcry against what was immediately branded a crass proposal to meddle in internal Arab affairs. In Cairo, Egyptian President Hosni Mubarak thundered "Whoever imagines that it is possible to impose solutions or reform from abroad on any society or region is delusional."[30] He and Jordan's King Abdallah rushed off to Europe to persuade G-8 members of the Arabs' case. Saudi Arabia's Foreign Minister, Prince Saud al-Feisal, scathingly (and revealingly) commented on the supposed parallel to the Helsinki Process:

> The results on the Soviet Union we all know. It was broken up, its people suffered deprivations, its people [were] the unhappiest people for at least two decades. So if this is presented as a lure to Arab countries, we really don't see much of a lure in the Helsinki Accords.[31]

A high Arab League official pointed sharply to the lack of reciprocity in a proposal that was designed to further U.S. security by aiding the war on terrorism:

> It is unacceptable to speak of any initiative or vision which ignores... the Palestinian cause... and to discuss security considerations without speaking of Israeli weapons of mass destruction.[32]

Faced by this fierce Arab reaction, as well as by considerable European skepticism over its proposed approach, Washington revised the initial GMEI guidelines. The new version amounted to a considerably watered-down suggestion for a common front in support of Middle East democratization. The result was visible at the June 2004 G-8 Summit at Sea Island, which produced what became known as the Broader Middle East and North African Initiative (BMENAI). The final product dropped any idea of the G-8 bypassing local governments to work directly with civil society groups. It also abandoned the notion of funding an NGO to monitor political reform. Moreover, it not only pledged that G-8 support for reform in the region would "go hand in hand with support for a just, comprehensive and lasting settlement to the Arab-Israeli conflict" but also acknowledged that "change should not and cannot be imposed from outside" and that "each society will reach its own conclusions about the scope and pace of change."[33]

Critics of the switch in Washington's drive for Middle East democratization were vocal. Ottaway and Carothers concluded that by taking "a soft-edged approach to promoting change in the Middle East, the administration has ended up with an initiative that is hollow at the core." In their view, "soft" approaches simply would not work

> ... in situations where entrenched power elites are determined to hold onto power and only interested in cosmetic reforms.... In such situations, which prevail in most of the Arab World, the central problem is... the absence of any real interest or will on the part of powerholders to carry out changes that will threaten their own powers.[34]

On the other hand, not all observers were so gloomy. Noting that in the wake of the leak of Washington's original GMEI proposal many Arab governments had sought to forestall the move toward foreign pressure by embarking on a variety of liberalizing steps and declarations of intent, some analysts argued that the whole affair had forced a fruitful internal reevaluation in the Arab World:

> ... the increasingly public and fertile discussion of reform across the region strongly suggests that liberals in the Arab World, long resigned to working within their flawed systems, are increasingly claiming an independent voice....[35]

Has the Bush administration's campaign for Middle East democratization led to a situation in which authoritarian regimes will once again tinker with no more than cosmetic reforms that ensure their holds on power, or will it unleash dynamics that will promote democratic development and thereby undermine the terrorist threat to the United States? The jury is still out on that one, and is likely to remain so for some years to come. Still, the most probable outcome is the former. While Washington's prescription for the Arab World therefore remains highly doubtful, what is far more certain is that the Bush administration did not err in identifying the stifling and oppressive conditions characterizing the region's political life as largely responsible for the terrorist challenge it confronts.

ASSESSING THE RESPONSE TO 9/11: THE LIMITS OF DISCOURSE

George W. Bush was reelected to the presidency in November 2004. By then, many might have found cause for worried dismay over the U.S. reaction to 9/11. On the one hand, the sweeping characterization of the enemy as no more than malevolent "terrorists" frothing at the mouth for American blood dominated most public discourse—and held no promise of an intelligent understanding of, and therefore defense against, those who would attack the country. On the other hand, and utterly amazingly, were opposing voices, raucously raised in the public forum, purveying the message that no terrorist threat existed. At times, the entire tenor of popular public reflection on 9/11 seemed almost surreal.

The national elections of 2004 should have provided some relief. They did not. The Democrats might have been expected to challenge the Bush administration's understanding of the causes of 9/11, the implications of 9/11, and the long-term meaning of 9/11 for American security but they didn't. Instead, the Democratic presidential candidate, John Kerry, packaged his case against the incumbent in tactical issues. Was the war in Iraq being correctly pursued? No, Kerry didn't think so. Should Washington do more to enlist its European allies in its War on Terrorism? Yes, Kerry thought so. Could the United States be better prepared against future terrorist attacks? Oh yes, Kerry was sure it could. What was missing were the deep and serious questions: had the United States so far correctly appraised the causes of the 9/11 attacks? Was the U.S. response congruent with, or moving toward congruence with, those causes? What were the requirements of long-term American security?

Although these questions did not become major issues in the 2004 presidential campaigns, basic aspects of the Bush administration's interpretation of 9/11 were soon challenged—not by leading spokespersons of the Democratic Party, but by members of the country's intellectual, scholarly, and public service communities. A look at a few of the more important works illustrates the range of reservations that generated opposition to the administration's reaction to 9/11

The late writer Susan Sontag was one of the first to place an oppositional voice in print. In a piece published by *The New Yorker* less than two weeks after the September 11 attacks, she bitterly criticized what she termed the "self-righteous drivel and outright deceptions being peddled by public figures and TV commentators." Sontag insisted that what was needed was "a lot of thinking" to understand the attacks and the "options available to American foreign policy." Instead, she charged, the reaction to 9/11 had become dominated by "reality-concealing rhetoric." In her view, the attacks were "undertaken as a consequence of specific American alliances and actions." Perhaps what most disturbed many people, however, was the scorn she heaped upon what had already become the common habit of branding the attackers "cowards":

> . . . if the word "cowardly" is to be used, it might be more aptly applied to those who kill from beyond the range of retaliation, high in the sky, than to those willing to die themselves in order to kill others. In the matter of courage (a morally neutral virtue): whatever maybe said of the perpetrators of Tuesday's slaughter, they were not cowards.[36]

Later, as the drive to war against Saddam Hussein's regime gained irreversible momentum, another major literary figure, Norman Mailer, attacked the administration's post-9/11 stand. In Mailer's view, the administration was guided by "Flag-Conservatism," an ideology he saw as combining America's Christian ethos with its national admiration for successful economic competitiveness: "Jesus and Evel Knievel."[37] Mailer argued that Washington's real objective was "world empire." He sought to explain the administration's foreign policy, and particularly its eagerness for war with Iraq, as consistent with both Flag-Conservatism's premises and view of contemporary American society. "Flag conservatism," he wrote, "is not madness but an undisclosed logic":

> From a militant Christian point of view, America is close to rotten. The entertainment media are loose. Bare belly-buttons pop onto every TV screen . . . . The kids are getting to the point where they can't read, but they sure can screw. One perk for the White House, therefore should America become an international military machine huge enough to conquer all adversaries, is that American sexual freedom, all that gay, feminist, lesbian, transvestite hullabaloo, will be seen as too much of a luxury and be put back in the closet. Commitment, patriotism, and dedication will become all-pervasive national values again (with all the hypocrisy attendant). Once we become a twenty-first century embodiment of the old Roman Empire, moral reform can stride right back into the picture.[38]

Some time earlier, the MIT-based academic Noam Chomsky, who is part polemicist, part scholar, and fully America's best known gadfly, also lambasted the dominant American outlook. Unlike Mailer, Chomsky did not see the problem as rooted in the particular ideology of the Bush administration. Instead, he found it in the enduring nature of America's presence on the world stage: "the U.S. is a leading terrorist state, as are its clients."[39] His case rested on a litany of examples of U.S.-linked violence in third world countries over the past four decades, ranging from peasant massacres in Indonesia, to the Contra's campaign in Nicaragua, to CIA-promoted car bombings in Beirut. Although noting that "nothing can justify crimes such as those of September 11," Chomsky concluded that the United States was not an "innocent victim," and that the 9/11 attacks were "indirectly" consequences of the terrorist nature of U.S. foreign policy.[40]

Chalmers Johnson, a respected specialist in Asian affairs and international relations who is now retired from the University of California, produced a carefully documented book charging that U.S. foreign policy had metamorphosed into a conscious pursuit of world empire well before 9/11: "The terrorist attacks of 9/11, the war against the Taliban, and Bush's 'war on terror,' merely provided further impetus for a plan that had been in the works for at least a decade."[41] Johnson's focus was global, not limited to the Middle East. His conclusions hinged on an analysis of the nature and implications of the worldwide expansion of U.S. military power in the latter half of the twentieth century and, particularly, since the Soviet Union's collapse. Unlike Mailer, Johnson did not attribute the basic force behind the search for empire to the conservative outlook prevailing under the Bush administration. While not discounting the force of ideology, he argued that U.S. imperial ambitions were the outgrowth of militarism, "the phenomenon by which a nation's armed services come to put their institutional preservation ahead of achieving national security or even a commitment to the integrity of the governmental structure of which they are a part."[42] In short, Johnson maintained that decades of growth of the American military establishment and that process' concomitant impact on the economic, social, political, and ideological foundations of the United States had forged a deeply rooted structural tendency toward world empire. This tendency was whipped into a full-blown drive by recent events, "the advent of the George W. Bush administration and . . . the assaults of September 11, 2001."[43]

Johnson's final assessment was gloomy. Having mounted "the Napoleonic tiger," the problem was "could we . . . ever dismount."[44] If not, he warned, the future would be "a state of perpetual war, leading to more terrorism against Americans wherever they may be and a growing reliance on weapons of mass destruction among smaller nations as they try to ward off the imperial juggernaut."[45] He saw only a small hope of escaping this fate:

> There is one development that could conceivably stop this process of overreaching: the people could retake control of Congress, reform it along with the corrupted elections laws that have made it into a forum for special interests, turn it into a genuine assembly of democratic representatives, and cut off the supply of money to the Pentagon and the secret intelligence agencies. We have a strong civil society that

> could, in theory, overcome the entrenched interests of the military-industrial complex. At this late date, however, it is difficult to imagine how Congress, much like the Roman Senate in the last days of the republic, could be brought back to life and cleansed of its endemic corruption. Failing such a reform, Nemesis, the goddess of retribution and vengeance, the punisher of pride and hubris, waits impatiently for her meeting with us.[46]

Zbigniew Brzezinski, the prominent academic who served as President Jimmy Carter's National Security Adviser, also issued a dire admonition, this time against relying on unilateral power to cope with the post-9/11 world: "A fortress on a hill can only stand alone, casting a menacing shadow over all beneath... [it] would become the focus of global hatred."[47] Brzezinski too was not prepared to accept the view that the terrorist assault on the United States sprang from the inherent malevolence of evil men. Instead, he saw it as part of the context of a historical development: "the massive worldwide political awakening of mankind and its intensifying awareness of intolerable disparities in the human condition."[48] In terms reminiscent of Clinton's allusion to "the dark side of global interdependence," he portrayed "global turmoil" as the threatening consequence of globalization's negative features, and implicitly castigated the Bush administration for a simplistic myopia that failed to perceive this:

> Recognition of global turmoil as the basic challenge of our time requires confronting complexity. That is the weakness of the issue insofar as the American political scene is concerned. It does not lend itself to sloganeering or rouse the American people as viscerally as terrorism. It is more difficult to personalize without a demonic figure like Osama bin Laden. Nor is it congenial to self-gratifying proclamations of an epic confrontation between good and evil on the model of the titanic struggles with Nazism and Communism.[49]

Brzezinski was especially critical of the administration's approach to national security. 9/11, he wrote, had exacerbated an ongoing debate that arose as the United States emerged as the world's sole superpower. The point at issue was whether the United States would "engage in a gradual, carefully managed transformation of its own supremacy into a self-sustaining international system, or... rely primarily on its own national power to insulate itself from the international anarchy that would follow its disengagement."[50] Brzezinski argued that Washington's unilateralist bent threatened to isolate the United States and undermine its security. He saw post-9/11 pressures for a new approach to the Middle East independent from America's traditional Western allies as particularly insidious:

> The terrorist strike of 9/11 has created the opening for those who feel strongly that the states that are somehow in conflict with Muslims—be they Russia, China, Israel, or India—should somehow now be viewed as America's natural and primary partners. Some even argue that America's goal should be to reorder the Middle East, using America's power in the name of democracy to subordinate the Arab states to its will, to eliminate Islamic radicalism, and to make the region safe for Israel. That perception is shared domestically in America by various right-wing neoconservative, and religiously fundamentalist groups. Fear of terrorism gives this orientation a powerful public appeal.[51]

Brzezinski's analysis of America's current options sprang from his historical perspective. History, he indicated, teaches that all dominant powers eventually decline, and the same will be true of the United States. The United States can either try to prolong its global predominance by imposing conditions on the rest of the world or, alternatively, it can encourage others to share U.S. interests in creating the international system's next phase. The former choice risks turning the United States into "a fortress on a hill." The latter offers the prospect of positive action to mold the international environment in ways congenial to the most enduring American values. In either case, Brzezinski's message indicated, a major problem in international politics will be to cope with globalization as a phenomenon having a deep "moral dimension."[52]

Critical books by two officials who served under the Bush administration captured much of the reading public's attention. Richard Clarke was Bush's Coordinator for Security, Infrastructure Protection and Counterterrorism until March 2003, when he resigned. In 2004, he published *Against All Enemies: Inside America's War on Terror*.[53] Clarke focused his most bitter criticisms of the administration's response to 9/11 on the decision to go to invade Iraq, "a completely unnecessary tangent."[54] Saddam Hussein's regime, he argued, had no vital connection with al-Qaeda, and by attacking Iraq, the United States had done just what

> ... al Qaeda said we would do. We invaded and occupied an oil-rich Arab country that posed no threat to us, while paying no attention to the Israeli-Palestinian problem. We delivered to al Qaeda the greatest recruitment propaganda imaginable and made it difficult for friendly Islamic governments to be seen working closely with us.[55]

Rather than enhance U.S. security, the Iraq war, he argued, undermined it:

> in fact, with our Army stretched to the breaking point, our international credibility at an all-time low, Muslims further radicalized

> against us, our relations with key Allies damaged, and our soldiers in a shooting gallery, it is hard to believe that America is safer. . . .[56]

Moreover, Clarke held that the objective of the administration's campaign against al-Qaeda, to seek out and eliminate Osama bin Laden and its other leaders, held no promise of victory over America's terrorist enemies. He recalled that, as portrayed in the film *The Battle of Algiers*, that strategy had failed the French, and he suggested another approach he felt would be more fruitful:

> We are likely to face the same situation with al Qaeda [as the French faced in Algeria]. The only way to stop it is to work with leaders of Islamic nations to insure that tolerance of other religions is taught again, that their people believe they have fair opportunities to participate in government and the economy, that the social and cultural conditions that breed hatred are bred out.[57]

Clarke's overall appraisal of the administration's performance in the face of 9/11 was caustic:

> The nation needed thoughtful leadership to deal with the underlying problems 9/11 reflected: a radical deviant Islamist ideology on the rise, real security vulnerabilities in the highly integrated global civilization. Instead, America got unthinking reactions, ham-handed responses, and a rejection of analysis in favor of received wisdom. It has left us less secure.[58]

American readers were also exposed to a book, *Imperial Hubris: Why the West is Losing the War on Terror*, whose romantically vague authorship ensured it would win attention.[59] It was a resounding critique of the war on terror, anonymously penned by someone described on its jacket as "a senior U.S. intelligence officer with nearly two decades of experience in national security issues related to Afghanistan and South Asia." The press soon identified the author as Michael Scheuer, a ranking CIA analyst who since 1996 had directed a secret unit charged with tracking Osama bin Laden. Scheuer's book, published with CIA approval, was both a plea for victory in the war signified by 9/11 and an unadulterated condemnation of the American reaction to that attack. The book's central message was that neither the American government nor public had yet understood the nature of the war they were fighting and, consequently, the enemy was winning. It decried the prevailing view of Osama bin Laden and his cohorts as bloodthirsty evildoers, describing them instead as motived by "love," deep and sincere love of their God, their religion, and their fellow Muslims. It was, the author argued, a love reciprocated by millions in the Muslim world who saw 9/11 as a heroic defensive measure against long-standing U.S. led aggression on the Islamic World. *Imperial Hubris* maintained that bin Laden and his followers, impelled by sincere religious conviction to defend any attack on the lands or peoples of Islam, were not waging war on the United States because of its values or lifestyles, but rather because of its actions. The goals of Washington's antagonists were broad, but not unlimited, and had nothing to do with Americans' pursuit of their own way of life within their own borders.

> The Islamists in Al Qaeda, in other similar groups and ordinary Muslims worldwide have been infected by U.S. policies toward the Muslim world. America's support for Israel, Russia, China, India, Algeria, Uzbekistan and others; its protection of multiple Muslim tyrannies; its efforts to control oil policy and pricing; and its military activities in Afghanistan, Iraq the Arabian Peninsula, and elsewhere—these are the sources of hatred spreading in the Islamic world.

Washington, its leaders, analysts, and pundits alike, have failed to recognize, or to admit, that such policies have provoked not "terrorism" but a widely spread Islamic insurrection that seriously threatens the United States. The author argued that, despite declarations to the contrary, America's leaders were not fighting a "war." Instead, the campaign against terrorisim was largely being pursued as a law-enforcement activity, an approach promising only defeat. He put the blame for this on a self-serving hubris that refused to see that all evidence pointed to sincerity and commitment on the part of bin Laden and his supporters, rather than to uncontrollable hatred and malevolence. This blindness, he said, is the result of an inability to accept or understand the mind-set of the enemy, which is rooted in both hatred and "a counterintuitive reality."[60] The author approvingly noted that some analyses of bin Laden had not lapsed into the more common mode of making him out to be a bloodthirsty madman but have, instead, portrayed him "as an innovative military man and warrior CEO." These, he said, are closer to an accurate, useable estimate of the man but still miss the "key element" that makes bin Laden "much more than just an intelligent soldier and a formidable CEO." What is missing is recognition of the "religious piety and faith" driving bin Laden and his followers. Western observers have failed to accord this very visible element the seriousness it deserves because they are too modern to bring themselves to believe that notions of "counterintuitive reality" can have such motivational power. Thus, much of Washington's reaction to 9/11 has futilely aimed at promoting an Islamic Reformation:

> Surely, we have concluded, if we drive and manage an Islamic Reformation that makes Muslims secular like us, all this unfortunate,

> nonsensical talk about religious war will end and Muslims will be eager to keep God in the same kind of narrow locker in which the West is slowly asphyxiating Him.[61]

In the view expressed by "Anonymous," the administration's failure to understand that it was not fighting terrorists but rather a growing generalized Islamic insurgency, along with its failure to understand the motivational wellsprings of that movement, led to very counterproductive measures. The invasion of Iraq was a "gift" to al-Qaeda, adding to the long list what Muslims have long perceived as anti-Islamic measures. He offered the following structural sketch of the insurrection that is fueled:

> It is . . . the Muslim perception that the things they love are being intentionally destroyed by America that engenders Islamist hatred toward the United States, and that simultaneously motivates a few Muslims to act alone and attack US interests; a great many more to join organizations like al Qaeda and its allies; and massive numbers to support those organizations' defensive military actions with prayers, donations, blind eyes or logistical assistance.[62]

The driving purpose behind the analysis presented by "Anonymous" was not an effort to condone America's Muslim enemies. It was, instead, designed "purely to ensure that America is prepared to defend itself."[63] The country, he said, "is in a war for survival . . . in terms of keeping the ability to live as we want, not as we must."[64] He ominously proclaimed that "nobody should be surprised when bin Laden and al Qaeda detonate a weapon of mass destruction in the United States."[65]

The critique of Washington's post-9/11 policies presented in *Imperial Hubris* was total and unrelenting. The Afghanistan War had been bungled, the Iraq War was totally unnecessary and wasteful. Both ventures had strengthened, not weakened, the Islamic insurgency. America's longstanding policies toward Islamic lands and peoples had given credibility to bin Laden's claims that the United States was attacking Islam. Regarding the last point, the author referred to Chechnya and Kashmir, among other places, as well as to U.S. support of authoritarian regimes throughout the Arab World. But he devoted most attention to America's relationship with Israel as a phenomenon lending plausibility to al-Qaeda's interpretation of U.S. intentions:

> Surely there can be no other example of a faraway, theocracy in-all-but-name of only about six million people that ultimately controls the extent and even the occurrence of an important portion of political discourse and national security debate in a country of 270-plus million people that prides itself on religious toleration, separation of church

> and state, and freedom of speech. In a nation that long ago rejected an established church as inimical to democratic society, Washington yearly pumps more than three billion taxpayer dollars into a nation that defiantly proclaims itself "the Jewish state" and a democracy—claims hard to reconcile with its treatment of Muslims in Israel, its limitations on political choice for those in the occupied territories, and the eternal exile it has enforced on those camped in the refugee diaspora across the Levant. At the UN and other international fora, the U.S. government stands four-square, and often alone, with Israel to free it from obeying UN resolutions and non-proliferation treaties; with US backing, Israel has developed and deployed weapons of mass destruction at the pace it desires. Objectively, al Qaeda does not seem too far off the mark when it describes the U.S.-Israel relationship as a detriment.

"Anonymous" did not disguise his hope that the United States would modify or abandon the policies that had inflamed the Islamic world. At a minimum, he argued, they should be rethought and debated in order "to begin a process toward something which America has lacked since the end of the Cold War: a clear definition of the national interest."[66] His own preference was drawn from the traditional conservative American outlook. Foreign policy should be strictly tailored to securing clear national interests; it should eschew missionary-like or altruistic campaigns:

> ... can it be proven that it would make a substantive—vice emotional—difference to U.S. security if every Hutu killed every Tutsi, or vice versa; every Palestinian killed every Israeli or vice versa; or if Serbs, Croats, and Bosnians exterminated each other to the last person? The brutal but correct answers are: we do not understand these conflicts, and none of them, regardless of who wins, endanger U.S. interests. All evoke empathy and stir emotion, but it is, as always, a cruel world, and each nation's one mandatory duty is to care for and defend itself.[67]

If, on the other hand, America should choose to retain its current set of foreign policies toward the Islamic world, it must—in the interest of its own survival—abandon its phony war on terrorism and fight a real one. The current combination of a law enforcement approach and a political effort to promote democracy in the Middle East will not work. Unless and until policy shifts occur, the author argued, the United States must accept that its struggle with al-Qaeda is "a plain old war" and act accordingly. We must accept, he maintains, that such a war, like all wars, will entail much bloodshed and destruction.

> Killing in large numbers is not enough to defeat our Muslim foes. With killing must come a Sherman-like razing of infrastructure. Roads and irrigation systems; bridges, powerplants and crops in the field; fertilizer plants and grain mills—all these and more will need to be destroyed to deny the enemy its support base. Land mines, moreover, will be massively reintroduced to seal borders and mountain passes too long, high or numerous to close with US soldiers... such actions will yield large civilian casualties, displaced populations, and refugee flows... this sort of bloody-mindedness is neither admirable nor desirable, but it will remain America's only option so long as she stands by her failed policies toward the Muslim world.[68]

In any case, asserted "Anonymous," there is no real option just now. For the moment at least, the enemy "wants war" and America has "no choice but to fight; it is the decision about policy that will determine the fight's length and cost."[69] And so long as America has to fight, he argued, it must escalate its military activity:

> Victory... lies in a yet undetermined mix of stronger military actions and dramatic foreign policy change; neither will suffice alone. Defeat for America... lies in the military and foreign policy *status quo* and the belief that our Islamic foes will be talked out of hating us and disappear if only we can teach them voting procedures, political pluralism, feminism, and the separation of church and state.[70]

The foregoing brief summaries of some of the more thoughtful and challenging expressions of opposition to the Bush administration's pursuit of the war on terror are merely illustrative. They show that these—along with other works not mentioned here—pointed to serious and sometimes profound grounds for questioning the nature, effectiveness, and purpose of Washington's chosen path. Ideally, such ideas should have provoked extensive discussion and debate. They did not, an outcome that can partly be attributed to the print media—books and intellectual articles—through which they were transmitted. While some—Chomsky's small book, *9/11*, and the books by Clarke and "Anonymous"—achieved significant sales among the reading public, that in itself reveals a drawback in contemporary America's political life. The "reading public" in the United States is not a significant portion of the wider society, and its standing continues to decline at an increasing rate. In the summer of 2004, the National Endowment for the Arts released the results of a study of American literary reading habits conducted by its research division. It was, noted NEA Chairman Dana Giola, not a report that the NEA was happy to issue.[71] It showed that "for the first time in modern history, less than half of the adult population now reads literature, and these trends reflect a larger decline in other sorts of reading. The report, he went on, reflected "our society's massive shift toward electronic media for entertainment and *information*" (emphasis added). Giola underlined the political implications of the accelerating decline in reading:

> ... print culture affords irreplaceable forms of focused attention and contemplation that make complex communications and insights possible. To lose such intellectual capability... would constitute a vast cultural impoverishment.
>
> ... The decline in reading, therefore, parallels a larger retreat from participation in civic and cultural life. The long-term implications of this study, therefore, not only affect literature but all the arts—as well as social activities... and even political engagement.[72]

Another reason why dissenting views failed to provoke wide discussion in the United States undoubtedly had to do with the post-9/11 development of a decidedly unreceptive climate in the public forum. The case of a tenured professor at the University of Colorado speaks volumes about why academics (tenured and untenured alike) may have preferred not to speak out on basic questions raised by 9/11. Given that the halls of academe are, theoretically, designed to house gadflies and other pesky nonconformists in hope that they will occasionally prod the broader society toward useful insights, a significant national resource may have been cowed.

Ward Churchill chaired the Department of Ethnic Studies at the University of Colorado when he was invited to deliver a lecture at Hamilton College in Clinton, New York. The talk was to be given in early February 2005. Some two months prior to the scheduled event a member of Hamilton College's faculty drew attention to an article Churchill wrote shortly after 9/11. An immediate uproar ensued, with significant numbers of voices demanding that Churchill's invitation be cancelled. Hamilton College initially sought a compromise. It tried, reported its president, "to alter the event by designing a panel discussion to include two Hamilton faculty members, so as to make certain that Mr. Churchill's views on 9/11 would be confronted."[73] Despite this, the anti-Churchill pressures mounted. Various media stories, including "several hostile segments on 'The O'Reilly Factor,'... led to more than 8000 e-mails and hundreds of phone calls to me and others at the College," said Hamilton's president.[74] By the end of January, Hamilton officials learned that Churchill had received "100 threats of violence." The college received similar calls, "with one person threatening to bring a gun to the event."[75] Hamilton College understandably decided that its first priority had to be "the safety and security of our students, faculty staff and the community in which we live." Churchill's appearance was cancelled.[76]

The University of Colorado was not offended by the treatment to which this tenured member of its own faculty was being subjected. On the contrary, the University of Colorado College Republicans organized a rally in opposition to Professor Ward Churchill. Nobody held a counterrally.

The Governor of Colorado, Bill Owens, decided it was appropriate for the state to take a strong position on the issue. He sent a congratulatory letter to the rally, offered his own critique of Churchill's work, and suggested that Churchill look for another job:

> I applaud every person on the University of Colorado campus who has come to speak out against the indecent, insensitive and inappropriate comments and writings of Ward Churchill.
>
> All decent people, whether Republican, Democrat, liberal or conservative, should denounce the views of Ward Churchill...
>
> No one wants to infringe on Mr. Churchill's right to express himself. But we are not compelled to accept his pro-terrorist views at state taxpayer subsidy nor under the banner of the University of Colorado. Ward Churchill besmirches the University....
>
> His resignation as chairman of the Ethnic Studies Department was a good first step. We hope that he will follow this step by resigning his position on the faculty of the University of Colorado.[77]

Owens' reference to the end of Churchill's chairmanship was correct. The furor had already caused the professor to take that step, which reportedly entailed a $20,000 drop in salary.[78] But this was hardly the end of the professor's troubles. Colorado's House of Representatives passed a resolution condemning Churchill because his article "strikes an evil and inflammatory blow against America's healing process." Colorado's Senate later passed an identical resolution.[79] Meanwhile, the University of Colorado also started to act on the case. "As a first step toward possibly firing him," reported the *Chronicle of Higher Education*, the institution's interim chancellor and two deans would "review the work of the professor."[80] A special meeting of UC's Board of Regents was convened to discuss the issue. The board approved the proposed investigation but left little doubt of its inclination toward prejudgement. Before the meeting ended, the Regents said that Churchill's published views had "brought dishonor" to the university and that the board wanted to "apologize to all Americans."[81]

Churchill had few defenders, or at any rate none whose voices achieved prominence.[82] Hamilton College President Joan Hinde Stewart explained her decision to cancel his appearance by proclaiming that "even as the threats of violence are abhorrent, the outcry concerning Mr. Churchill's deplorable statements concerning the victims of 9/11 is understandable."[83] The American Association of University Professors opted for a detached stand upon which to base its principled position. It proclaimed "that any questioning of Mr. Churchill's future at Colorado should be done by the faculty and should ensure the professor due process. Also, the association cautioned that Mr. Churchill should not face harsher standards because of the subject of his remarks."[84]

What was there in Churchill's short (approximately 5,000-word) article to convert so many established mountains on the American social landscape—from Fox News' Bill O'Reilly, to two respected institutions of higher learning, to the State of Colorado—into angry volcanoes that were so determined to immolate the career of a hitherto obscure professor of ethnic studies?

Ward Churchill identifies himself as a Native American, though controversy surrounds his ethnicity.[85] Decidedly a politically radical thinker, he was once associated with the American Indian Movement (AIM) but broke with that group. He obtained a BA and MA from Sangamon State University, an institution founded in the Vietnam era as an alternative to mainstream higher education which has since been incorporated into the University of Illinois. Churchill's work largely focused on the historical experience of Native Americans in the United States. He had, therefore, long been preoccupied by issues such as genocide and oppression, concerns which led him to conclude that the American Indian people continue to be colonized victims of the United States.

The article that propelled him to infamy, "Some People Push Back: On the Justice of Roosting Chickens," was an intemperately written, and sometimes almost childishly vulgar, piece that is readily available on the Internet.[86] The article made several questionable points as well as some highly doubtful ones. But neither style nor content satisfactorily explain the massive reaction against Churchill. One can only conclude that the intensity of the furious assault was largely caused by the thrust of the article's overall message. This was conveyed through its main points, which unfolded as follow:

Churchill accused the United States of having waged a persistent genocidal campaign against Iraq, a campaign which, among other things led to the deaths of some half a million Iraqi children. He buttressed his assertion by citing UN Assistant Secretary Denis Halladay's contention that the post-1991 Gulf War embargo against Iraq constituted "a systematic program of deliberate genocide."[87] Churchill argued that the American public was "hardly unaware" of the situation, but greeted the news "with yawns." In his view, the few Americans who did protest against U.S. policy toward Iraq during the 1990s tried to ensure that "nobody went further than waving signs as a means of 'challenging' the patently exterminatory pursuit of Pax Americana."[88] Thus, those who attacked the United States on

9/11 did not initiate a war with America: "they finally responded in kind to some of what this country has dispensed to their people as a matter of course."[89]

As Churchill saw it, "the 9/11 attackers did not license themselves to 'target innocent civilians.'"[90] The personnel who died at the Pentagon "were military targets, pure and simple." Those killed in the World Trade Center, he argued, "formed a technocratic corps at the very heart of America's global financial empire," a status that Churchill clearly felt made them also legitimate targets. The paragraph in which these remarks appeared was the one most often referred to by Churchill's detractors. It will be looked at more closely below.

On the basis of the foregoing, the article went on to argue that "the men who flew missions against the WTC and the Pentagon were not cowards";[91] that 9/11 constituted an "act of war, not 'terrorist incidents'"[92]; that FBI and CIA efforts to counter the threat to the United States "will be nil"[93]; that the 9/11 attackers had "given Americans a tiny dose of their own medicine"[94]; that the perpetrators of 9/11 sought to send Americans a message "as uncomplicated as 'stop killing our kids, if you want yours to be safe'"[95]; and that there is little chance of this message being heeded because "a far higher quality of character and intellect would have to prevail among average Americans than is actually the case."[96]

Churchill's final, and major point, had already been made in the article's title:

> Looking back, it will seem to future generations inexplicable why Americans were unable on their own and in time to save themselves, to accept a rule of nature so basic that it could be mouthed by an actor, Lawrence Fishburn, in a movie, The Cotton Club.
>
> "You've got to learn," the line went, "that when you push people around, some people push back."
> As they should.
> As they must.
> There is justice in such symmetry[97]

To understand the vehemence of the reaction to Churchill's article, its most widely cited paragraph must be taken into account. The WTC victims were, he wrote, "civilians of a sort."

> But innocent? Gimme a break. They formed a technocratic corps at the very heart of America's financial empire—"the mighty engine of profit" to which the military dimension of U.S. policy has always been enslaved—and they did so willingly and knowingly. Recourse to "ignorance"—a derivative, after all, of the word "ignore"—counts as

> less than an excuse among this relatively well-educated elite. To the extent that any of them were unaware of the costs and consequences to others of what they were involved in—and in many cases excelling at—it was because of their absolute refusal to see. More likely, it was because they were too busy braying incessantly and self-importantly, into their cell phones, arranging power lunches and stock transactions, each of which translated, conveniently out of sight, mind, and smelling distance, into the starved and rotting flesh of infants. If there was a better, more effective, or in fact any other way of visiting some penalty befitting their participation upon the little Eichmanns inhabiting the sterile sactuary of the twin towers, I'd really be interested in hearing about it.[98]

Governor Owens called for Churchill's dismissal from the University of Colorado on grounds that "we are not compelled to accept his pro-terrorist views at state taxpayer subsidy . . . " But which of the points in Churchill's article constituted "pro-terrorist views"? Susan Sontag had blasted the popular characterization of the 9/11 attackers as "cowards." Norman Mailer had railed against the drive for an American Empire. Noam Chomsky condemned the course of modern American foreign policy as that of "a leading terrorist state" and proffered a list of American-linked violence in the third world to support his claim. Chalmers Johnson's work insisted that the United States was undergoing a process of overreaching imperialism, and that there was small chance of democratic processes stopping it. Zbigniew Brzezinski had argued that the post-9/11 environment requires "confronting complexity," and indicated that this is a requirement which the American political scene does not handle well. Richard Clarke had decried the war on Iraq as an unnecessary invasion of a country that "posed no threat to us" and as a measure that undermined American interests. The CIA analyst, "Anonymous," presented—but did not share—anti-American views that are widely held by terrorists and non-terrorists in the Muslim world. He also clearly saw the terrorist campaign as a response to actions taken by the United States in that area.

Each of these points was in some way woven into Churchill's article. Are they all "pro-terrorist views"? If so, should all those having them be silenced? Surely this cannot be desired (or can it?) for that would not only impoverish America's intellectual life but also make the country limit debate that is in the interest of enhanced security.

Ward Churchill's real sin in today's America was not that he took positions similar to some of those voiced by Sontag, Mailer, Chomsky and the others, nor even that his article presented a fairly clear picture of the terrorists' view of America. It was, rather, that he not only presented but shared the terrorists' outlook. This sin was compounded by Churchill's undisguised and obscene reveling in the deaths of the Americans who died on 9/11.

As bothersome as this is, there is no getting around the fact that defeating the terrorists requires understanding the terrorists—and that means listening to them. It is counterproductive and self-defeating to silence their spokesmen. Moreover, it would be pure folly and hubris—to use an apt term employed by many of the authors just discussed—to believe that our enemies have nothing worthwhile to say, that there is not an iota of substantial reason for their hatred of us, that there is nothing we might do in nonmilitary terms to help defeat their campaign against us. In short, it behooves us not only to listen to them but to hear them.

This is why the onslaught on Ward Churchill was so destructive, and it is supremely ironic that the real danger of Churchill's poorly thought out little essay lay not in what it said but in the reaction to it. For the piece itself suffered from a fatal contradiction that rendered it worthless from the outset as a guide to any sort of analytical or moral understanding of 9/11: Churchill could glory in the deaths of the Americans who died that day only by dehumanizing them, thereby falling into the very crime he claimed those same dead had perpetrated against Iraqis. To "hear" the terrorist view is not necessarily to be swayed by it.

As of this writing, the full outcome of the "Churchill Affair" is not yet known. In late June 2006 he received notice from the Chancellor of the University of Colorado that the institution would move to dismiss him from the faculty. Churchill was scheduled to defend himself before a university committee in late January 2007.[99] While it is unclear whether the tenured professor will keep his position, it is a foregone conclusion that at least some academics in Colorado uneasily wonder what Governor Owen and others see as the limits on what may be said or written about 9/11-related matters. The fate of the professor in New York who invited Churchill to speak at Hamilton College suggests that such concerns have probably spread far beyond Colorado itself. In mid-February 2005, Nancy Rabinowitz resigned as director of the Kirkland Project for the Study of Gender, Society and Culture, a position she had held since the Project's foundation in 1996. Rabinowitz, a tenured professor of comparative literature who had served Hamilton for twenty-seven years, said she resigned "under duress," adding that "what the Project needs now is someone more adept at the kind of political and media fight that the current climate requires."[100]

THE MISGUIDED CONSERVATIVE DEBATE OVER ISRAEL

By the onset of Bush's second term, there were two other realms in which opposition to his administration's approach to the post-9/11 world were being loudly expressed. The first grew out of what was initially an intramural quarrel among American conservatives, who formed the president's natural constituency. However, it soon developed into a much wider debate. The issue that generated the controversy was Israel, or, better said, Israel's standing in the priorities of U.S. national interests. The second was played out in the mass media. It was driven by much passion and little informed thought. Although it strongly pressed its own opposing interpretation of 9/11, its real target was not so much the White House view of that event as the president himself. This section looks at the first of these, reserving for the next a discussion of the second.

Patrick Buchanan, former Nixon speechwriter and head of the Reagan White House's communication office, is a leading conservative spokesman who by end of Clinton's presidency had twice bid for—and failed to obtain—the Republican Party's presidential nomination. Buchanan sees himself as a "traditional conservative" whose outlook on foreign affairs is linked to that of Robert Taft or—to go back even further in American history—to the post-Enlightenment pragmatism that shaped the views of Washington and Jefferson. Buchanan defended an isolationist and unilateralist position on U.S. foreign policy.[101] By the 2000 presidential elections, he had abandoned the Republican Party and became the presidential candidate of the American Reform Party, the alternative party founded earlier by Ross Perot.

In accepting the ARP's nomination, Buchanan accused both major parties of having led the country into behaving "like the haughty British empire our fathers rose up against...."[102] He promised that his presidency would "no longer squander the blood of our soldiers fighting other countries' wars or the wealth of our country paying other countries' bills."[103] Buchanan aimed a sharp remark at those who argued that the United States should accept the responsibilities of a hegemonic or imperial role in world affairs: "To hell with empire; we want our country back."[104]

Buchanan would develop these themes more strongly in the face of 9/11 and the looming invasion of Iraq.[105] In an essay entitled "To Hell With Empire," he dealt more extensively with the Middle East, directly challenging the administration's understanding of the sources of terrorism.

> We Americans have been behaving like the Roman Empire. Between 1989 and 1999, we invaded Panama, smashed Iraq, intervened in Somalia, invaded Haiti, launched air strikes on Bosnia, fired missiles at Baghdad, Sudan and Afghanistan, and destroyed Serbia. We imposed embargoes on Libya, Iran, Iraq and dozens of other states. The Iraqi sanctions may have caused the deaths of 500,000 children....
>
> No doubt, in every instance, America acted out of good and noble motives, but can we not understand how others might resent the "Dirty Harry" on the global beat?
>
> The blow-back has been an Arab-Islamic resort to the last weapon of the weak....

> Why did Osama bin Laden target America? Not because we are a democracy but by his own testimony, because he wanted American infidels off the sacred soil of Saudi Arabia . . . . The terrorists were over here because we are over there.[106]

In the same essay, he singled out the American connection with Israel and the role of Paul Wolfowitz as largely responsible for the imperial drift of U.S. foreign policy in the Middle East.

> Israel looks out for Israel first, and Americans must start looking out for America first. Because our interests as a world power are broader and greater, and may conflict with the annexationist agenda of [Israeli Prime Minister Ariel] Sharon, America must first make known to the Arab and Islamic world that Israel does not have a blank check from the United States. We can no longer give preemptive absolution to an Israeli regime that could drag America into a war of civilizations with the Arab and Islamic world—and there's reason to believe that is exactly what Ariel Sharon has in mind.
>
> It also seems that this is what some Americans are hoping for. Among them is Paul Wolfowitz, Pentagon author of the *Wolfowitz Memorandum* of 1992 . . . , a scheme for American empire . . . .[107]

Other voices soon took up the theme. An article by Paul Schroeder, a prominent professor of diplomatic history at the University of Illinois, referred to what the author called "possibly the unacknowledged real reason" for the impending war against Iraq: "security for Israel."[108] Schroeder argued that of various suggested reasons for "the planned war," the "more plausible" was:

> . . . that this plan is being promoted in the interests of Israel. Certainly, it is being pushed very hard by a number of influential supporters of Israel of the hawkish neoconservative stripe in and outside the administration (Richard Perle, Paul Wolfowitz, William Kristol and others), and one could easily make the case that a successful preventive war on Iraq would promote particular Israeli security interests more than general ones.[109]

Writing in *The Nation*, Jason Vest noted that two pro-Likud, Washington-based think tanks, the Jewish Institute for National Security Affairs (JINSA) and the Center for Security Policy (CSP), now had "dozens of their members [in] powerful government posts."[110] They had, he said, woven together and worked for an agenda that had "support of Israel right at its core."[111] These individuals sought to promote the idea that "there is no difference between

U.S. and Israeli national security interests, and that the only way to assure continued safety and prosperity for both countries is through hegemony in the Middle East."[112] Vest charged that the effort was "underwritten by far-right American Zionists (all of which help to underwrite JINSA and CSP)" in a milieu "where ideology and money seamlessly mix."[113] Internationally renowned columnist Georgie Anne Geyer flatly concluded that the "real intention of the administration's war party—whose policies and mission were often identical with those of the far right and expansionist Likud party of Ariel Sharon in Israel" was to "'reconfigure' the Middle East in a way favorable to Israel's long-term security."[114] Near the end of 2002, the columnist and commentator, Robert Novak, branded the upcoming conflict in Iraq "Sharon's War."[115]

By the end of Bush's first term, at least two members of Congress had taken similar positions. Their shared status as Democrats left no doubt that Patrick Buchanan's reservations about the Bush administration's policy toward Iraq and the Middle East were not the preserve of right-wing American politics. Representative James Moran, of Virginia, attacked the administration on the eve of the war but also heavily criticized what he saw as the Jewish community's role: "If it were not for the strong support of the Jewish community for this war with Iraq we would not be doing this.... The leaders of the Jewish community are influential enough that they could change the direction of where this is going and I think they should."[116] In the spring of 2004, with U.S. forces still dying in Iraq, South Carolina's Senior Senator, Ernest F. Holling, published an article, "Why We're in Iraq." He pointed to Israel and its neoconservative supporters in the United States:

> Led by Richard Perle, Paul Wolfowitz and Charles Krauthammer, for years there has been a domino school of thought that the way to guarantee Israel's security is to spread democracy in the area. Wolfowitz wrote: "The United States may not be able to lead countries through the door of democracy, but where that door is locked shut by a totalitarian deadbolt, American power may be the only way to open it up." And on another occasion: "Iraq as 'the first Arab democracy'... would cast a very large shadow, starting with Syria and Iran but across the whole Arab World."[117]

Both politicians came under immediate and strong attack. The White House and leaders of both major parties rebuked Moran, while Jewish leaders charged that he was "hostile to Jews and Israel."[118] Moran promptly issued various apologies.[119] Although Hollings came under similar fire, the elderly senator was scheduled to retire from public life at the end of the year. Rather than apologize, he spoke out in the Senate, reaffirming his position while denying anti-Semitic inclinations or intentions: "We are losing the war on terror because we thought we could do it militarily under the domino policy of President Bush. That is my point. That is not anti-Semit[ic].... When you want to talk about policy, they say it is anti-Semitic."[120] The octogenarian senator's defense was reportedly dismissed by Jewish leaders who claimed Hollings had always differed from his party's stand on Middle East issues and that his recent comments reflected "a confused politico nearing retirement."[121]

The controversy over the Jewish role in post-9/11 U.S. policy spread rapidly, reaching half a world away to involve Israelis on both sides of the issue. In the summer of 2004, Israel's former Ambassador to the United Nations, Dore Gold, attacked what he called a "Wartime Witch Hunt" that sought to blame Israel for the Iraq War. Gold argued that "by 2003 the Iraqi Army had been severely degraded in both military manpower and equipment." He concluded that it was therefore "ludicrous" to claim, as was being done by some in the United States, "that the *primary* interest of the Bush administration in going to war with Saddam Hussein was to defend Israeli security interests."[122] In contrast, the veteran Israeli peace activist and war hero, Uri Avnery, affirmed that the toppling of Saddam Hussein's regime had been a victory for "the small group that initiated this war—an alliance of Christian fundamentalists and Jewish neo-conservatives... from now on it will control Washington almost without limits."[123] The goal of this alliance, he argued, was not only "an American empire, but also... an Israeli mini-empire, under the control of the extreme right and the settlers [in occupied Palestinian lands]." Avnery had little patience with those who argued that "all this is good for Israel... [because] Never before have Jews exerted such an immense influence on the center of world power."[124] He worried that the Americans would someday "go home," but that Israelis would have "to live with the Arab peoples." Washington had already shown that its "understanding of Arab realities is shaky."

> Wolfowitz and Co. may dream about a democratic, liberal, Zionist and America-loving Middle East, but the result of their adventures may well turn out to be a fanatical and fundamentalist region that will threaten our very existence.[125]

Once the war he had warned against was launched, Patrick Buchanan attacked the claim that anti-Semitism figured in opposition to the Bush administration's policies:

> ... it is the charge of "anti-Semitism" itself that is toxic. For this venerable slander is designed to nullify public discourse by smearing and intimidating foes and censoring and blacklisting them and any who would publish them. Neocons say we attack them because they are Jewish. We do not. We attack them because their warmongering threatens our country even as it finds a reliable echo in Ariel Sharon.

.... They charge us with anti-Semitism—i.e., a hatred of Jews for their faith, heritage, or ancestry. False. The truth is, those hurling these charges harbor a "passionate attachment" to a nation not our own that causes them to subordinate the interests of their own country and to act on an assumption that, somehow, what's good for Israel is good for America.[126]

Having, so to speak, cleared the decks in this way, Buchanan unloosed the volley of his real message on the Iraq war: that "a cabal of polemicists and public officials seek to ensnare our country in a series of wars that are not in America's interests." This cabal, he continued, was "deliberately damaging US relations with every state in the Arab World that defies Israel or supports the Palestinians' right to a homeland of their own."[127] Its purpose was "to conscript American blood to make the world safe for Israel."[128]

Buchanan concluded by agreeing that America had, and should honor, "a moral commitment" to Israel's right to "peace and secure borders." However, he argued:

... U.S. and Israeli interests are not identical. They often collide, and when they do, U.S. interests must prevail. Moreover, we do not view the Sharon regime as "America's best friend."[129]

In late 2004, Norman Podhoretz, published a lengthy piece in *Commentary*. Entitled "World War IV: How It Started, What It Means, and Why We Have to Win," it laid out the neoconservative case. Its final section, "History's Call," went to the root of the neocon outlook: the presumed awareness of an imperative of History's Process: "Now," Podhoretz concluded:

... our "entire security as a nation"—including to a greater extent than [at the Cold War's onset] in 1947, our physical security—once more depends on whether we are ready and willing to accept and act upon the responsibilities of moral and political leadership that history has yet again so squarely placed upon our shoulders.[130]

The article directly confronted the claim that the war on Iraq had been fought for Israel as a result of a largely Jewish cabal. Podhoretz charged that Buchanan, Novak, and others had developed a theory of the Iraq War that "inescapably rested on all-too-familiar anti-Semitic canards—principally that Jews were never reliably loyal to the country in which they lived, and that they were always conspiring behind the scenes... to manipulate the world for their own nefarious purposes."[131] The anti-Neocons' theory, he retorted, was inherently ridiculous, first, because "quite apart from its pernicious moral and political implications" it

> . . . asked one to believe the unbelievable: that strong-minded people like Bush, Cheney, and Rice could be fooled by a bunch of cunning subordinates, whether Jewish or not, into doing anything at all against their better judgment, let alone something so momentous as waging a war . . . in which they could detect no clear relation to American interests.[132]

In the second place, Podhoretz pointed out, the "purveyors of this theory" based their claim on evidence that "consisted of published articles and statements in which the alleged conspirators openly and unambiguously advocated the very policies they now stood accused of having secretly foisted upon an unwary Bush administration."[133]

Buchanan, Novak, and many others would no doubt have denied that their view of the dynamics that led the administration into war on Iraq constituted any sort of "theory," and much less one resting on the two general propositions that Podhoretz correctly branded as "all-too-familiar anti-Semitic canards." It was, however, also true that others, whose thinking was far more likely to rest precisely on the anti-Semitic premises cited by Podhoretz, also accused the administration of fighting a war "for Israel." Thus, Mark Weber's essay, "Iraq: A War for Israel?" was prominently featured on the Web site of the Institute for Historical Review, a California-based organization that since 1978 has dedicated itself to challenging standard accounts of the Nazi extermination campaign against European Jewry.[134] Far more extreme voices joined in. Former Ku Kux Klan leader David Duke made a typical accusation: "Traitors to the United States have allowed a terrorist nation [Israel] to control the United States Government."[135]

Notwithstanding the intensity it sometimes achieved, the "debate" over Israel's place in U.S. national interest failed to capture much attention among the broader American public. Many conservatives presumably followed it, moved largely by their feelings about the neoconservative ascendancy within the Republican Party. The rantings of David Duke and his ilk were apparently ignored by all but his established minor following, and much the same seemed true of the marginal Institute for Historical Review.

In fact, the argument never became a real debate because the principals failed to come to grips with the fundamental issue dividing them. Instead, their battle stayed at the superficial level of different policy preferences. They spoke past, rather than to, one another: "Yes, Israeli and U.S. Interests are Identical" vs. "No, They Are Not."

What was utterly missing was any focus on the criterion to be applied in determining whether Israeli and U.S. interests were essentially similar. Had the discourse veered in this direction, it would quickly have posed a choice between two strikingly different perceptions of reality. On the one hand, there was the Neoconservative certainty that History has a clear direction and purpose, and that they had identified it. By extension, of course, this carried the equal conviction that, as Bush told the West Point graduates, "moral truth is the same in every culture, in every time, and in every place." From this perspective, so long as one accepted the Neocons' claim to have captured the key to History, it was fully possible—nay, required—for any fully and totally patriotic American (Jewish or non-Jewish) to accept the administration's view of the nexus between the national interests of Israel and the United States.

The competing view of reality was what Bill Clinton characterized as "what most of us believe": the belief "that no-one has the absolute truth." From this vantage point, it was very possible—indeed, probable—that countries would have unique visions of national interest, the corollary being that even the closest of international ties would probably involve the need to cope realistically with sometimes sharply different goals. Sadly, that basic point of contention did not figure in the post-9/11 "debate" over Israel. Clinton's thesis about "what most of us believe" was not tested. Its validity still remains an open question.

The Insidious Popular Debate

There was a final venue in which opposition to the administration was voiced. Unfortunately, it was almost certainly here that most Americans were exposed to "debate" over—or at least different points of view on—Washington's reaction to 9/11. Perhaps rather than "exposed," it should be said that most Americans had these differences "imposed" upon them, for the venue was the mainstream mass media, as represented by the ubiquitous cable and satellite TV networks and the film industry. While I cannot claim to have conducted or found a content-analysis of relevant discourses in the media, and while—to be fair—there clearly were occasions on which mainstream networks offered viewers serious critiques of prevailing policies and discussion of alternative viewpoints, the dominant fare did not dwell on such fundamental questions as why 9/11 occurred or what it implied. In the setting of the mass media, the most representative "debate" came in the form of the contrast between Fox News, one of the most watched networks, and the widely run anti-Bush mouthings of Michael Moore, the aging, baseball-capped, cherubic figure who pushed himself into the role of an anti-administration icon. Fox enjoyed a seemingly endless herd of "talking heads" who could barely rise above explaining the motivations of America's terrorist enemies in terms of innate "savagery" or "barbarism." Moore, in his guise as a self-proclaimed political authority, incessantly drove home the idea that "there is no terrorist threat." The theme was reinforced by his cinematic efforts, particularly the widely viewed and mindlessly Bush-bashing "documentary" *Farenheit 9/11*. Seconding Moore's efforts on the big screen by mid-2004 was *The Village*, written and directed by M. Night Shyamalan. The film, a poor makeover of Arthur Miller's *The Crucible*, allegorically promoted the same message: "there is no terrorist threat." There could not have been a more erroneous or dangerous idea.

There is no reason to dwell on the dangerous falsity of the Moore/Shyamalan position. The very real threat of a non-state actor employing nuclear, radiological, chemical, or biological weapons of mass destruction against the United States has long been recognized and increasingly documented, particularly since the Soviet Union's collapse.[136] Two excellent recent works, respectively by Graham Allison and Stephen Flynn, should be required reading for all who wish to understand the perils facing today's United States.[137]

OVERVIEW

Any assessment of the consideration given to the American response to 9/11 is forced to focus on its limitations. The basic questions were quickly addressed by the Bush administration and its supporters. Yet, intellectuals, public servants, academics, and artists of various sorts were not slow to challenge the prevailing wisdom that emanated from Washington. Even some politicians struck out against the premises that shaped the administration's understanding of 9/11.

These skeptics did manage to provide the opportunity for a thorough debate over the fundamentals. However, not much more than that could be claimed, for the opportunity was not fully seized. America's mainstream post-9/11 discourse flowed along the channels charted by the administration in the wake of the attacks: the terrorists were impelled by pure hatred of the values for which the United States stood; their defeat lay in the spread of freedom and democracy.

This conceptual foundation produced the actions that comprised the U.S. response to 9/11, the war on terrorism. By the end of Bush's first term, Washington could point to various achievements. The Taliban had been routed and a fledgling new regime was in place, a regime that was at least pledged to the development of democracy in Afghanistan. Saddam Hussein's government had been destroyed, the dictator himself captured and imprisoned, and Iraq was in the throes of a bloody struggle, which the administration viewed as the birthpangs of democracy in the Arab World. Finally, the United States and its allies had waged an offensive campaign against al-Qaeda around the world. Al-Qaeda operatives were captured or killed throughout the Arab World as well as in North America, Europe, and Asia.[138] By the summer of 2004, CIA calculations allowed President Bush to claim that 75 percent of al-Qaeda's leadership had been eliminated.[139]

Such results may well have occurred, but their true import remained very cloudy. In the absence of firm knowledge about al-Qaeda's force structure, the significance of body counts could not be known. The same, of course, was true of al-Qaeda's losses at the leadership level. The political futures of Afghanistan and Iraq obviously still remained uncertain.

Above all, however, the Bush administration's proclamation of a global campaign for democratization places in high relief a pressing question: can the drive to democratic development be jump-started by outside intervention? This, of course, is precisely what the United States is attempting to do by occupying Iraq. For all of Bush's assurances that the commitment to promote democracy did not "seek to impose our form of government on anyone else," the policy he launched was predicated on the premise that American intervention could alter the cultural foundations of targeted societies in ways amenable to democratic development.[140] This placed strict limits on the meaning of his repeated, and ostensibly complacent, assurances that "representative governments in the Middle East will reflect their own cultures."[141] What Washington really meant was that it would accept those elements of Middle East political culture that were conducive to open democratic processes while it would reject those it deemed antidemocratic.

Donald Rumsfeld made this clear shortly after the demise of Saddam Hussein's regime when he flatly indicated that the United States would not allow any Iranian-like fundamentalist Islamic government to come to power in Iraq.[142] In this sense, Bush's dismissal of those who questioned whether "this country, or that people, or this group are 'ready' for democracy" was empty, not to say less than forthright, rhetoric. For the Bush administration itself clearly accepted the reservations implied by such questions. Where it differed from many of those who raised the issue was by rejecting any assumption that fundamental social change is a mysterious historical process that requires time. Bush and his chief lieutenants believed the process could be externally induced and brought to fruition by force. Thus, the president and his chief lieutenants frequently pointed to Germany and Japan as societies once dominated by anti-democratic consummatory values that had been converted into stable democracies.[143] The point is valid in itself; the historical record cannot be denied. But that record should be heeded completely. Quite apart from Brzezinski's observation that the use of post-World War II Germany and Japan as examples of imposed democracy "ignores historically relevant facts,"[144] another reason for caution is in order. The attractiveness of the examples becomes even more dubious when it is recalled that the war which produced those democratic conversions cost over four million German and nearly two million Japanese lives, not to mention the additional millions of Allied dead, the destruction of the physical infrastructures of Germany and Japan and, finally, the nuking of Hiroshima and Nagasaki.

By the onset of his second term, Bush was ready to raise the stakes of his commitment to worldwide democratic revolution. He did so on the basis of a very sound argument: that the security of the United States "increasingly depends on the success of liberty in other lands."[145] In light of the very real destructive power that technology now potentially puts at the disposal of relatively small groups whose political environments have helped turn them to terrorism, Bush's prescription for achieving security carried compelling logic:

> We will encourage reform in other governments by making clear that success in our relations will require *decent treatment of their own people.* (emphasis added)[146]

The main problem here is one of choice, not of diagnosis or prescription. By 2005, the administration had already firmly singled out Syria and Iran as states failing "in the decent treatment of their own people," and therefore as friendly environments for the cultivation of terrorism. With the security of the United States cast—as it should be—in terms of the potentially menacing consequences of unresponsive and repressive governments on a global scale, the issue was stark and unsettling: Washington's current determination to plant and nurture the seeds of democracy on a worldwide scale implied an unendingly fallow field of governments "failing in the decent treatment of their own people" that would have to be tended with the blood and bones of American troops.

The question is whether there is a better option.

By way of moving toward an answer, it will be useful to review the attacks of 9/11 at a fairly abstract level, one that enhances the possibility of capturing the essence of what transpired without becoming mired in specifics that—because they are open to various interpretations—tend to becloud, more than clarify, the events of that day.

On September 11, 2001, nineteen young men violently hijacked four civilian airliners over the United States and then attempted to crash them into pre-identified targets of symbolic value. The hijackers were determined to cause large loss of life, including their own. Three of the hijacking groups succeeded in reaching their targets, two planes hitting the twin towers of the World Trade Center in New York and the third crashing into the Pentagon. Action by passengers on the fourth plane caused it to crash, short of its target, into a Pennsylvania field.

The nineteen hijackers were not all citizens of the same country, but they were all Arabs and therefore shared the history of the Arab World. They were recruited and sent on their mission by an organization whose active membership, though not precisely known, undoubtedly constituted only the tiniest fraction of that region's inhabitants. Nonetheless, the act of terror perpetrated on 9/11 led to reactions in the Arab and Muslim worlds that in various ways indicated significant and widespread sympathy for the attack.

The hijackers acted in full knowledge that they themselves would die. They were motivated by an ideology that, once internalized, seared them with a worldview that not only steeled them for their own deaths but also gave them certainty that their fatal mission served a purpose more real than any bound by the limits of earthly life. *They* called this cause Islam. Other Muslims—probably a majority—differed. That was inconsequential to the hijackers themselves, who viewed their attack as a heroic act of war and themselves as heroic warriors.

The 9/11 event was beyond question the most striking example of a type of warfare known as "asymmetrical conflict," hostilities waged between sides distinguished by a remarkably large imbalance in power. Nineteen members of a relatively tiny group of Middle Eastern malcontents launched an attack on major centers of the world's most powerful state. No conflict in history comes even close to matching this sort of asymmetry. Yet asymmetric conflicts have been with us for aeons, or at least since tiny Melos confronted mighty Athens. Can examples of such confrontations tell us something useful about today's search for international security? It is likely that they can, or at least that such is the case with regard to a type of asymmetrical conflict that came to be waged in widely different parts of the developing world in the closing years of the twentieth century.

If this is so, then a more useful answer than the president's explanation of "What Happened" on 9/11 is the following: What happened on September 11, 2001 was an act of asymmetrical war.

Part II

A Type of Asymmetrical Conflict

Chapter 3

Mexico's Zapatista Rebellion

On a thunderously rainy night in the summer of 1995, I found myself in a Mexican jungle, sitting in the open-air kitchen of a tiny wooden shack speaking with "Chapo."[1] At my side were the two other participants in what we jokingly called my "research honeymoon." One was my recent bride, Conchita Añorve, a Mexican architect and artist. The other was Carl Money, a young aide to a member of the Texas State Legislature who had been sent to look into some of the same things in Chiapas that interested me. Carl became the third member of our tripartite honeymoon at the behest of a close associate of the activist Bishop of San Cristóbal, Samuel Ruiz, the cleric who was then trying to mediate a peaceful settlement of the Zapatista Rebellion.

The man to whom I spoke, a Tzeltal Maya, was the leading Zapatista in one of the remote Valleys where the rebels exercised control. He stood calmly on the earthen floor, upon which several children played with even more puppies, while his mother and wife prepared the evening meal over a wood fire.

He was in his early thirties, short, dark, and soft-spokenly eloquent. He was dressed in blue jeans and a sparkling-clean, white T-shirt that rather incongruously sported the legend "RODEO DRIVE" in two-inch black letters across his chest. "Chapo" spoke of his commitment to the rebellion. He had no obvious desire to die—indeed, he very much seemed to enjoy life. Yet, his remarks sprang from an acceptance of the high probability that he would soon be dead. His mother tended the fire but frequently smiled at him glowingly. The immense pride she had in her son was plain. His wife stood silently in a darkened corner, occasionally handing the mother some item on the menu.

> Yes, they can kill me and they can kill other leaders. It would not matter... poverty and misery will keep producing others like us. It is better to lose a life such as this while fighting for change.[2]

"Chapo" had good reason for concern. As we spoke, some 60,000 Mexican troops encircled the Chiapas Highland valleys into which he and his fellow Zapatistas retreated after their unexpected offensive eighteen months earlier had placed them briefly in control of several urban centers in the Chiapas Highlands, including the major city of San Cristóbal de las Casas.[3] In the standoff that followed the initial wave of combat, the valleys—and parts of the Lacandón Jungle to which they led—remained under Zapatista control as convoluted negotiations between the Mexican government and the rebels intermittently dragged on. It was in San Cristóbal that the offer to tour "the Conflict Zone" had been made some days earlier.

We met Dr. Raymundo Sánchez Barraza in his austere office in the equally austere building that is the Bishop's Palace in San Cristóbal. Originally from the central Mexican state of Guanajuato, Sánchez Barraza had settled in Chiapas some five years earlier and quickly made a name for himself in local community development efforts. Soon after the rebellion broke out, he joined a small group that helped Samuel Ruiz, the Bishop of San Cristóbal de las Casas, develop and implement a mediation strategy. Officially called the National Intermediation Commission, the group was better known by its Spanish acronym, CONAI. Bishop Ruiz's enemies among the established Chiapaneco elite viewed Raymundo Sánchez Barraza as a particularly radical and dangerous foe of the status quo.[4] With the Bishop away for a lengthy spiritual retreat, I spoke to Sánchez of my own concern. I worried that Ruiz's enthusiasm for reform in Chiapas might lead the Zapatistas to overplay their hand in the ongoing negotiations. "If the Mexican Army is unleashed," I commented, "it will be the Indian population in the Conflict Zone who gets hurt."

"It is not that easy," replied Sánchez, "the Indians know that territory, the Army doesn't... and believe me, it is very rough terrain there. You should see it."

"Can you arrange that?"[5]

He could and did, and he arranged for Carl—who proved to be a delightful and wonderfully observant companion—to accompany us.

"Chapo" had spoken at length of his own experiences and hopes. His comments frequently touched on his children—the tots playing at our feet—and his anger at the possibility that their lives would be no more than a replay of his own. He just as often praised the Zapatista Movement for its "calls for dignity and for self-respect, and for the demand for respect by others."[6]

While he contemplated his own death, and even that of his children, his confidence in the ultimate victory of justice as he saw it was unshaken. "Chapo's" comments were consistently reiterated by other Zapatistas as we worked our way down the valley to the Lacandón. I do not recall seeing any firearms during that journey, but there was no doubt that some were stashed in the villages and settlements through which we passed. There was even less doubt that they were no match for the tanks, assault rifles, and heavy machine guns displayed by the Mexican troops on the Conflict Zone's perimeter.

MARGINALIZED VIOLENT INTERNAL CONFLICT

The Zapatista Rebellion raised a compelling question: What was it that made perfectly sensible and intelligent men and women initiate a conflict under circumstances that virtually assured their own destruction, yet also gave them a firm conviction in the eventual victory of their cause?

During the years that followed my initial visit to Chiapas, I concluded the answer lay in the interaction of three broad factors. These were, first, the "structures" (prevailing patterns of behavior and relationships) that formed the insurgent group's sociopolitical context; second, "cognitive factors"—that is, the mobilizing ideology (or worldview) that underlay the insurgency; and finally, historical and current forces exerted upon the insurgent group by its local, national, and international environments.

Furthermore, these same analytical categories seemed to help explain at least two other asymmetrical "Third World" conflicts of the 1990s, which—as elaborated below—shared distinguishing characteristics with the Zapatista Rebellion. The insurgent groups in these latter cases were very different from the one I encountered in Chiapas, and those same differences made the similarities among the insurgencies themselves more compelling. The additional insurgencies were those waged in the 1990s by the *Gama'a al-Islamiyya* in Upper Egypt and the Ogoni in Nigeria's Niger Delta.

The three conflicts unfolded in widely different ways. Egypt's, for example, was the bloodiest and most deadly; Mexico's insurgents displayed signs of sophistication in the realm of public relations that made their fight unique; finally, Nigeria's Ogoni Uprising was a relatively minor upheaval in a state whose national integrity has faced far more serious challenges. In terms of social context, the conflicts were also distinct. The one developed in an Islamic environment influenced over millennia by a desert-riverine tradition. The other took root and flowered in the verdant highlands of a Meso-American environment whose inhabitants were heavily influenced by pre-Columbian and Roman Catholic worldviews. The final conflict developed in the steamy swamplands of sub-Saharan Africa's Niger Delta and involved a people whose outlook was shaped by animism and a variety of Christian beliefs. These very differences made similarities in the confluences of the sociopolitical and cognitive structures that marked these conflicts all the more interesting.

As decolonization proceeded in the last half of the twentieth century, violence became the hallmark of domestic politics in what was often called the "Third World." Tribal and ethnic conflicts, as well as separatist struggles and civil wars were all too frequent. Nearly forty years ago, the well-known political scientist Samuel Huntington warned that political processes in developing states were in danger of being replaced by armed conflicts.[7] Subsequent events appeared to bear out that gloomy warning to such a degree that by 1978 some scholars were predicting that the Third World would probably soon see "literally hundreds of revolutionary organizations—nonstate actors—seeking the means to lever themselves into power. . . ."[8] Sixteen years after this unsettling suggestion, UN Secretary General Boutros Boutros-Ghali devoted his entire 1994 annual report to the relationship between development and conflict, arguing that "the lack of economic, social and political development is the underlying source of conflict."[9] Boutros-Ghali pointed out that fifteen of the twenty-seven UN efforts to cope with conflict in 1994 involved exclusively domestic hostilities, and that all but one of these were in Third World states in Asia, Latin America, the Caribbean, Africa, and the Arab World. Many of the remainder dealt with conflicts of a mixed internal-international nature.[10] He also stressed that the cases of third-world domestic violence in which the UN intervened were but a sample of a much larger problem. This was partly due to the reluctance of national governments to accept international initiatives in their own territories and partly to the increasing reluctance of Security Council members to countenance such initiatives.[11]

It was, perhaps, because the world had become so inured to political violence in developing areas that observers long failed to notice the emergence in the late twentieth century of a new type of domestic political conflict in such disparate regions as Latin America, the Middle East, and sub-Saharan Africa. The postdecolonization wave of Third World political violence had largely found its sources in secessionist, tribal, and ethnic frictions. None of these categories suited the Zapatista Rebellion, the *Gama'a al-Islamiyya's* campaign in Egypt, or Nigeria's Ogoni conflict. In the eyes of these latest insurgents, they themselves struggled to uphold the "true" values of the state, and did so on behalf of the vast majority of their fellow citizens. Their enemy was not, then, the state, but rather the incumbent government, whom insurgents accused of having corrupted the state's real values. They therefore did not justify their own struggle by exclusive claims on behalf of any particular group within the state, but rather in terms of what they perceived as justice for the overwhelming bulk of the state's inhabitants.

I have elsewhere given this type of conflict the label "Marginalized Violent Internal Conflict" (MVIC).[12] Admittedly, this is an unfortunate and awkward designation. Yet, it has the merit of going to the heart of the matter. For the conflicts to which it refers are indeed linked to marginality in fundamental ways. First, they find expression among people who have been decidedly marginalized—that is, excluded from sharing the economic, political, and social benefits of national development efforts within the state. Second, geography and the limitations of prevailing technology have historically marginalized the heartlands of such groups from the centers of national political, economic, and cultural life. Finally, the balance of armed power in the conflicts launched by the insurgents so heavily favored national authorities that the incumbent regimes could only see the military challenge as a marginal nuisance, although one that might carry more serious political or economic threats.

Despite the differences in their cultural settings and ideological outlooks, the range of common features surrounding the conflicts launched by Mexico's Zapatistas, Egypt's *Gama'a al-Islamiyya*, and Nigeria's Ogoni was striking. In addition to the points mentioned above, these included various other commonalities that will be made evident in the following pages. However, a key common source of tension must be stressed at the outset: each group felt essentially threatened. This fear of an *essential* threat involved much more than mere anger and discomfort over deprivation. It was, at bottom, a fear of a loss of identity, a loss of existence as understood by members of the group.

It must be kept in mind that the dynamics of MVIC led real men and women to opt consciously for armed conflicts that by all objective criteria of military balances of power could only result in their own defeat or death. That the syndrome repeated itself in the closing years of the twentieth century in the Middle East, Africa, and Latin America should have told us something about the dynamics of the world we presently inhabit.

In short, it is easy enough to see retrospectively that Mexico's Zapatista Rebellion, Egypt's fight against the Upper Egypt-based *Gama' al-Islammiya* and Nigeria's violent confrontation with its Ogoni should have been a stark warning that military power itself will not necessarily deter attack; that something in the human makeup can lead individuals to challenge unchallengeable odds, and to do so with the calm certainty that victory will ultimately be their's. The question is whether or not this "wakeup call" will be heeded, and become a real "turning point" in perspectives that until now continue to determine the dominant reaction to 9/11.

The emergence of MVIC conflicts in the 1990s was related to, but not simply caused by, the widespread shift to neoliberal economic development strategies that began to spread in the Third World in the 1970s.[13] This shift marked the eclipse of the previously favored "command economy" strategy, which relied on government as the main engine of economic growth. The essence of the new approach was faith in market-driven economic development. Although there was much scope for variety in the nature and pace of specific policy steps, the neoliberal development revolution gave a common orientation to those countries who participated in it (which by the 1990s had come to include almost all developing states). This was typically characterized by a sharp reduction in government's role as director of the national economy—which generally meant curtailing the regulatory, planning and, above all, productive functions of government. Deregulation, reliance on market forces, and divestiture of state-owned enterprises became the new key economic tools. Moreover, the neoliberal approach usually entailed reducing or eliminating government subsidies to producers and consumers. Finally, it also gave heavy emphasis to attenuating protective policies that had been designed to shield the national economy from international competition. The goal of neoliberal development is to spur economic growth through productive efficiency and rationally competitive integration into the global economy. The hope is that a growing economy will benefit all sectors of the national populace.[14]

Perceptive observers soon warned that well before the realization of such expectations, the combined impact of neoliberalism and the technological revolution in communications could lead to the de facto social, economic, and political disenfranchisement—and ensuing embitterment—of vast numbers of people. By the late 1980s, David Apter's profound focus on the Third World led him to raise the looming spectre of the "superfluous man"—those whose social existence would prove incapable of contributing positively to the demands of neoliberal economies. He described the plight of such marginalized groups as follows:

> Marginalization . . . is a condition resulting from prolonged functional superflousness. [Marginals] are deprived of virtually all the roles of which functioning society is composed . . . . Considered by the rest of the population as pariahs, morally and even perhaps biologically distinctive they . . . remain more or less permanently on the perimeters of society . . . .[15]

The prospect, of course, was that marginals would not fade quietly into the dusk of history but rather burst forth in a discourse of violence.

Ten years later, another sociologist—Manuel Castells—produced a monumental and widely acclaimed study of our era, *The Information Age*.[16] Noting that a key feature of contemporary life is "the sudden acceleration of the historical tempo," Castells pointed to the same phenomenon that had alarmed Apter, and made more explicit the probable consequences:

> . . . people all over the world resent loss of control over their lives, over their environments, over their jobs, and, ultimately, over the fate of the Earth. Thus, following an old law of social evolution, resistance confronts domination, empowerment reacts against powerlessness, and

alternative projects challenge the logic embedded in the new global order.[17]

REBELLION IN CHIAPAS

On January 1, 1994—the date of Mexico's entry into the North American Free Trade Association (NAFTA)—some two to four thousand fighters of the *Ejército Zapatista de Liberación Nacional* (EZLN) seized several municipalities in the Highlands of Chiapas. This was accomplished with relatively little bloodshed and the rebels were quick to pledge that no harm would befall civilians, including tourists. The event took most observers by surprise. Only eight years earlier, Alan Riding, a very sensitive and perceptive student of Mexican affairs, had lamented the multifaceted oppression of Chiapas' Indians but concluded that anything resembling uprisings of previous centuries "could not occur today."[18]

Because the bulk of Zapatista fighters came from Chiapas' marginalized Mayan population, the Rebellion did bear some resemblance to earlier Indian insurrections. Yet, it also differed fundamentally from all such historical examples. While the demand for indigenous rights figured prominently in the Zapatista position, the Rebellion's justification and aims were cast in terms of inclusive national values. In their own eyes, the rebels were acting on behalf of all Mexicans. The enemy was not the Mexican state but rather the Mexican government—an institution the Zapatistas saw as a self-serving and self-perpetuating clique that had long since betrayed Mexico's true national and cultural values. Among their specific demands, the initially successful rebels called for the resignation of Mexico's government, a return to the 1917 Mexican Constitution, and free and fair democratic elections.

Of the five relatively important towns taken by the Zapatistas, San Cristóbal was the most removed from the lower slopes of the Highlands. The other four municipal centers were nearer to, or on the edges of valleys leading to the Lacandón Jungle, the rain forest that stretches to the Guatamalan border. They were also far smaller than San Cristóbal. Two, Altamirano and Chanal, contained less than 5,000 inhabitants each. Ocosingo and Las Margaritas had populations of not much more than 10,000 individuals. San Cristóbal fell to the Zapatistas with little bloodshed, although two civilians were killed during the first hours of the city's occupation.[19] Other towns were taken at more cost. The assault on Altamirano took the lives of the local police chief and several members of his small force, as well as that of a high-ranking EZLN officer. Chanal's nine-man police force offered a brief defense of the municipal palace, but surrendered when at least one of its members was mortally wounded. Several policemen were also killed during the occupation of Las Margaritas, where according to some reports they inflicted heavy casualties on Zapatista forces before being overwhelmed.[20] The fight for Ocosingo is generally recognized as the most bloody encounter in the rebellion's opening hours. Some sources claim that as many as eighty policemen lost their lives, although others put the figure much lower.[21]

The Zapatistas had no intention of battling the Mexican Army for possession of the occupied towns. The EZLN began to withdraw from San Cristóbal in the early evening of January 2, just over twenty-four hours after having taken the city. Altamirano was abandoned on January 4. The withdrawals from Las Margaritas and Chanal came almost simultaneously or shortly afterward. In each case, the redeployments were effected in time to avoid entrapment by the Mexican Army. Things again went differently in Ocosingo. While most of the occupying EZLN contingent departed in good order on morning of January 4, a sizeable number was still present when government forces arrived that afternoon. Encircled by infantrymen and paratroop units, many rebels retreated to the town's central market and were soon caught in the deadly trap. Although some managed to escape during the night, all accounts agree that the Zapatistas took their heaviest casualties in Ocosingo, where sporadic fighting continued until January 6.[22]

Even disregarding the events at Ocosingo, the withdrawals from the other towns did not signal the end of the EZNL's combat operations. The forces that exited San Cristóbal on January 2 attacked an army base on the city's outskirts later that same day. Evidently hoping to capture the base's arsenal, the rebels showed particular determination against that target, futilely attacking it nine times during the next week. During that same period clashes between the Mexican Army and Zapatista forces occurred in various parts of the lower Highlands area.

Nonetheless, the military balance quickly shifted decisively as the Mexican state brought its resources into play. On January 4 and 5, the Air Force went into action, bombing and rocketing wooded hillsides within sight of San Cristóbal. Columns of troops, bringing tanks and light artillery, moved into the area from bases near one of Chiapas' chief tourist attraction, the Mayan ruins at Palenque, and the neighboring states of Tabasco and Campeche.

But the Army tended to move slowly and cautiously, hampered by a limited highway network and, once off the few main arteries, by Zapatista roadblocks and the fear of ambush at every twist and bend in its passage through the mountainous territory. Not until the morning of January 12 did Mexican commanders report that they had regained control of all the Highland towns taken by the insurgents. The next day, January 13, a cease-fire went into effect. To all intents and purposes, the armed rebellion was over, replaced by a prolonged political process that has still not been definitively concluded. The Rebellion and ensuing political process highlighted deep divisions, both within Mexico and in Chiapas. Mexico's civil society mobilized rapidly to push for a peaceful settlement, while elements within the government long agitated for military action. At the same time, the Zapatista movement divided Chiapanecos. The divisions were not limited to that between the rebels and the state's ruling oligarchy. They also extended to

Chiapas' Indian communities. Although the Zapatistas' success in keeping secret their planned offensive while they mobilized several thousand fighters indicated that they enjoyed at least tacit support from the Highland Indian communities, the following months and years would show that significant numbers of Indians opposed the insurgency.[23]

The Zapatista withdrawal after the cease-fire took two forms. Some troops, fully rebels but not the EZLN's standing core, disappeared into their home villages and settlements—most, but not all, of which were located in the small valleys sloping down to the Lacandón Jungle from Ocosingo, Altamirano, and Las Margaritas. These were the *milicianos*, the Zapatista militia. *New York Times* correspondent Tim Goldman provided a striking eyewitness account of the militia's "redeployment":

> Virtually all of the several dozen rebels interviewed in the past few days said they had come from towns like Altamirano and Oxchuc and more dismal hamlets in the pine forests and jungles beyond...
>
> On the edge of Altamirano this afternoon, two young rebels appeared to have simply taken off their bandanas and uniforms, showered and settled in the wooden shack of one of their relatives, waiting to fight another day.[24]

Other Zapatista troops, members of the standing force—the *insurgentes*—moved as units farther into the valleys and jungle. There, under the sheltering foliage of the Lacandón, in the small village of Guadalupe Tepeyac—soon to be renamed Aguascalientes—EZLN established its command center. It was from Aguascalientes that the rebellion's most visible spokesman, Subcomandante Marcos, quickly captured the attention of Mexico and the world. The mysterious, green-eyed figure in the black balaclava had already charmed and intrigued members of the world press during the first hours of San Cristóbal's occupation. Obviously not an Indian, the Zapatista leader first revealed the wit, passion, and intelligence that would make him famous when he reassured worried international tourists in San Cristóbal that no harm would befall them, and then kept his promise. Marcos was eventually identified as Rafael Sebastián Guillén Vicente, a thirty-five-year-old academic and native of Tampico. Even before the withdrawal from San Cristóbal, Marcos had strongly hinted that the Zapatistas saw armed conflict as a catalytic tool to promote revolutionary change through a national political process. Insurrection, he declared, had been chosen because "they left us no other way." It was not, he added, the "only way, nor do we think it is above all others." The most oppressed part of an oppressed national population had given the nation "a lesson in dignity," that should be heeded. "Liberty and democracy" would provide the solutions to Mexico's problems.[25] A few days later, an official EZLN communiqué expanded on these remarks:

> ... our Zapatista troops initiated a series of political-military actions whose primordial objective is to make known to the Mexican people and the rest of the world the miserable conditions in which millions of Mexicans, especially we Indians, live and die.
>
> Our countrymen's grave conditions of poverty have a common cause: the lack of liberty and democracy....
>
> ... we ask for the resignation of the illegitimate government of [Mexican President] Carlos Salinas de Gortari and the formation of a government of democratic transition... [and] we aim to unite all of the Mexican public and its independent organizations so that, through all forms of struggle, there will be generated a national revolutionary movement in which there is place for all forms of social organization that with honesty and patriotism seek the betterment of our Mexico.[26]

The full cost in human lives of the Zapatistas' military campaign remains unknown. Some early estimates placed the total number of dead at 1000 or more, but later accounts considerably reduced these figures. A 2002 overview of the 1994 insurgency argues that between 200 and 1000 persons were killed, a conclusion that only reinforces the issue's cloudiness.[27] Whatever the actual body count was, the violence of January 1994 severely jarred Mexico's political system. After more than six decades in power, the country's ruling party, the Institutional Revolutionary Party (best known by its Spanish acronym, PRI), was facing a serious crisis of legitimacy that went far beyond the Chiapas Highlands. The intertwined ills of the PRI's corruption, autocratic style, and mismanagement of the nation's economy had fallen increasingly heavily on Mexico's articulate middle classes since the 1970s. An economic collapse in the early 1980s—which would be followed by more than a decade of periodic financial crises—crowned these achievements and progressively alienated growing sectors of the middle and upper economic classes from the PRI's banner.

The PRI itself was riddled by bitter internal divisions. The result was that the Zapatistas' condemnation of the Mexican government resonated effectively, and quickly, within the country's civil society. President Carlos Salinas de Gotari's difficult position was made even harder because national elections were scheduled to be held in August. He opted for a political response instead of a military offensive. By mid-January, he had not only accepted the cease-fire but also agreed that the Bishop of San Cristóbal, Samuel Ruiz Garcia, should serve as mediator. Within months the Bishop organized and won recognition for the legally mandated CONAI, a small group whose members he picked as advisors. In addition, Salinas appointed a former mayor of Mexico City, Manuel Camacho Solís as the government's official negotiator with the Zapatistas. These steps were later complemented by the creation of a special multiparty commission of Mexico's Congress, the Commission of Concord and Pacification (COCOPA).

Encircled in what became known as the "Conflict Zone," the Zapatistas waged a highly successful public relations campaign, aimed at both Mexican and international public opinion. Marcos, an extremely skilled writer, produced a series of widely read commentaries ridiculing the government's initial efforts to brand the rebellion as inspired by foreign forces, attacking Mexico's authoritarian political system, and repeating the Zapatistas' call for the establishment of a true democracy. In August 1994 the Zapatistas held the first of several "consultations" with the broader Mexican public. This took the form of a National Democratic Convention, which convened in the Zapatista-controlled village of Aguascalientes. Over 6,000 individuals undertook the arduous journey to the remote location. They represented a broad sector of Mexican civil society, including NGOs, political parties, and the press.

In the meantime, efforts to find a peaceful solution limped along, frequently threatened, but never collapsing totally. Bishop Ruiz's initial mediation managed to produce an agreed list of talking points and—even more importantly—established the precedent of negotiations between the government and the insurgents. These significant achievements were all the more notable for occurring within a wider context that was quickly turning 1994 into Mexico's "year of chaos." The impact of the PRI's ongoing internal rot could no longer be hidden. In March, the party's presidential candidate, Luis Donaldo Colosio, was assassinated. The arrest of his killer, officially described as a deranged individual acting under his own impulses, did nothing to dampen speculation that Donaldo Colosio had died as a result of a top-level conspiracy. The party's new candidate was Ernesto Zedillo, a relatively unknown and rather colorless technocrat who nonetheless sometimes had strong opinions. In July, Camacho Solís accused Zedillo of sabotaging the talks with Zapatistas and resigned as the government's chief negotiator. Several months later, in September, the PRI's Secretary General, and President Salinas' former brother-in-law, José Francisco Ruiz Massieu was gunned down in Mexico City. This time the trail led directly to the President's elder brother, Raul Salinas, who was eventually convicted of having masterminded the crime. Although Carlos Salinas was never officially linked to the assassination, well-informed sources cite strong evidence that he participated in the decision to murder Ruiz Massieu and that his office funded the assassination.[28] Finally, shortly after Salinas departed office on December 1, 1994, it was discovered that his administration had steered Mexico into yet another major financial crisis.

Mexico's new president, Ernesto Zedillo, was initially inclined to settle the Zapatista issue militarily. In February and March 1995, he unleashed an offensive against Zapatista-controlled areas in Chiapas, ostensibly to allow the Army to serve arrest warrants on the insurgents' leaders. The leaders avoided capture and the same considerations that had inclined his predecessor toward a political approach now swayed Zedillo. The offensive was called off. Mexico's Congress passed a measure entitled "The Law for Dialogue, Reconciliation, and a Just Peace in Chiapas" and charged a multiparty legislative commission (COCOPA) with conducting the new negotiations. There followed a series of meetings among representatives of the government, the Zapatistas, CONAI, and COCOPA, which laid the basis for substantive peace talks.

Although the Zapatista agenda for the negotiations included such topics of national significance as "Democracy and Justice" and "Welfare and Development," government negotiators were largely successful in limiting discussion to purely Indian issues, rather than allowing them to delve into areas of broader national concern. The inevitable result was that apparent progress, coming in the form of what was known as the San Andrés Accords, was made only on the question of "Indigenous Rights and Culture." Near the end of 1996, the multiparty Congressional Commission, COCOPA, produced its "final" proposal of constitutional reforms on Indigenous Rights and Culture. The Zapatistas accepted the proposal. The government at first also accepted COCOPA's proposal, but soon had second thoughts and rejected it.

This marked the end of substantive formal negotiations between the Mexican government and the EZLN. Discussions among CONAI, COCOPA, and the Zapatistas continued, though in light of the government's position they led nowhere. In mid-1998, Bishop Samuel Ruiz resigned from CONAI, accusing the government of having rendered useless further attempts at mediation. Following his resignation, CONAI disbanded itself. COCOPA pledged to continue working for a peaceful settlement but reliable sources portrayed that body as dispirited and suffering from internal dissention and a lack of coordination.[29]

As if anticipating this dreary outcome to its formal negotiations with the Mexican government, the EZLN had devoted much earlier effort to building national and international support for its demand for a democratic revolution. In addition to constant appeals to international opinion, the EZLN fostered the birth of two political pressure groups within the Mexican political system. The first was what became known as the National Indigenous Congress, while the second was the Zapatista Front for National Liberation (FZLN). Both organizations were acknowledged as parts of the EZLN's efforts to lay the groundwork for its own transition from an armed guerrilla movement to a politically Zapatistas' oriented, pro-democracy civil movement. However, true to the Zapatistas insistence that they did not seek political power, neither group became a political party. Their aim, instead, was to work within Mexican civil society to press for democratic and constitutional reforms. While the Indigenous Congress was to focus on the plight of the country's Indian communities and, particularly, exert pressure for government adoption of the San Andrés Accords, the Zapatista Front would seek to mobilize all "systematically marginalized and oppressed" groups within Mexican society.[30]

Mexico's national mid-term elections in the summer of 1997 sharply underscored the PRI's downward slide. In a departure from what had been the case for nearly seventy years, the ruling party lost its majority in the Chamber of Deputies. The political impasse between the government and Zapatistas was not broken during the remainder of Zedillo's term in office. In the Conflict Zone, Zapatistas proceeded to set up "autonomous" municipalities and villages, which were locally governed on a fully participatory basis. Despite sporadic incursions by the Mexican military, the EZLN held to the cease-fire. EZLN did the same in the face of even more deadly provocations by local paramilitary forces. The growth of these bands of hired thugs became a major source of instability in the Chiapaneco countryside during the 1990s. Organized, it was widely believed, by Chiapas' local ruling elites or by the state's PRI—which essentially amounted to the same thing—and countenanced, if not financed, by the national government, paramilitary bands attacked Zapatistas and their sympathizers with impunity. Their most horrific accomplishment came on December 22, 1997, at the village of Acteal, where forty-five unarmed Tzotzil Indians, mainly women and children, were massacred. The butchery reportedly went on for four hours, within sight of a police post.

Mexico's national elections in 2000 were the most honest the country had experienced, for which outgoing President Ernesto Zedillo could rightfully claim much credit. For the first time in over seventy years, the PRI failed to win the presidency. The new president was Vicente Fox, a former state governor and Coca Cola executive who had run under the banner of the center-right National Action Party (PAN). The PRI, however, was by no means eclipsed. It remained the largest party in both houses of the federal Congress.

Fox assumed office exuding confidence that he could quickly resolve the Zapatista problem. For their part, the Zapatistas now looked hopefully toward an acceptable settlement with Mexico City, but made the resumption of negotiations contingent on three demands: the release of all Zapatista prisoners, the closure of military bases bordering Zapatista strongholds, and, finally, implementation of the San Andrés accords. Fox promptly took significant steps toward meeting the first two requirements but asked for time to deal with the last, on grounds that constitutional change had to come through an act of Congress. With Fox having submitted the proposed legislation to Congress, the EZLN leadership received government approval to organize a caravan to Mexico City, where Zapatistas hoped to convince the Congress to accept the measure, which was based on COCOPA's final proposal for constitutional change. What became known as the "Zapatour" covered some 3,000 kilometers, passed through twelve of Mexico's thirty-one states, and arrived to a tumultuous popular welcome in Mexico City on March 11, 2001. Marcos and other leaders addressed an estimated 100,000 cheering supporters in the capital's main square. Despite the opposition of a majority of congressmen from Fox's own party, PAN, the legislature finally agreed to hear the masked Zapatista leaders, whose speeches were broadcast live to the nation by television and radio.

In the end, Congress passed a modified version of the measure submitted by Fox. However, its provisions for Indian autonomy were so watered down and at variance with COCOPA's 1996 proposal that the EZLN immediately rejected it.

In the following years, the Fox administration relegated the Zapatista problem to the backburners of its attention. While the military presence on the borders of the Conflict Zone was significantly reduced, it was not eliminated. And although government support for anti-Zapatista paramilitary groups appeared to taper off, the paramilitary threat remained alive.[31] In early 2005, Samuel Ruiz—having retired and been granted the honorific Bishop Emeritus of Chiapas—and his former colleague, Bishop Raul Vera López, publicly called on the federal government to act on the ongoing problem posed by paramilitary groups in Chiapas. Saying that the Zapatista movement had become "primarily a social and political group," the Bishops charged that its supporters were still being subjected to armed attacks. "Paramilitary groups have not been disarmed and continue to be organized," charged Ruiz.[32]

During the years of Fox's more or less benign neglect, the EZLN focused on consolidating its autonomous presence in Chiapas. By 2005, there were thirty-eight autonomous Zapatista municipalities in the state, reportedly giving the Zapatistas political control of more than 15 percent of Chiapas' territory and embracing an estimated population of some 100,000 people.[33] Life in the autonomous region was not easy, but the Zapatistas were slowly attempting to develop a viable infrastructure that emphasized education, health care, and participatory agricultural cooperatives. The latter, particularly a cooperative devoted to the production and sale of organic coffee, helped finance the Zapatista attempt to develop an autonomous existence. Further financial support came from a variety of Mexican civil society organizations and national as well as international NGOs.[34]

More than a decade after the outbreak of the Zapatista Rebellion, it was still not clear just what the insurgency accomplished, though it was obviously not a sterile event in Mexico's recent history. At a minimum, the Rebellion had placed the plight of Mexico's Indians, some 10 percent of the country's inhabitants, on the national agenda. Then too, the Zapatistas' success in mobilizing widespread support from Mexican civil society was probably a factor that helped weaken the PRI's once iron grip on all significant aspects of national politics, thereby helping Mexico develop a more truly democratic system. While the Zapatista movement (including the EZLN and the FZLN) still clung to its original objective of promoting democratic change on behalf of all Mexicans, the practical focus of its efforts had come to dwell on reversing the marginalization—defined in economic, political, and cultural terms—afflicting Mexico's Indians. This—partly the result of government negotiators' steady refusal to discuss issues of overall national relevance, and, presumably, partly a consequence of the fact that "Indian issues" were of primordial concern to the bulk of the EZLN's forces—raised the question of whether the Zapatistas' broader national demands were still relevant. Ernesto Zedillo's claim that the PRI's loss of a majority in the Chamber of Deputies in 1997 proved that radical approaches to political reform were unnecessary in Mexico, may have been seen as optimistic rhetoric at the time. However, following the PRI's subsequent loss of the presidency, his point may have to be reevaluated.

Four obvious conclusions emerge from any consideration of Mexico's Zapatista experience. The first is that the marginalization of the country's Indian communities, and of its urban and rural masses, has not been overcome. The second is that claims for greater social justice and political inclusion have been firmly placed on the nation's political agenda. The third is that the threat of a renewal of violence on the part of the EZLN and its supporters has not been eliminated. The fourth is that the governments that ruled Mexico since 1994 managed, for whatever reasons, to avoid choosing to settle the Zapatista issue via the bloody road of simply employing military means.

The current existence of autonomous municipalities in much of Chiapas is an anomaly that must someday, somehow be settled. The question awaiting an answer is whether this will occur pacifically and politically, or through force. The very fact that the question still exists more than a decade after the Rebellion was launched gives some hope that the passage of time may promote changes in interests and perceptions on all sides that will help produce a political solution.

Structural and Cognitive Elements

The roots of the Zapatista Rebellion lay in Chiapas' history. Relevant factors were Chiapas' socioeconomic structure, including the cognitive frameworks at the structure's base, and the encounter between that structure and outside factors beyond anyone's control. Historically, topography and distance set Chiapas apart from much of Mexico's experience. From the outset, of course, it shared with Mexico, or New Spain, as the colony was then called, the *encomienda* system—the post-*conquistador* practice of land grants, through which members of the conquering Spanish newcomers not only received land but also the legal right to exploit the labor of indigenous communities living on the land. The colonizers established their cities, of which San Cristóbal remains the best example, and in the countryside took the best lands, excluding Indians—save for necessary labor—from both. The latter were steadily pushed to less hospitable territories: the mountains, the valley slopes, and the jungles.

The progressive isolation of Indian communities mirrored the more general isolation of Chiapas itself. For the non-Indian colonial powers in Chiapas were themselves isolated, both by distance and a colonial structure that, by at times assigning Chiapas administratively to the Captaincy of Guatemala rather than to New Spain, helped separate them from the centers of events in Mexico. Mexico won its independence in 1810. Chiapas declared its own independence eleven years later, but opted to join the Mexican Republic in 1824. A major Chiapaneco leader of the time appraised the decision in these semiprophetic words: "It is good. The only thing is that [with Chiapas] being so far from the center, the government will forget about it."[35] Mexico never really "forgot" Chiapas—the state offered too much wealth for that—but it proved all too willing to allow Chiapaneco society to develop on its own terms so long as the state's wealth continued to contribute to the national economy. As Chiapenco scholar David Dávila has noted, "wealth is created in the state, but the Chiapanecos remain poor."[36]

By the late twentieth century, Chiapas played a key role in Mexico's economy. Agriculture, the state's dominant pursuit, was not limited to subsistence enterprises. Agricultural products such as bananas, coffee, cocoa, and soy injected more than $150 million dollars into the Mexican economy in 1994. At the same time, Chiapas provided some 55 percent of the country's hydroelectricity, while also annually producing some 20 million barrels of crude oil as well as significant amounts of natural gas and sulfur.[37]

The problem, of course, is that the wealth generated by these resources has always flowed strictly along the lines of the highly stratified social system that evolved in Chiapas after the Conquest. The descendants of the first Spanish colonists continue to preside over this stark social configuration, at the top of which figure "Ladinos," those claiming (not always accurately) a purely European ancestry, and, at the bottom, the region's Indians. Over the centuries, Ladino landowners and peasants pushed the original Indian inhabitants to less productive areas. The prevailing Ladino view of the Indian was—and remains—overtly and strongly rascist, based on the conviction that the Indian is by nature not only inferior but also characterized by a potentially dangerous childishness.[38] The Chiapaneco elite also cling to a negative stereotype of their counterparts in other parts of Mexico. Widely characterized by non-Chiapanecos as provincial and somewhat crude, Ladinos return the favor by voicing perceptions that paint the former as effete "outsiders" who do not understand the realities of life.[39]

The Revolution that produced Mexico's 1917 Constitution did not substantially alter Chiapas' socioeconomic structure. The Chiapaneco elite found its place in the clientalistic chains forged by the PRI as Mexico's postrevolutionary political system was consolidated. In return, for supporting the federal government, this elite was permitted to extend its own control of the local state government through similar clientalistic arrangements. At the lowest level, these resulted in tangible benefits—often the lucrative right to sell liquor—for village chiefs (*caciques*) who supported the status quo.

By the 1990s, the Ladino's iron grip on the state's economy and politics had produced horrendous conditions. According to official Mexican figures, Chiapas had a population of 3.2 million inhabitants, of which 855,000 were economically active. Yet, 19 percent of the latter received no income.[40] Of just over 655,000 Chiapanecos who did receive earned income, 52 percent received less than the nationally mandated minimum wage. The situation was even worse in the Highlands, where the Zapatista Rebellion was born. In that area, 59 percent of the nearly 104,000 economically active population received no income, while 63.6 percent of the region's gainfully employed earned less than the minimum wage.[41] Not surprisingly, the relatively greater economic deprivation of the Highlands in comparison with the dismal profile of the state itself was mirrored by other, equally depressing, social indicators. Embracing an area of 75,634 square kilometers, Chiapas had 14,613 kilometers of roads, only 22 percent of which were paved.[42] The most casual encounter with the Highlands provided ample proof that little of the paving found its way to that area. Poverty and the very limited infrastructure of roads and bridges did much to exacerbate deficiencies in basic services such as health care and education.

A related difficulty in this respect was the fact that most of the region's population was dispersed among micro-villages and settlements. Here, again, the Highlands reflected in more acute form a general condition in the state. According to Mexico's 1990 census, Chiapas' population resided in 16,442 recognized settled entities (*localidades*). However, more than 12,000 (74 percent) of these were occupied by less than 100 persons. On the other hand, while 99 percent of recognized towns contained less than 1,000 inhabitants, three cities—Tuxtla Gutiérrez, Tapachula, and San Cristóbal de las Casas—together accounted for nearly 16 percent of Chiapas' population.[43]

This bleak statistical picture found its reality in a rugged mountainous terrain that is broken by steep valleys, which at their upper levels are adorned by coniferous forests and, on their lower slopes, by abundant semitropical vegetation. In this setting, usually lacking the most elemental amenities of running water, electricity, and drainage, are scattered multiple communities whose members' primary aim is to secure the necessities of daily subsistence. Mornings see women and children trudging into the forest or semi-jungle to collect firewood and water. Men go out somewhat later to take up sundry chores—chopping and stacking firewood for the next day's collection, clearing small patches of undergrowth for *milpas* (cornfields) or tending existing fields. Midday and afternoons witness the continuation of these activities and the initiation of others. Women deal with the multiple demands of homemaking, child-rearing and supplementary, though important, productive activities—tending vegetable gardens or engaging in minor animal husbandry. Evenings bring brief moments of relaxation—a time for gossiping, complaining, sometimes planning, sometimes laughing, sometimes quarreling. Then the village sleeps; and then, with the dawn, the endless routine begins anew.

Such, essentially, is the daily reality that statistics point to as the life of many of Chiapas' people, and particularly of those in the Highlands. But this is no reliable routine enacted by a robust peasantry gleaning a simple, but satisfactory, livelihood from the soil. The bulk of activity is devoted to survival farming, and the margin between livelihood and disaster remains perilously thin. The inherent precariousness of it all is heightened by a lack of adequate basic health care. Malnutrition is endemic and enhances the prevalence of disease. Tuberculosis, cholera, malaria, typhoid, trachoma, dengue, and digestive ailments are rife. Leprosy is not uncommon in some parts.[44]

Chiapas' several Indian communities—of which all but one are of Maya origin—have suffered most from the state's rampant inequities. From the Highlands to the Guatemalan border, the main Indian groups are the Tzeltal, Tzotzil, Lacandón, and Tojolabal. As late as the mid-1990s, nearly 24 percent of the Highland's population could not speak Spanish.[45] The harsh realities of poverty and powerlessness produced massive social deterioration. Alcoholism, violence, sexual abuse, and similar ills plagued Indian communities.[46] Mexico's postrevolutionary establishment of communal landholdings *(ejidos)* generally did not provide the Indians with more fertile or extensive fields than in the past, and the few attempts that were made to develop new lands were usually soon frustrated by members of the local elite who wished to extend their own holdings.[47]

On the night his forces took San Cristóbal, Subcomandante Marcos noted that the average age of the EZLN's troops was only twenty-two.[48] The young men and women who constituted the bulk of the Zapatista fighters had been shaped not only by the poverty-stricken conditions of Indian life in Chiapas but also by the rich, intricate, and vibrant Indian culture that still permeates the indigenous Highland communities. Vestiges of pre-Columbian Maya culture are visible in the daily lives of modern Chiapas' Indians, and are readily found in culinary tradition, clothing, and important patterns of social behavior that determine personal status.[49] However, the most important elements of precolonial Maya influence are in the sphere of religion. Evon Vogt, the anthropologist who initiated the "Harvard Chiapas Project" in the late 1950s, has recalled how his first impressions regarding the religious life of a Tzotzil community (Zinacantán) changed over the years. It became, he wrote, "more and more apparent that Zinacantecos were not Catholic peasants with a few Maya remnants left in the culture, but rather that they were Maya tribesmen with a Spanish Catholic veneer—a veneer that appears to be increasingly thin as we do fieldwork with the culture."[50]

The Highland Maya are predominantly Roman Catholics, but this is more nominal than anything else. Tourists visiting San Cristóbal will generally make the short trip to the Tzotzil town of San Juan Chamula, where they will visit the local church in order to witness a clear example of the Highland Indians' syncretistic melding of Catholicism with pre-Columbian religious beliefs and practices.[51] Generally, the church's statuary will be adorned with small mirrors and other articles that are unusual to orthodox Catholic eyes. Shamans and their patients will be scattered in groups around the stone floor, and each site is marked by intricate patterns of candles as well as by large bottles of soft drinks and *aguardiente*. Sometimes Marlboro cigarette cartons appear among such offerings. The Shamans chant or mutter their incantations in low voices. Photographs are strongly discouraged.

But Chamula is only the tip of a much larger cultural iceberg. Vogt and other anthropologists have shown that pre-Columbian beliefs and rituals, combined with the "thin veneer" of Catholicism, prominently figure in virtually all aspects of the Highland Maya's daily life, serving as a unifying social force at all levels. Birth, courtship, marriage, child-rearing, and death, as well as moving into or building a new house, planting and harvesting crops, recovering from or preventing illness and ensuring supplies of water are only some of the areas in which the practice of the Highland religion regularly figures.

The Mayan cosmology underpinning these practices is vast and complex, with myriad gods, spirits, and saints, many of whom dwell in mountains and lakes and require frequent propitiation. The Shaman is therefore a needed figure in the community, and there are many. In addition to conducting rituals related to the issues mentioned above, Shamans serve to interpret dreams, provide protection from "evil" counterparts, or witches, who supernaturally attack innocent victims, and—since disease is attributed to distortions in, or loss of parts of, the multifaceted human soul—to cure illnesses.[52]

The Highland Maya cosmos is one in which the supernatural and natural blend, and interact in an ongoing process of accommodation and reaccommodation. Ancestors, spirits, gods, and saints constantly relate to the individual and the community, sometimes helping, sometimes hurting. The miraculous—the manipulation of mundane forces by supernatural means—is part and parcel of daily experience.

Writing in 1970—about the time most of Subcomandante Marcos' Zapatista troops were born—Vogt described how this cosmological view is transmitted:

> During the age of socialization there is little formal instruction... about the sacred values of the culture or about the ritual procedures and prayers that are learned and performed by any competent adult. Sacred stories about the gods and their activities are sometimes told around the hearth.... Experiences involving beliefs about the "souls" are often shared in conversation. But even more learning takes place by virtue of the fact that people live in one-roomed houses, and hence

> when a shaman comes to diagnose an illness, or returns later to perform a curing ceremony, small children observe the proceedings as a matter of course. When the children are very small, they sleep through the all-night ceremonies. But as they become older, they stay awake longer and longer, and are called upon to help with the ceremonies. The boys are pressed into duty as assistants for the shamans. The girls help their mothers to prepare the ritual meals. In addition, children are taken to ceremonies in the [town's] Center, beginning at an early age. By the time Zinacantecos become adults they have learned an immense range of ritual procedures and prayers for ceremonies.[53]

While the force of traditional outlooks is clear, few of Chiapas' rural population failed to experience nontraditional ways of life, or false hopes of modernizing change, prior to the 1994 Rebellion. During the 1970s, the Highlands became the primary focus of the central government's attempts to include Mexico's Indian communities in national development efforts.[54] Although corruption and inefficiency severely limited their long-term impact, federal funds poured into the region at a rate surpassing those of resources allocated to other areas of the country for similar purposes. In the 1980s, events beyond Mexico's borders caused the national government to devote even more resources to Chiapas. By 1982, a steady influx of refugees from Guatemala, many of whom were Indians engaged in an ongoing war against the Guatemalan regime, caused Mexican ruling circles to fear that Chiapas' rural population might be contaminated by radical activism.[55] A major result was an upsurge of federal funding. The "Chiapas Plan" was a two-track effort to increase the region's security by enhancing Mexico's ability to project force into the area and, on the other hand, to defuse chances of domestic unrest by promoting economic development. The ensuing large-scale investments in state projects such as hydroelectric plants, oil exploitation, and road development brought welcome opportunities for employment.[56] Unfortunately, these opportunities would be short-lived.

The economic crises that began to grip Mexico in the 1980s and the country's turn to neoliberal policies severely affected the already precarious conditions of the small farmer in Chiapas and, particularly, in the Highlands. Declining federal investment in rural development led to the reduction or elimination of governmental organizations and programs designed to help peasant and Indian farmers. However limited or ineffective such aid had been in the past, its reduction further increased the level of misery in Chiapas. So too did decreases of subsidies to the agricultural sector and—particularly—the elimination of subsidies to coffee producers.[57] The peasants' plight was augmented as the liberalization of Mexico's trade policies led to an influx of cheaper foreign agricultural products into the domestic market. At the same time, the termination of large-scale government projects and the privatization of major agricultural concerns reduced employment opportunities for peasants. All this contributed to a thoroughly dismal outcome: between 1980 and 1990 the economically active population in the Highlands receiving less than the minimum wage increased by 122 percent.[58] Hopes that only a few years earlier had been bright were dashed.

A bitter twist was added to the problems that engulfed Chiapas in the 1980s by the fact that the overall picture of the state's agriculture during the same period showed significant gains made by large landowners who benefited from the De la Madrid administration's "Chiapas Plan."[59] However, the most striking step in the liberalizing drive to rationalize agriculture and facilitate movement toward agro-industry came in 1992, when the modification of Article 27 of the Mexican Constitution effectively halted land reform and permitted the sale of *ejido* land distributed under the old order. Many years later, Subcomandante Marcos described the impact this measure had on the EZLN's recruitment:

> The impact on the communities that were already Zapatistas was, to say the least, brutal. For us (and note that I am no longer distinguishing between the communities and the EZLN) land is not a commodity... it has cultural, religious and historical connotations that are not necessary to explain here. At any rate, our ranks grew through geometric progression.[60]

THE FORMATION OF THE EZLN

It was in the context described above that the EZLN originated, recruited its membership, and mobilized for the offensive that greeted 1994. The movement's development can be traced to efforts launched some twenty years earlier by Bishop Samuel Ruiz. Ruiz was thirty-six years old in 1960, when he arrived in San Cristóbal. The city's Ladino elites—who proudly call themselves "*Coletos*"[61] —were initially charmed by the newcomer but felt betrayed after a few years when he became actively concerned with the economic and social plight of his Indian flock. A leading member of the Coleto community—whose most rascist members were, by the mid-1990s, calling themselves *Auténticos Coletos*—recalled the young bishop as an initially promising addition to San Cristóbal's established way of life:

> ... it fell to me to welcome Samuel Ruiz. He was a very tranquil man and dined and had coffee in the most honorable homes of San Cristóbal. Yes, in those days he passed his time with *Auténticos Coletos*! But then he slowly began to change. I think it's always been important for him to seek fame.[62]

Ruiz confirms that his first years in San Cristóbal were marked by early impressions that began to crumble as he started perceiving the harsh realities beneath the colonial city's elegant surface:

> When I arrived . . . I saw the churches full of Indians . . . only later did I become aware of these people, of the sad reality [and that] provoked a process of conversion in me.[63]

Learning the local Indian languages, Ruiz set out to discover what it meant to be an Indian in Chiapas, visiting even the remotest parts of his far-flung diocese, then the largest in the world. The exercise led him to an activist, Theology of Liberation, view of the Church's mission. Years later, a priest who served under Ruiz put the core of this vision succinctly:

> In this diocese . . . we have taken a stand for the poor—not excluding the rich, but inviting them to make a radical change and to be for and with the poor in the society. We've been literally going out to the people, walking with the people, being in their villages, eating the food they give us. Instead of encouraging people to accept suffering in this life in hope of a better life after death, we are saying that the reign of God starts now.[64]

Ruiz's application of Theology of Liberation was carried out by religious workers in his diocese as well as by Indian lay catechists, the latter being trained in San Cristóbal before being deployed to their home villages. The resulting network of religious and lay community development workers was largely in place by 1974. In the early 1970s, Ruiz's efforts were seconded by radical young Mexicans who arrived in Chiapas in flight from the country's security forces. These individuals, augmented by a second generation of young radicals who joined them in the early 1980s, mobilized peasants in pursuit of objectives that were very similar to those pursued by the local Catholic hierarchy. The former's more militant approach led to the EZLN's foundation in 1983. Nonetheless, the Theology of Liberation adhered to by Bishop Ruiz and the Marxist orientation of the newcomers remained largely compatible. The result was that the two collaborated for several years in setting up a series of interlocking peasant organizations.[65]

During the 1980s, Chiapas' elites vigorously used state and national institutions to intimidate (and frequently liquidate) peasant activists. This intensified strains between Church-linked and Marxist-oriented activists in the budding peasant movement, with the latter steadily gaining adherents to the view that armed struggle was necessary. In the early 1990s, the two trends split. The EZLN may still have retained ties to national Marxist revolutionary groups. If so, the links appear to have been broken sometime prior to EZLN's 1994 offensive.[66] However, Samuel Ruiz's nonviolent followers' sympathy for the EZLN remained strong and members of the EZLN visibly continued to hold the Bishop virtually in awe. These close ties undoubtedly help explain not only the Zapatistas success in preserving secrecy as they mustered their forces on the eve of 1994, but also the relative ease with which the movement subsequently accommodated itself to political, instead of military, action.

The Zapatista Rebellion provides an opening wedge to an understanding of the asymmetrical conflict that blossomed on 9/11. Among the Rebellion's most obvious and important lessons are two, each of which is reinforced and extended by the examinations of the nearly coterminous insurgencies in Egypt and Nigeria that follow in the next two chapters. The first of these is that human beings, if faced by what they deem to be intolerable situations, will eventually choose to fight, regardless of the odds against them. The second is that such a choice is dependent on—or at least facilitated by—a cognitive framework, a mind-set, that finds reason to doubt that objective, empirical evidence defines the limits of the real or the possible.

CHAPTER 4

UPPER EGYPT AND THE *GAMA'A AL-ISLAMIYYA*

Herodutus gave us the pithy statement that Egypt is "the gift of the Nile," an observation as true today as when it was first written some 2,500 years ago. Demography provides definitive proof. While Egypt's national territory extends over some 597,000 square miles, less than 5 percent of its surface area is habitable. Crowded into that limited strip is an estimated population of seventy million, whose existence is made possible by the great river.

From it origins in the highlands of equatorial Africa, what becomes the Nile forms Egypt's vital spine as it courses the nearly 1,000 miles between the Sudanese border and the Mediterranean Sea. For approximately half this distance, the river pursues its northerly flow through a narrow valley that is ridged by desert escarpments to both the east and west. The eastern plateau comprises the desolate mountains of the vast desert that runs to the Red Sea and then stretches through Arabia and into the subcontinent. The western escarpment is the gateway to the enormous Libyan, or Sahara, Desert that crosses the African continent to the Atlantic Ocean. Since time immemorial, this narrow strip of the southern Nile Valley—Upper Egypt—has been distinguished from the northern half of Egypt, or Lower Egypt. Lower Egypt is formed by the Nile's lotus-shaped delta, which takes form just to the north of the country's capital, Cairo.

THE SETTING

Whether under Pharaonic, Ptolemaic, Roman, Byzantine, Mamluk, Ottoman, French, British, or modern Egyptian rule, distinctions between Upper and Lower Egypt have always been present. In the late twentieth century, these differences were to contribute to the campaign that a fundamentalist Islamist movement known as the *Gama'a al-Islamiyya* (the Islamic Group) waged against the regime of Hosni Mubarak, Egypt's third president since the country achieved real self-determination just over fifty years ago. This last point is worth stressing, for despite frequent politically motivated rhetorical claims, and even more frequently shouted touristically oriented sales pitches, to the effect that "Egypt is a 6,000-year-old country," the reality is that full Egyptian rule over Egypt was ended by the second Persian occupation in 343 B.C. and not really restored until the final vestiges of British colonial rule were shattered by Gamal Abdul Nasser in 1952. Today's Egypt, an ancient political entity, is still a relative newcomer to the task of trying to build a modern state.

Mohammed Ali, the Albanian Ottoman officer who in the early nineteenth century seized power and founded the dynasty that held sway until Egypt's monarchy was abolished in 1952, sought to modernize the country's army and economy. In doing so he fixed his gaze northward, determined to emulate the advanced states of Western Europe. Under his long rule (1805–1848) sweeping changes occurred. Although his attempts to industrialize Egypt ultimately failed, Mohammed Ali eliminated the Mamluks and, along with them, their landed baronies. Private landholdings became possible. By depending on an administrative system that relied on local peasant village headmen (*Omdahs*), Ali's reforms helped further the growth of a small but relatively prosperous class of landed peasant notables. At the same time, however, he and his descendants relied so heavily on the practice of giving large land grants to influential court favorites, tribal leaders, and others who could be counted on to serve as local supports of the government's authority, that by the late 1800s the Egyptian peasantry's position was increasingly precarious. As Egyptian political economist Nadia Farah Ramsis notes, "a class of large landowners formed the base of the political system."[1]

In the latter half of the nineteenth century, the global demand for Egyptian long staple cotton spurred an even greater concentration of landholdings. Yet, the country's potential wealth proved no match for economic mismanagement. Unable to cope with its international debt, Egypt was occupied by the British in 1882 and essentially ruled by them until the early 1920s, when it received a limited measure of independence. Under London's direction, "Egypt became a huge farm, dedicated to the production of cotton for British mills."[2]

A major part of Mohammed Ali's effort to modernize Egypt was his readiness to accept the presence of non-Muslim foreigners in Egypt, an attitude also adopted by his successors. Between 1838 and 1881, Egypt's resident foreign population mushroomed from an estimated 8,000–10,000 to some 90,000.[3] Concentrated in the cities of Alexandria and Cairo, the foreigners—Greeks, Italians, French, British, and sundry others—soon dominated the country's commercial and financial life. Members of the Egyptian elite quickly adapted to the new cultural influence. Often equally at home in Arabic, English, and French, they enthusiastically sent their offspring to study in Europe and to participate lucratively—it was hoped—in Egypt's burgeoning links to the world economy. Many of the gloriously optimistic signs of this attitude are still available to any casual observer who takes the trouble to scrutinize what can be seen today in Cairo or Alexandria. For beneath the inevitable grimy patina left by Cairo's smoggy atmosphere and the erosion caused by Alexandria's confrontation with the Mediterranean's seaborne air lie countless examples of Belle Epoch architecture, which still express the hopes of that bygone age.

The architecture also represents another phenomenon. In its drive to modernize, Egypt's turn-of-the-century elite not only looked abroad but also turned its back on the country's masses, the peasantry. From the mid-1800s to the mid-1900s, the plight of Egypt's peasants steadily worsened, a trend most glaringly reflected in patterns of land ownership. While the consolidation of large landholdings grew steadily, small peasant holdings shrank through fragmentation with each passing generation. By 1952, 0.5 percent of landholders were classified as large landowners, who together held fully one-third of the country's cultivated land. On the other hand, "75 percent of all rural property owners were peasants farming less than one feddan" (a *feddan* is 1.038 acres).[4] These small landowners accounted for only 13 percent of cultivated land. In short, the bulk of Egypt's population remained "rural, poor and illiterate."[5]

The full extent of poverty in contemporary Egypt remains somewhat controversial, though nobody denies that it burdens a significant portion of the country's population. The Egyptian government acknowledges that just over 20 percent of Egyptian families are mired in poverty, but other observers argue that the figure is vastly higher.[6] A World Bank study finished in 2002 concluded that between 16 and 17 percent of Egypt's population live in poverty, though it warned that the country's economic slowdown at the end of the 1990s may have fueled an increase in poverty rates.[7]

Poverty typically brings a variety of social ills in its wake, a rule to which Egypt is no exception. Egyptian youth, a group comprising some 13 million individuals, was the focus of a 1997 Population Council study that produced disturbing results. Based on a survey of over 9,000 individuals between the ages of ten and nineteen, the study found that over half the males (and almost as many females) suffered from anemia and that fully half of those surveyed had parasitic infections. Such conditions, the study noted, helped explain why "the growth of many adolescents is stunted and their sexual maturation is delayed." Not surprisingly, the survey also found that child labor was rampant, often technically in violation of Egyptian law. Over half the male sample engaged in income-generating activity, and half of those did so in violation of laws supposedly governing minimum working age and maximum work hours per week. Fully 40 percent of the male sample worked seven days a week.[8]

The implications of poor nutrition, poor health, and overwork for the education of Egypt's new generations are dire. Although recent years have seen significant progress in the spread of literacy, approximately 35 percent of the population remains illiterate. Between the pressures of poverty at one end and limitations on the educational experience of the young at the other, the threat of an enduring vicious circle is very real.

Coping mechanisms among Egypt's legions of poor, more visible in rural areas and among communities of rural origin that have migrated to urban areas, include what many nineteenth-century Western observers branded as the hallmark of the Egyptian peasant, "fatalism." Looked at more closely, however, this so-called fatalism breaks down into at least two component parts, which together contradict those early stereotypical attributions of passive acceptance or apathy to the Egyptian peasant. Certainly religion, Islam, as well as Christianity among Egypt's minority Coptic community, has promoted a heavy reliance on the belief that "God disposes," and just as certainly this belief helps make grinding poverty bearable for millions of believers. Yet, the religions of Egypt's rurally rooted masses—whether Islam or Christianity—are not the same as those practiced by their more sophisticated urban coreligionists. Instead, what prevail among this sector of society are better labeled as forms of folk religion, an Islam and Christianity imbued with saints and holy places, and with miracles and the ever-present possibility of divine intervention in the problems of daily life. It is also marked by ritual practices and people who are believed to facilitate such intervention. Thus, the village healer will be relied upon to cure illnesses resulting from spirit possession and local shrines will receive ritualized petitions for supernatural help in overcoming problems that may include a wide variety of issues, ranging from health to personal relations.[9] Rather than implying a fundamentally passive attitude, the folk religions of Egyptian peasants are decidedly proactive.

The pall of poverty and its attendant ills affects all parts of Egypt, but is not evenly spread. Perhaps the most striking feature of the World Bank's 2002 study was its finding that between 1996 and 2001 rural as well as urban poverty increased in Upper Egypt, while it generally declined in lower Egypt. By 2002, Upper Egypt contained some 40 percent of the country's population, or some 28 million people, but was home to some 70 percent of its poor.[10]

Far from the traditional centers of Egypt's political, economic, and cultural life—Cairo and Alexandria—Upper Egyptians evolved the traditions, outlooks, and patterns of speech and social interaction that still give them a unique character within the national context. Upper Egypt is known in Arabic as the *Sa'id*; its inhabitants as *Sa'idis*. Long famous in the Arab World for their irrepressible sense of humor, Egyptians won their comedy crown largely on the basis of an endless repertoire of *Sa'idi* jokes, virtually all of which portray *Sa'idis* as mentally stunted country bumpkins. *Sa'idis*, on the other hand retain their own negative sterotypes of Lower Egyptians, who are generally seen as lacking in honesty, manhood, and honor.

Egyptian anthropologist Reem Saad correctly reminds us that generalizations about Upper Egyptian society must be made with care, and that even those that are on the whole valid should be understood as having scope for significant variations at the local level.[11] Nonetheless, despite the intensity of localized social patterns, broader generalizations applicable to *Sa'idi* society are possible. One of these, as Saad herself notes, is "the condition of being on the [national] periphery, and the deep bitterness engendered as a result of this"—a reaction that by and large cuts across divisions of class or social group.[12]

Yet another general characteristic of Upper Egyptian society is its highly stratified nature. The social pecking order is rigid and cast in terms of tribe, clan, and family. Social mobility tends to be determined by one's place in these groups. Although the criteria for determining social groups may vary from locale to locale, their importance in forming a relatively inflexible scale of identity that defines the individual's status, and hence life opportunities, is common to the region.[13] As there are significant numbers of Copts in Upper Egypt, religion too must be cited as one such factor. Within the broader, overwhelmingly Islamic, context of Upper Egypt—as is true of Egypt as a whole—Copts are generally seen and treated as second-class citizens. This, however, does not necessarily mean that they automatically occupy the lowest position in Upper Egyptian social hierarchies. With roots in the area going back to pharaonic times, local Coptic communities may enjoy a higher social status than more recently arrived groups.[14]

Another common feature of Upper Egypt is the high social value given to honor and to loyalty to one's tribe and family group. Such values underlie and help explain both the feud, as a prevalent Upper Egyptian practice, and the evolution of localized processes of conflict management and resolution, practices that national authorities in Upper Egypt have found expedient to countenance in the application of Egypt's legal code.[15]

Such pragmatism has traditionally been part and parcel of the mechanisms through which Cairo sustained its authority in Upper Egypt, a process that involved securing the support of prominent locals—whether tribal leaders or village notables. In return, of course, Cairo's policies were careful to support the positions and interests of local elites. This clientalistic pattern has remained essentially unchanged since the days of Mohammed Ali. While the nature of local elites has varied, particularly since the Nasserist revolution of 1952, the political dynamic has not.

Nasser's land reform helped alter Upper Egypt's social structure. Although large landowners frequently found ways to retain control of their holdings, redistribution provided some relief for the area's peasants. This, however, was tenuous—particularly in light of Egypt's booming population. When it is recalled that in the century between Egypt's first census in 1882 and its 1986 census the country's population increased from 6.7 million to over 48 million, and that today it stands at an estimated 70 million, it is clear that pressure on land ownership has been overwhelming.[16] In Upper Egypt as well as elsewhere, land fragmentation has resulted in peasant landowners coming to rely for their livelihood on nonagricultural work—when they can get it. Under Nasser, the government bureaucracy became the avenue to gainful labor, prestige, and security. Within the politicized environment of post-1952 Egypt, the so far enduring dominance of single-party authoritarian regimes has ensured that the party controls entry to the bureaucracy.[17]

The fading hope that land could provide an escape from poverty, coupled with the Nasserist focus on industrializing Egypt—but not industrializing the *Sa'id*—inevitably led to massive internal migration by Upper Egyptians. Cairo and, just to its south, Helwan, soon bulged under the influx of tens of thousands, and then more, of *Sa'idis*. The influx of villagers into Egyptian cities and towns, which by the 1970s led increasingly to the "ruralization" of Egypt's urban life, came to provide fertile fields for antimodernist, fundamentalist movements. Urban mosques often became centers for the recruitment of rural migrants into militant organizations.[18]

In the 1970s, the quadrupling of oil revenues by the Middle East's oil-rich states led the Saudis, Kuwaitis, Libyans, and the rulers of the United Arab Emirates to embark on vast infrastructural projects that required unskilled labor. Egyptian peasants, many from Upper Egypt, responded in their millions. More than one million Egyptians were working abroad by 1980. Within three years, this figure reached an estimated 3.2 million.[19] The termination of infrastructural projects, combined with the decline in oil prices after 1986 as well as political events in the Arab World, particularly Iraq's 1990 invasion of Kuwait, drastically reduced the viability of temporary labor emigration as an option for Egypt's struggling peasantry.

In the late 1950s, Nasser's regime began to expand Egypt's system of higher education by building new universities in the provinces, including the University of Assiut in Upper Egypt. By 1964, the government promised employment to all university graduates. With university degrees as tickets to secure government jobs, young *Sa'idis* flocked to the new halls of academe. It was a good move for the first generations of students, but one that quickly became questionable as the bureaucracy bloated beyond any reasonable limits. Within a decade, government policy shifted to allow ministries to impose quotas on their hiring needs. Education no longer promised young Egyptians an escape from poverty.

As shown by the World Bank's 2002 study, Upper Egypt's poverty has increased over the past few years, in contrast to the relative improvement that has been seen in Lower Egypt. The marginalization of the *Sa'id* contributed materially to the domestic unrest and violence that Egypt suffered in the 1990s. Current trends that further differences between Upper Egypt and the rest of the country do not bode well. In 2003, one of the most penetrating analysts of Egyptian affairs, Robert Springborg, put it this way:

> Saidi, or Upper Egyptian identity, has grown apace as the region has failed to keep pace with the development of the remainder of the country. Saidi identity is intermixed with religion and tribalism/familism, creating a lethal brew that Cairo considers as seditious and has responded to accordingly. In the Hobbesian world of Upper Egypt only two things are certain. The first is that whether Islamist, tribalist, or regionalist, the motivating ideology is stridently anti-governmental. The second is that unlike Christian or Islamist/modernist identities and political movements, the Saidi identity and the individuals and groups that seek to translate it into political action lack extra-Egyptian connections. Theirs inevitably is a rural revolt, against which massive firepower can be deployed indiscriminately and successfully, for the world does not aid the insurrectionists, even by recognizing their plight. But Saidi identity is unlikely to be eradicated by force, whereas it probably would be tempered were the region to be more thoroughly and profitably integrated into the national political economy.[20]

The *Gama'a al-Islamiyya*

Egyptian political scientist Maye Kassem notes that while Islamic values had figured prominently in Arab political thought of the late nineteenth and early twentieth centuries, it was only with the creation of the Muslim Brotherhood in the1920s that "Political Islam in its contemporary, participatory and popular form emerged. . . ."[21] The Brotherhood began and grew as a truly grassroots movement, successfully portraying itself as the champion of anticolonialism, Egyptian and Arab nationalism, and the Islamic values that alone could mobilize sufficient strength to overcome the corrupting influences of European imperialism and its local elite acolytes. Its goal was to bring about the rule of Islamic Law, or Sharia. The two decades that preceded the collapse of Egypt's monarchy in 1952 were politically volatile in Egypt, marked by rising levels of universal resentment of Britain's ongoing presence in the country, the weakening of the British Empire in World War II, and growing tensions—and ultimately war—in Palestine. With its populist, activist, nativist message, the Brotherhood benefited from this heady atmosphere. While the government and established political parties struggled to cope with the harsh realities of the 1930s and 1940s, the Brotherhood remained an oppositional political movement, untainted by the inevitable compromises required of dominant political players or the scandals and defeats associated with those in power. Its appeal grew accordingly, as did its political importance.

Even under the monarchy, Egypt's rulers—although fully recognizing a fundamental incompatibility of interests with the Brotherhood and alarmed by its ability to "mobilize mass support and organization"—occasionally sought to enlist the movement as an ally in their own domestic struggles. This early pattern was followed by each of the three "authoritarian presidencies" erected on the monarchy's grave after 1952.[22] Gamal Abdul Nasser initially offered cabinet positions to the Muslim Brotherhood, hoping to use the movement as a counterweight to the displaced elites who had been the former monarchy's mainstay. When the offer was rejected, his regime temporarily adopted a live-and-let-live policy, allowing the Brotherhood to conduct its activities undisturbed. The honeymoon was short-lived. Following a failed attempt on Nasser's life in 1954, the regime ruthlessly clamped down on the Brotherhood, executing several of its leaders and jailing thousands of its members.

When Anwar Sadat assumed the presidency following Nasser's death in 1969, he too tried to use the Islamic movement as a resource against those who might have prevented him from consolidating his position, Communists and—as he set about reversing his predecessor's populist and socialist policies—Nasserists. But Sadat was presiding over a different era, one that was above all shaped by Egypt's total defeat at Israel's hands in the war of 1967. A major consequence of that event, in Egypt and throughout the Arab World, was that the established actors of the old order were severely discredited, particularly in the eyes of the younger generations. This reaction extended to the Muslim Brotherhood. Even before the defeat, some Egyptian Islamists had found the Brotherhood insufficiently militant and begun to organize new and more radical groups. This process accelerated in the post-1967 years. Maye Kassem's interview with a former radical Islamist leader of the period elicited this explanation: "The Muslim Brotherhood had just come out of Nasser's prisons, they were worn out and just wanted to make peace with the government."[23]

Throughout much of the 1970s, the Sadat regime countenanced, and to a degree actively supported, the growth of the Islamist movement, particularly within Egypt's universities. Various groups emerged, a minority of which were oriented toward militancy. In 1974, one such group, the Islamic Liberation Organization carried out an unsuccessful but bloody attack on the Technical Military Academy in Cairo.[24] While the flourishing Islamist groups differed on various questions, particularly those related to how their objectives should be pursued, they shared a fundamental common cause, "the implementation of *sharia*," that is, the rule of Islamic Law, in Egypt.[25] "Islam is the solution," became more than a rallying slogan—it developed into a virtual mantra for those convinced that Sharia was the remedy for all the country's ills.

By the late 1970s, Sadat's international policies were rapidly eroding his support at home. Islamists, who generally supported the 1979 Islamic Revolution in Iran, were horrified when Sadat offered Egyptian hospitality to the deposed Shah.[26] Even more offensive were Sadat's moves on the stage of Great Power politics. He had not only distanced Egypt from its long-time superpower champion, the Soviet Union, but also openly, persistently and, ultimately, successfully endeavored to place the country under the wing of the United States. By way of doing so, he abandoned the Arab struggle against Israel and, in 1979, signed a peace treaty with the Jewish state. Egypt paid for this by being ostracized from the Arab World. The regime paid by becoming ever more isolated from the Egyptian public. It all redounded to the benefit of militant Islamists, fueling equally their rage and their ability to attract new adherents. One such group, *Tanzim al-Jihad*, better known simply as the Egyptian *Jihad*, wove a widespread network that included both university and nonuniversity groups in various parts of the country. It was ironic that as the Muslim Brotherhood turned increasingly to a political path that eschewed violence, the *Jihad*—along with other extremist Islamic groups—found theoretical direction in the legacy of one of its members, Sayyid Qutb. Qutb had suffered imprisonment, torture and, finally, execution under the Nasser regime in the 1960s. However, he produced various works propounding the notion that Islamic duty called for the overthrow of regimes that substituted God's law, Sharia, by their own.[27] Under this inspiration, the *Jihad* emerged as the leading radical Islamist movement of the late 1970s and early 1980s.

By then, but too late, Sadat had become alarmed at the Islamists' strength. In 1981, his security forces lashed out, arresting and imprisoning hundreds of Islamists. The *Jihad* retaliated within a month. Having infiltrated elements of the Egyptian Army, it orchestrated Anwar Sadat's assassination under circumstances that could not have been more public: the president was shot dead by members of the very units he was reviewing at an annual military parade.

Hosni Mubarak succeeded Sadat to the presidency and for several years enjoyed a period of relative quiescence on the part of militant Islamists. This may have been partly due to the sweeping crackdown on Islamists that immediately followed Sadat's assassination. In part, it may also have resulted from the regime's wish not to exacerbate relations with Islamists any more than was absolutely necessary while Mubarak secured his new position.[28] In the meantime, the Muslim Brothehood—by now dedicated to political means—was assiduously creating the network of alliances with established parties that by the end of the 1980s would make it "the largest opposition force in parliament."[29] It really didn't matter much. By the time Mubarak decided to adopt a less tolerant approach to Islamist activity, seeds that had been planted more than a decade earlier would begin flowering into the Upper Egypt-based insurgency that would preoccupy his regime for most of the 1990s.

In 1985, Egypt's linkages to the globalizing economy led to a project that, after being filtered through the Cairo regime, eventually impacted directly on the country's peasants. The project was a drastic revision of laws governing landholdings; in short, a reversal of the land reform carried out under Nasser three decades earlier. The objective was to rationalize Egypt's agricultural sector by enabling large holdings, thus helping to make the country's agricultural products more competitive on the world stage. It was a touchy and controversial move, one that became a key national issue around which a very prolonged debate erupted. In the end, after seven years, the Mubarak regime prevailed. The law, enacted in 1992, effectively repealed statutes governing tenancy after a further five-year grace period. It was branded by its opponents as "the law for throwing out tenants from their land." This neoliberal measure, as Reem Saad comments, profoundly disturbed what the rural poor considered "an important basis of moral and political order."[30]

THE *GAMA'A*'S INSURGENCY

No single event marked the onset of the insurgency waged by the *Gama'a al-Islamiyya* against the government of Egypt in the 1990s. However, by 1992 it was clear that Mubarak's regime was facing a determined and sustained armed challenge that, while based in Upper Egypt, had the capacity to carry out attacks throughout the country. At the time things reached this pitch, the regime's security resources were formidable. Egypt's military, numbering nearly half a million, was increasingly being armed with up-to-date American equipment, one result of Anwar Sadat's determined drive to ally Cairo with Washington. Moreover, the country's vast security forces, born under Nasser and retained, expanded and ever more relied upon by his successors, were themselves estimated to number well over 300,000 individuals.[31]

Nobody really knows what the *Gama'a*'s operational strength was at that time, though it was surely far below that of the Egyptian state. A 2004 Report for Congress prepared by the Congressional Research Service opined that "at its peak" the *Gama'a al-Islamiyya* probably counted on "several thousand militants."[32] In the early 1990s, some observers speculated that the *Gama'a* might have been able to field as many as 10,000 fighters.[33] This significant imbalance of power did not prevent the *Gama'a* from waging an insurgency that proved both frustrating and costly to the government. Between 1992 and 1997, the group conducted a series of attacks, largely in Upper Egypt, against police posts, government officials, and foreign tourists. This last, which involved at least thirty attacks on buses, trains, and boats, was particularly damaging in light of Egypt's heavy dependence on the tourism industry for scarce foreign currency. As early as 1993—though by then only three foreign tourists had been killed—the country's tourism sector had been devastated.[34] Much worse was to come.

From the start, it was evident that the *Gama'a*'s fighters, however small a minority of the population they may have been, enjoyed a significant degree of at least tacit support within Upper Egypt. The *Gama'a*'s presence in the countryside was not hidden, and at times actually dominant. Press accounts of the period amply demonstrate the extent to which the group prevailed in rural areas. The following, relating events in "a tiny village in Upper Egypt," is typical of such reports:

> Since March [1992], clashes between villagers and security forces have claimed two dozen lives. Farming is the only occupation... the district boasts few jobs and fewer public services.... It is fertile soil in which to recruit ardent young men for the Islamic League [*Gama'at al-Islamiyyah*], with their aura of romance and their programmes of spiritual betterment and practical activism.
>
> In recent years the membership of such leagues has swollen into the thousands. In a dozen villages league enthusiasts have made themselves into enforcers of order and the providers of service.[35]

The *Gama'a* did not limit its campaign to the countryside, although Upper Egypt remained the insurgency's focal point. Having extended its network to other areas of the country, particularly the poverty-ridden slums of Cairo, into which tens of thousands of Upper Egyptians were packed, it launched attacks in the nation's capital—again, largely focusing on government officials and tourists, though now including Egyptian intellectuals it considered to be "un-Islamic." Among these last were the liberal writer Farag Foda, murdered in 1992, and the Egyptian Nobel Prize-winning novelist, Naguib Mafouz, who, though severely wounded, survived an attack in 1994. Cairo was also the scene for various attempts, some successful, to assassinate high government officials and to kill foreign tourists. As the *Gama'a* generally relied on bombs and automatic weapons, innocent bystanders were also frequently killed.

Mubarak's regime met the insurgency with inflexible harshness. In 1992, the government decreed that terrorist cases would be tried by military courts. Amnesty International described the military courts' procedures as falling "far short of international standards for fair trial."[36] Over the next seven years, these courts would hand down ninety death sentences.[37] Egyptians were to become inured to the sight of condemned militants greeting their sentences with joyous outcries and songs. The regime's response in the Greater Cairo area was draconian. In December 1992, thousands of troops cordoned off and searched the entire neighborhood of Imbaba, a sweltering labyrinth of run-down buildings on the Nile's west bank and home to hundreds of thousands of poor immigrants from the countryside, many of whom were from Upper Egypt. The *Gama'a*'s presence in parts of the neighborhood had grown considerably in recent years. Led by an illiterate former-electrician-turned-Sheikh, one Gaber Mohammed Ali, the *Gama'a*'s true believers had effectively taken control of parts of Imbaba, particularly the district known as al-Muneera al-Gharbiyya, which held some 300,000 people.[38] In the process, they made life difficult for their neighbors:

> Stories were told of how Gaber's foot soldiers, bearded young men who wore white crocheted skullcaps and white *gallabiyyas*, had formed vigilante squads intent on enforcing Islamic morality. When locals hired belly dancers for their wedding parties, as popular custom dictated, Gaber's so-called *emirs* declared the dancers *haram*—forbidden under Islamic teaching. They gave the bride and groom a stark choice: get rid of the dancers or we will do it for you. Beer and hashish, often the highpoints at local weddings, were ruled immoral. The *emirs* burned video shops and hair salons, also declared sacrilegious, and warned women not to leave their homes without the *hijab*, the Islamic shawl that covers the hair, neck, and shoulders.
>
> Sectarian conflict between Coptic Christians and Muslim extremists contributed to the violence in Imbaba in the three months before the [government's 1992 incursion] In September, a Christian butcher had shot and seriously wounded a Muslim who wanted him to slaughter a chicken while reciting the Koranic injunction, "God is Great." The incident sparked a wave of sectarian clashes. Muslim militants defaced Christian religious portraits hanging in the streets, wrecked shops owned by Christian Copts, and burned churches.
>
> When the militants were not applying their religious and moral codes directly to Imbaba's residents, they were engaging in Islamic agitprop. Every Tuesday, they organized meetings along al-Buhi Street, a main thoroughfare, between the afternoon and evening prayers to condemn the failings of the Egyptian government. In the evenings, they lined up television sets in rows along the street to replay videos of the 1981 assassination of President Anwar Sadat. They hung banners with the signature of *al-Gama'a al-Islamiyya* to convey their message: "First it was Sadat... and tomorrow it will be whoever dares to oppose Islam," read one popular poster.[39]

The government's five-week siege of Imbaba netted hundreds of prisoners, most of whom were subsequently released with no charges having been filed, and broke the militant Islamists' hold on the area. The majority of the neighborhood's inhabitants seemed to see this as a mixed blessing at best. Having suffered the indignities of house-to-house searches, and manhandling and sometimes arrest, by the invading troops, their ambivalence was perhaps understandable. One Imbaba resident who experienced the government's intervention, put it like this to a curious journalist: "the hell of the *Gama'a* was better than the heaven of the police."[40]

In Upper Egypt, government forces pursued the insurgents relentlessly, occupying and searching villages and burning sugarcane fields in hope of flushing militants into the open and denying them cover for ambushing tourist-bearing trains, buses, and riverboats. When security forces and police started detaining relatives, including women, of suspected militants, the violence took on an additional twist. In accordance with Upper Egypt's strict social code, the vindication of personal honor now figured as a driving force behind the escalating violence. Targeted assassinations of police and security agents followed.

An additional feature of the violence that wracked Upper Egypt in the 1990s came in the form of attacks on members of the region's numerous Coptic community. Amnesty International reported that "scores of Coptic Christians were deliberately and arbitrarily killed by members of the *Gama'a al-Islamiya*" as the violence in Upper Egypt raged between 1992 and 1998.[41] While the *Gama'a* did not launch a generalized campaign against Egypt's main and most ancient Christian denomination, Amnesty International's investigation establishes that the Copts' traditional second-class status rendered them particularly vulnerable as the *Gama'a*'s militant version of Islam took to arms. Religious ideology combined with Upper Egyptian culture and the material requirements of the *Gama'a*'s insurrection, to produce this outcome. Thus, the *Gama'a*'s first attack on Copts, in mid-1992, involved the slaying of thirteen members of a single Coptic family in a town near Assiut, and was explained by the *Gama'a* as an act of revenge for the earlier killing of two Islamists by members of that same family.[42] On other occasions Copts were killed after having been accused by *Gama'a* members of revealing to authorities the names and whereabouts of Islamic militants.[43] Then too, the *Gama'a al-Islamiyya* saw Copts as legitimate targets for fund-raising. In part, this took the form of armed robberies of Coptic gold and jewelry shops, in the process of which Copts were sometimes killed. It also frequently took the form of extortion: specific sums of money were demanded as the price for not killing individual Copts or their family members. Those who were slow to pay or flee the area sometimes paid with their lives, or with those of their kin.[44]

It was, however, also evident that for at least some *Gama'a* militants, Copts were legitimate targets simply because of their religion. This attitude was visibly embarrassing to the *Gama'a*'s leadership, as shown by its reaction to the most blatantly religiously-motivated killing of Copts during this period. The event occurred on February 12, 1997, in Abu Qerqas, a town near Minya in Upper Egypt. Five masked *Gama'a* militants burst into St. George's church and opened fire on a group of unarmed young Copts who were there for a weekly religious gathering, killing ten of them. The pogrom disconcerted the *Gama'a al Islamiyya's* leaders:

> Two days after the massacre *al-Gama'a al-Islamiyya* issued a vaguely-worded statement, on the one hand denying responsibility, but also acknowledging the possibility that some members of the group, cut

> off from the leadership of the group, may have carried out the attack. "In a situation like this . . . ," according to the statement, "excesses were bound to happen," then adding that it also did not rule out the involvement of government forces or "Zionist quarters" in the massacre.[45]

Perhaps the "excess" at Abu Qerqas convinced part of the *Gama'a* leadership that the insurgency was losing direction, or perhaps the Egyptian government's consistently hard-line response convinced them that their approach was misguided, or perhaps it was a combination of both things that led to a split at the organization's upper echelons. In any case, five months after Abu Qerqas, five imprisoned leaders of the *Gama'a al-Islamiyya* publicly called for the organization to halt violent activity.

Mubarak's regime was unimpressed. From the insurgency's start, the government had rejected any notion of dialogue with the militants. Indeed, one interior minister, Abdel Halim Moussa, who showed signs of interest in such an avenue had been promptly sacked in 1993.[46] Then, in November 1997, came the terrible event that finally caused the insurgency to wither—not so much because of the government's predictable and immediate reaction, as because of the tidal wave of sheer revulsion that engulfed the Egyptian public and, at least for a while, thoroughly discredited the *Gama'a al-Islamiyya.*

Tours of Upper Egypt's ancient monuments generally get started early in the day, a way to beat the heat and still have time to return to the hotel or cruise ship for a cooling drink, good lunch, and perhaps an early afternoon nap. By 9:00 a.m. on November 17, 1997, the temple of Hatsepshut, across the Nile from Luxor, was already swarming with tourists. As they made their way through the multileveled, colonnaded splendor of the 3,400-year-old memorial to the ancient queen, the multinational visitors were suddenly attacked by six *Gama'a al-Islamiyya* gunmen disguised as policemen. The assailants took their time, shooting first, then finishing off the wounded with long knives, and in some cases pausing to mutilate the bodies. When the attack—which lasted about an hour—was over, fifty-eight foreign tourists and four Egyptians lay slaughtered. All the assailants escaped, only to be hunted down and killed by Egyptian authorities later.[47]

Among the dead foreigners were citizens of Bulgaria, Colombia, France, Germany, Great Britain, Japan, and Switzerland.

The Egyptian government reacted swiftly to the Luxor tragedy, vastly increasing security measures at touristic sites, ensuring that tourist groups were closely monitored and traveled with armed guards, and even providing a ten-day antiterrorist training course for tour guides.[48] Predictably, however, none of these measures prevented an immediate and drastic downturn in the country's tourist industry. Although the industry suffered greatly during the remainder of 1997 and throughout the next year, it recovered by the end of 1999.[49] But if the *Gama'a*'s terrorist assault in Luxor resulted in only this limited damage to Egypt's vitally necessary tourism, its impact on the *Gama'a* itself was devastating.

It is difficult to gauge Egyptian public opinion. Under the country's successive authoritarian regimes, associational groups have been so constrained that it is almost hopeless to look there for signs of what Egyptians are thinking. Egypt's press, while relatively free in an Arab context, has long functioned under stringent controls. Limits on the public questioning of the government's hard-line response to the *Gama'a al-Islamiyya* were strict. Moreover, there exist no polls of Egyptian public opinion in the 1990s from which data can be gleaned to determine the public's outlook on the government's struggle with the *Gama'a*.

However, there is indicative evidence to support the impressionistic conclusion of many observers who lived in the country during that period: that in the first years of the *Gama*'s campaign, significant portions of the Egyptian public sympathized with the organization's demand for a polity under Sharia and—while not necessarily agreeing with the *Gama'a*'s violent path—were not supportive of the government's oppressive reaction. This could hardly have been otherwise in a country where it was generally conceded that the Muslim Brotherhood would emerge as the government's most serious challenger were free elections to be held. Limited empirical support for this portrait of Egyptian public opinion comes in the form of an unpublished MA thesis written by Jeongmin Seo, an energetic young Korean graduate student at the American University in Cairo. Jeongmin's work indicates that even the small proportion of Egyptians who initially supported the *Gama'a*'s violent approach steadily dwindled as the violence progressed.[50]

Luxor produced a sea change in Egyptian opinion, sweeping away virtually any vestige of sympathy for the *Gama'a*. Egyptians of all social levels and every political outlook rushed to condemn the attack, and to try to explain to every foreigner they could find that "Islam" could never condone such an atrocity. What they usually seemed unable to understand was the proof before their eyes: that a type of Islam had not only condoned, but urged, precisely that type of atrocity.

The split in the *Gama'a* became a glaring gap after Luxor, with the main leadership apparently united in publicly condemning the attack as a "violation" that was "more damaging to the *Gama'a* than for the Egyptian government."[51] But no amount of public relations damage control would restore the *Gama'a al-Islamiyya*'s position in Egyptian eyes at that point. By early 1998, the *Gama'a*'s leaders in Egypt reconfirmed an earlier pledge, issued just after the Luxor massacre, to abandon the use of violence. While the government continued to arrest, try, and sometimes execute *Gama'a* members during that year, only a few relatively minor armed clashes occurred. To all intents and purposes, the *Gama'a*'s insurgency within Egypt had ended, or at least been suspended. It had cost Egypt dearly. The tally included some 1,300 dead, mainly militants and members of security forces, and thousands wounded.

Seven years would pass before another fatal Islamist attack against tourists was carried out in Cairo. In April 2005 a young university student, killed himself, two French nationals, and an American when he exploded a homemade bomb in a street near the ancient al-Azhar Mosque. The *Gama'a al-Islamiyya* promptly issued a statement, entitled "Random Explosions Do Not Safeguard Religion or Reform States," condemning the attack as "an irresponsible act that undermines the image of Islam, and places the country in a vicious circle of chaos and unrest."[52]

It is, of course, not at all clear what this means for the future. The imponderable issue is whether the *Gama'a* is sincere and resolute in its declared rejection of violence or whether it is cynically buying time for a more propitious moment to resume its militant campaign in Egypt. Although thousands of *Gama'a* members, and quite a few leaders, have been released from custody since 2003, Egyptian security forces continue to keep a wary eye on the group and its sympathizers.

On the other hand, it is extremely clear that at least part of the *Gama'a*'s leadership remains thoroughly committed to promoting its view of the Islamic cause through violence in Egypt and beyond that country's borders. The split that began to tear the organization apart in 1997 was played out between leaders who remained in Egypt and others who had already sought refuge abroad, largely in Pakistan and Afghanistan. It was the latter who opposed the Egypt-based leaders' move toward a unilateral cease-fire and a renunciation of violence. Indeed, many analysts believe the more extreme foreign-based *Gama'a* leadership ordered the Luxor massacre.[53]

In 1998, this element of the *Gama'a* leadership joined with Ayman el-Zawahiri, a founder of Egypt's militant *Jihad* group who would subsequently emerge as a major figure in al-Qaeda, to support Osama bin Laden's proclamation of an "Islamic International Front to Fight Jews and Crusaders," one of whose tenets was that every Muslim had a duty "to kill Americans and their allies, both civil and military."[54] With this, as Maye Kassem notes, it became evident that while the Mubarak regime had "gotten the upper hand" in its struggle with Islamists, that achievement "contributed toward shifting the conflict into the international arena."[55]

THE DYNAMICS OF MILITANCY

The nature, shape, and motivating impulses behind the *Gama'a al-Islamiyya*'s five-year war against Egypt's government can be understood only by taking into account the movement's Upper Egyptian roots and attributes. Although the *Gama'a*'s campaign was obviously part of the broader wave of Islamic militancy that assailed Mubarak's regime in the 1990s, it retained a distinctly *Sa'idi* character. This was not only evident in the "honor killings" that added to the mayhem of those years and in the tacit support villagers gave to militants in the cane fields, but also in the pressures and motives that led its fighters to challenge the regime's superior forces.

The *Gama'a al-Islamiyya* developed in the early 1970s as a movement among students at Assiut University, which also had campuses in the other Upper Egyptian cities of Sohag, Qena, and Aswan. Its founders, influenced by the cause of the Muslim Brotherhood and the thought of Sayyid Qutb, were simultaneously moved by regional concerns and their own status within the Sa'id's social structure. Mamoun Fandy, a graduate of Assiut University and "one of the first generation of peasant farmers' sons to benefit from Nasser's educational reforms," was a classmate of many of the *Gama'a*'s founders. He recalls that the movement was marked from its inception by an Upper Egyptian peasant—or *fellah*—character, which was indicative of most of the membership's social status.[56] At that time the *Gama'a* had links to, and a degree of overlapping membership with, other militant Islamic groups in Egypt, including the *Jihad*, whose members assassinated Anwar Sadat in 1981.

In 1980 Egyptian sociologist Saad Eddin Ibrahim examined the latter group and concluded that Islamic militants came mainly from nonrural environments and lower middle-class backgrounds.[57] This finding, which focused on *Jihad* and other militant groups based in Lower Egypt, was not applicable to the *Gama'a*. This was not surprising, as the *Gama'a* was still a nascent group when Ibrahim conducted his research and was not mentioned in the article. In 1996, Ibrahim published another analysis entitled "The Changing Face of Islamic Activism."[58] Ibrahim found this altered visage because in comparison to militants of the 1980s, those of the 1990s proved to be "younger and less educated . . . [many coming] from rural, small town and shantytown backgrounds."[59]

This reflected the rise of the *Gama'a al-Islamiyya* to prominence as Egypt's preeminent militant Islamic group in the 1990s. Ibrahim's findings support Mamoun Fandy's account of the *Gama'a*'s growth, which argues that the motive force behind the organization's wide appeal in Upper Egypt lay in the frustrations that were rampant at the lowest levels of that society—that is, among the most marginalized in this most marginalized region of Egypt.

An academic and a scholar but not a trained anthropologist, Fandy offers an analysis of Upper Egyptian society based on his personal experiences and observations while "growing up in Kom al-Daba', a southern Egyptian village, and . . . as both a student and teacher at Assiut University from 1977 to 1986."[60] He posits a broad tripartite layering as the key to Upper Egypt's social stratification. A traditional hierarchy, he tells us, dictates the status of tribes and groups in the region. At its apex are the *Ashraf*, tribes claiming descent from the Prophet, whose members will not intermarry with other groups. Below the *Ashraf*, are the *Arabs*, whose members trace their lineages to the first tribes from the Arab peninsula to have settled in Egypt. At the bottom of the social order are the *Fellahin*, who are believed to descend from Egypt's pharaonic population and whose forebears accepted Islam only at the point of a sword.[61] Anthropologists who have studied Upper Egypt may question the applicability of Fandy's categories to all parts of the region.[62] However, they will not question his description of Upper Egyptian society as highly and rigidly stratified; nor will they challenge his assertion that the region's peasants traditionally have been—and remain—on society's lowest rungs. Nor will they, or anyone else, question the commonplace point that Cairo's authority in the *Sa'id* has for centuries depended on clientalistic relations with local notables, and that these relations have served, on the one hand, to protect the regional power structure and, on the other, to ensure the area's amenability to control by Egypt's central government.

By the late 1970s, the catalogue of ills suffered by the Upper Egyptians was inflicting a particularly harsh toll on the most marginalized. It had been the *fellahin* who responded most enthusiastically to the promise of Nasser's educational reforms, and they were the most frustrated when that promise withered. It was the *fellahin* who flocked to accept temporary manual labor in oil-rich Arab states, and it was they who suffered most as those opportunities dwindled. Additional frustration was piled on this sector of *Sa'idi* society by the prevailing social rules. University degrees, they found, could not match family connections when it came to obtaining either government employment or positions in the local private sector. Nor did money amassed abroad necessarily lead to an improved social status once they returned home.[63]

Religion increasingly provided the means for securing prestige and expressing discontent. For some, the educated, this direction was found through encounters with the works of Sayyid Qutb, the Muslim Brothers, and the burgeoning radical Islamist groups in other parts of Egypt. For others, the majority, it was discovered through spending extended periods of time working in the religiously conservative Gulf States, especially in Saudi Arabia, where they were exposed to a puritanical, but egalitarian, version of Islam. Many returning workers spent their money on religious projects. Thus, the construction of private mosques proliferated in Upper Egypt, providing both unchallengeable prestige in the region's Islamic setting and platforms for the spread of socially conscious religious anger. Specifically, the mosques served as fora allowing embittered *fellahin* to "use their own version of Islam to restructure the rules that govern southern society."[64] By way of demonstrating the point, Fandy points to the different emphases that came to distinguish the *Gama'a*'s Islamic discourse from that of the *Sa'id*'s dominant groups. The latter, he points out:

> ... have focused on Islamic sayings that endorse their superiority. According to them, the Prophet said, "Those of you who were superior before the coming of Islam are your superiors after it." They also recite

> the Quranic verse that says: "We raised some of you above the others by different degrees."[65]

In contrast, the *Gama'a al-Islamiyya*'s discourse made use of Islamic verses that, in Upper Egypt's context, propounded a revolutionary social message. This alternative message had "as its center the Prophet's saying: 'All are equal in Islam: no difference between Arab and non-Arab except *taqwa* (piety).'"[66]

By the 1980s, the *Gama'a*'s efforts had spread far beyond university campuses, extending into the villages of Upper Egypt and Cairo's vast slums. A *Gama'a* activist subsequently described the movement in terms that tried to distinguish it from its Lower Egyptian counterparts:

> In the south there is only one Islamic force: al-Jama'a al-Islamiyya. Unlike Jihad groups, composed of clusters of secret organizations with different names ... that have no mosques or social relations, we are a social force that conducts our works in the open through our mosques and our relations with the larger society.

In its contacts with *Sa'idi* society, the *Gama'a* wore its fundamentalist religious cloak lightly. It did not, for example, oppose the Sufi groups that have a major presence in Upper Egypt, despite the fact that the Sufi approach to Islam is viewed as heretical by the ultraorthodox. Fandy provides a telling vignette of the ease with which *Gama'a* leaders blurred distinctions between their fundamentalist inclinations and the "mixture of paganism, Christianity and Islam," that is one of the region's cultural realities:

> ... during the fifteen-day Sidi Abu Al-Hajaj festival in Luxor, a festival in which thousands of Egyptians honor the Muslim saint Abu Al-Hajaj, the local people still carry the sun boats from the Karnak temple to the temple of Luxor, where the saint's shrine is located. In fact, one of my high-school classmates, who later became the *emir* [head] of one of the Islamic groups at the school of engineering at Assiut University, still takes his 65-year old mother to the festival. While her son preaches that there is no mediation between people and God, the mother clings to the shrine and kisses the walls, asking Abu-Hajaj to intervene with God to speed her recovery from arthritis. The mother's practice is against everything that her son supposedly believes in.[67]

The *Gama'a al-Islamiyya*'s ideology was never elaborated in a comprehensive way, though in 1984 imprisoned leaders made an effort in this direction by publishing a manifesto that identified the organization's goal as the establishment of a Califate along lines of that established after the Prophet's death.[68] This did nothing to clarify the movement's concept of

Egypt's role in a new Islamic order. On the whole, the *Gama'a*'s objectives were nationally oriented and voiced intermittently over the years in statements that overwhelmingly concentrated on the establishment in Egypt of Sharia as the law of the land. The group just as consistently directed its ire at the Egyptian regime, which it accused of persistently and maliciously betraying true Egyptian values.

Indeed, the *Gama'a*'s concentration on Egypt was repellent to some members of other militant Islamic groups whose long-term concerns focused less on national issues and more on the fate of the *Umma*, the broader community of Islam. As late as 1992, one of the leaders of the group that attacked Cairo's Military Technical Academy in 1974, a man who obviously had joined the Jihad, disparaged the *Gama'a*'s approach:

> The sa'idis call themselves al-Jama'a al-Islamiyya. This group does not consider those who rule Egypt non-Muslims. This group believes that the Egyptian state as is can be adjusted to be Islamic. Jihad is the group's means to bring about these adjustments. The Cairo Jihad, on the other hand, sees everything in Egypt as un-Islamic.[69]

Galvanized into insurrection by the multiple forms of marginalization inflicted upon Upper Egypt, the *Gama'a al-Islamiyya* represented a part of that society who found its ultimate refuge, purpose, and self-worth in an ideology that still clung to the state as its potential saviour.

The *Gama'a al-Islamiyya*'s campaign against the Egyptian government reinforces the Zapatista Rebellion's lessons that chronic marginalization can eventually promote the option of launching an asymmetrical conflict against all odds, and that possibilities of such a decision increase when the insurrectionary ideology is linked to a worldview that sees empirical reality as subordinate to the dictates of a higher transcendental reality. However, it also carries the lesson that unleashing political militancy on the basis of such an ideology can be an extremely dangerous double-edged sword—one as potentially fatal to its wielder as to its intended victim. The prompt demise of the *Gama'a* in the wake of the Luxor Massacre established that point.

Chapter 5

The Niger Delta's Ogoni Uprising

Squat and disheveled, Port Harcourt sprawls alongside the Bonny River, a distributary of the Niger that empties into the Gulf of Guinea on Nigeria's Atlantic coast some thirty miles away. It is a deep water port and the Delta's major city. Founded by administrators of the British Empire in 1912, Port Harcourt retains only minimal traces of what must once have been a comfortably pleasing colonial town. Today, these are to be found mainly in the residential neighborhoods that housed the country's British masters. Yet, the walls that still shield yesterday's colonial bungalows, and even the houses themselves, now have a tired and tattered look. For the most part, contemporary Port Harcourt is a collection of garbage-strewn, potholed streets bordered by open sewers and low, dilapidated buildings. The streets themselves are eternally clogged by chaotic traffic composed of motor vehicles, bicycles, pedestrians, and occasional small herds of cattle, all in ferocious competition to advance the next few meters. But Port Harcourt's rather bedraggled appearance is deceptive, for the city is the hub of the Delta's great oil industry, and the price of a single room in any of its few modern hotels is easily within range of what one would pay for centrally located lodging in Washington, D.C., or Paris. Typically, the guests in such places are not locals but rather foreigners or wealthy Nigerian businessmen from other parts of the country. The people of the Delta have not benefited from the wealth it produces.

On the morning of November 10, 1995, nine shackled prisoners were removed from the military barracks in Port Harcourt and taken to the walled compound of the city's prison. They were not told either their destination or the purpose of the short trip. Once at the prison, they were ordered to sit on a bench in a holding cell, at the far end of which was a door. At approximately 12:00 noon, one of the prisoners, Kenule Beeson Saro-Wiwa, was taken from his seat and escorted through that doorway. It was then that he saw the gallows and learned his execution was at hand. Local lore subsequently had it that the gallows' trapdoor repeatedly refused to function with Saro-Wiwa's weight upon it, springing open only after he asked the Ogoni Spirit to facilitate his death.[1]

The sentences passed on the nine men executed that day had been handed down a week earlier, not by Nigeria's established judicial system but by a "Special Tribunal" whose judgments could not be appealed. Despite an outpouring of calls for clemency from the international community, the sentences were rapidly approved by Nigeria's central government, then under the military dictatorship of General Sani Abacha. An equal flood of international condemnation came on the heels of the executions. British Prime Minister John Major summed up the prevailing view when he branded the proceedings at Port Harcourt as nothing less than "judicial murder." Protestors demonstrated in front of Nigerian embassies and consulates throughout the world and the country was suspended from the British Commonwealth.

It is impossible to know with certainty when Ken Saro-Wiwa first set out on the path that eventually took him and his colleagues to the gallows. It could, perhaps, be argued that the moment was that of his birth in the Ogoni town of Bori. Scion of a prominent and wealthy family, Saro-Wiwa was an exceptionally intelligent child. At the age of thirteen he won a scholarship to Government College, Umuahia, then Nigeria's finest school. Excelling at his studies, Saro-Wiwa was the only Ogoni student at Government College during the seven years he remained there. He recalled, however, that it was when he subsequently enrolled in the University of Ibadan, where there was only one other Ogoni student, that "the fact that I was an Ogoni, [that] I was on the periphery of the nation began to imprint itself on my mind."[2] Saro-Wiwa would go on to become a successful businessman, television producer, internationally recognized poet, playwright, novelist, and, finally, a charismatic political activist. In the course of this varied career, he also held high administrative positions in the Rivers State government.

THE OGONI

The Ogoni from which Saro-Wiwa sprang formed one of at least 250 tribal/ethnic groups inhabiting Nigeria when the country became independent in 1960.[3] With a national population estimated to exceed 100 million in 1990 and over 130 million in 2003, Nigeria is the most populous state in Africa. The Ogoni, by the latter year thought to number approximately 500,000, constitute a tiny minority of only 0.38 percent of Nigeria's overall population. The Ogoni People have traditionally inhabited a small area in

Nigeria's southeastern corner, just to the east of Port Harcourt. Ogoniland, comprising only some 400 square kilometers, is very much a part of the Delta; a flat, low-lying area of fertile soil, swamps, lush tropical vegetation, and creeks and streams. It is speckled with villages, in most of which palm-thatched mud huts predominate. Near the villages are small cultivated fields of cassava, melons, and yams—with the 10- to 12-foot bamboo stakes that offer the plants' vines a gateway to sunlight. Around and in the villages, various sorts of fruit trees and palms abound, as do flocks of chickens, small numbers of goats, and countless children. Basic amenities such as running water, indoor toilets, and electricity are generally absent.

The Ogoni's origins remain obscure. Part of their oral tradition has them springing from the earth itself at some ancient point when the Great Mother "came down from the sky."[4] Yet, the same source also indicates that the Ogoni may have moved to their present territory after migrating from other areas. Archeological evidence has been insufficient to provide definitive answers, though linguistic evidence clearly links the Ogoni language to regions lying to the south of their current land. By the time the British entered Ogoniland in 1901, the Ogonis had almost certainly been there for several centuries, during which they developed a complex and smoothly functioning socio-political structure. That traditional social organization largely persists to this day. Divided into four main groups—the Khana, Tai, Gokana, and Eleme—the Ogoni are also split into six kingdoms, of which three (Nyo-Khana, Ken-Khana, and Babbe) are found among the Khana, while the Gokana, Tai, and Eleme have kingdoms of their own.[5] These groups speak different, but mutually intelligible, dialects. Alongside this traditional form of tribal organization, Ogoniland is also sectioned in accordance with the political and administrative structures of Nigeria's Rivers State, in which it is located. Thus, Ogoniland includes (since 1976) the Local Government Authorities (LGAs) of Eleme, Gokhana, Khana, and Tai.[6]

A major unifying element among the Ogoni is religion. Their traditional religion was, and remains, animistic and strongly marked by ancestor worship. Saro-Wiwa described this traditional outlook as follows:

> To the Ogoni, the land on which they lived and the rivers which surrounded them, were very important. They not only provided sustenance in abundance, they were also a spiritual inheritance. The land is a god and is worshipped as such. The fruit of the land, particularly yams, are honored in festivals and, indeed, the Annual Festival of the Ogoni is held at the Yam Festival. The planting season is not a mere period of agricultural activity: it is a spiritual, religious and social occasion. "Tradition" in Ogoni means in the local tongue *(doonu Kuneke)* the honoring of the land (earth, soil, water) . . . . To the Ogoni, rivers and streams do not only provide water for life—for bathing, drinking,

> etc.—they provide fish for food, they are also sacred and are bound up intricately with the life of the community, of the entire Ogoni nation.[7]

Early British commercial interests in the Niger Delta were linked to the international traffic in slaves. After Britain outlawed the slave trade in 1807, her merchants found that the Delta produced other lucrative products. Chief among these was palm oil, which by the 1830s had important industrial applications in the fabrication of dyes and varnishes. Missionaries soon followed the merchants. While Christianity made quick and extensive inroads among Nigeria's coastal populations, traditional religious outlooks were not eclipsed. This was particularly true of populations of the more remote areas, including the Ogoni, who were among the last of the Delta's people to come under British influence. Beliefs in the Ogoni Spirit, the powers of ancestors, and local spirits inhabiting streams, groves, and particular geographic areas remained vital parts of everyday Ogoni life—albeit increasingly combined with a professed commitment to Christianity. This did not change when informal British penetration yielded to the more formal establishment of London's "Protectorate" over the Delta. As recently confirmed by Nigerian researcher John Agbonifo's work on the Ogoni, "the belief in supernatural protection is strong, and there is an admixture of the Christian faith and folk religion."[8]

The extension of British administration over Nigeria inevitably impacted on local social structures. In the predominantly Muslim north, where the missionary activities that paved the way for the imperialist venture had been limited, London's approach favored "indirect rule," which not only allowed local potentates to retain their positions but also tended to preserve the social status quo. In the south, missionary schools produced a growing cadre of culturally adaptable anglophones who served to fill clerical and intermediary positions of use to British administrators and private businessmen alike. While those benefiting from missionary education were generally the sons of local notables, the common educational background injected a bond that transcended the pattern of traditional social relations. This, however, did not override the traditional and class-conscious social structure that prevailed in the part of the Delta that would subsequently become Rivers State.[9] Under both the colonial regime and, after 1960, that of the Nigerian state, the Ogonis' social structure remained "composed of six autonomous kingdoms, and a retinue of Chiefs, under a paramount Chief [or king] ..."[10] Following independence, the various chiefs and kings received monthly stipends from the Nigerian government. With the discovery of oil in Ogoniland in the late 1950s, these local elites forged direct ties to foreign oil companies, typically as various sorts of contractors. This dual support from the state and international oil firms quickly became the basis of the elites' local power.

In the context of the broader Nigerian society around them, the Ogoni were looked down upon. A minority among the predominant Igbo ethnic group in southwest Nigeria, the Ogoni were perceived as primitive and uncivilized. Indeed, at least in the environs of Port Harcourt, the very term "Ogoni" was considered an epithet and not until the last part of the twentieth century would most Ogonis identify themselves as such. On the other hand, the Ogoni generally held negative stereotypes of the more dominant surrounding ethnic groups, who were usually portrayed as dishonest and untrustworthy.[11]

The modern formation, or perhaps better said, reaffirmation, of Ogoni identity is linked to the efforts of Ken Saro-Wiwa and his colleagues in the movement he founded in the 1990s. Thus, Ledum Mitee, current leader of the Ogoni movement and a friend and close associate of Saro-Wiwa, recalls that only a few years ago, Ogonis preferred to identify themselves as members of the tribe's subgroups—Khana, Gokhana, Eleme, etc.[12] Indeed, a 2002 study found that most members of the Eleme subgroup still prefer that identification in lieu of "Ogoni."[13] Nonetheless, the rapidity and effectiveness with which Saro-Wiwa's efforts successfully mobilized an active, identity-based political consciousness among the great majority of Ogoni demonstrates that the roots of their ethnic awareness were not deeply buried. It is also telling that this response came overwhelmingly from the Ogoni masses, who by all criteria had to be labeled the most marginalized of the marginalized in Nigeria's southeast corner.

Ambivalent or negative reactions to Saro-Wiwa's movement came from individual elites whose ties to the government and oil companies guaranteed them privileged positions, or from subgroups that for various reasons were similarly substantially less marginalized. Thus, Eleme leaders, and many of the Eleme subgroup, were less than enthusiastic about the Ogoni movement, largely because they had hopes of maximizing the political benefits of their territory, which hosted "some very important federal oil-based establishments (two refineries, a petrochemical industry, a fertilizer company and a gas turbine)."[14]

Events among the Ogoni must be understood in the context of Nigeria's volatile post-independence political history. Initially established as a federation of three regions, the Muslim-dominated north, and the predominantly Christian eastern and western regions, Nigeria's efforts to build a functioning democratic state failed miserably. Ethnic rivalries and suspicions, particularly among the country's three major groups—the Hausa-Fulani, the Yoruba, and the Igbo—produced the first of successive military coups in 1966. Since that date, Nigeria has more often than not been ruled by military regimes. By 2006, military governments had held sway a total of thirty years, as opposed to only sixteen years of civilian rule. If the current presidency of Olusegun Obsasanjo transfers power peacefully at the end of its second term in 2007, it will mark the first such occasion in over forty years.[15]

The culmination of ethnic tensions came in 1967, when the Igbo of the eastern region, hoping to take the oil-rich southern Delta with them, embarked on an unsucccessful secessionist war in hope of creating the state of Biafra. By that time, military leaders had moved to reduce the growing fears of Nigeria's many minority groups by replacing the regional system with a federal state structure—an arrangement that in theory promised greater local say in the formulation of national policies. The theory did not work out in practice. Despite the eventual expansion of Nigeria's states to today's thirty-six, Nigerian politics remains largely the preserve of the country's dominant ethnic groups and the powers of state governments remain dependent on, and decidedly inferior to, those of the central government. The most prominent evidence of this is found in the progressive reduction of the states' share of oil revenue. By 1993, the original revenue-sharing format, which allocated some 20 percent to local regimes, had been reduced to the point that states received only some 3 percent of revenues generated in their territories.[16]

The debilitating impact of ethnic rivalries on Nigeria's political development has been matched by that of unrestrained corruption at all levels of government. Civilian and military regimes alike have enthusiastically functioned on the principal that the main purpose of public service is self-enrichment. Extensive sophisticated networks of client-patron relationships have grown up to ensure that public trust is efficiently converted to private gain.[17] The tragedy, of course, is that at its birth the country possessed natural and human resources that were the envy of most emerging states of the 1960s. The human resources were corrupted, cowed into silence, exiled, or killed; the material resources have been plundered, squandered, and so poorly administered that Nigeria currently ranks among the world's most impoverished countries. According to United Nations figures in 2004, Nigeria's per capita Gross Domestic Product (GDP) was the equivalent of only $860, about half of those respectively reported for such well-known economic basket cases as Bangladesh and Haiti. Indeed, of the 177 countries categorized by per capita GDP, Nigeria was ahead of only ten. Significantly, all of these even poorer states were in sub-Saharan Africa.[18]

The extent of Nigeria's oil wealth only underscored the obscenity of the situation. It is estimated that since the early 1970s, Nigeria's oil revenues have totaled some $280 billion.[19] Massive government investments in non-productive prestige projects, along with monumental and ubiquitous corruption, dissipated the nation's patrimony in just a few decades. A 1999 article in the *Sunday New York Times Magazine* provides revealing insights into the working of corruption at the micro-level of local government officials and "influentials" in the Delta's oil-producing areas. The writer, Norimitsu Onishi, spent some days observing the daily routine of one Leonard Hutto, then the Port Harcourt-based superintendent of the Chevron Corporation's production in the Delta. Hutto estimated that he spent "at least 60 percent of his time on community relations." What this meant in practice was very heavy engagement in the fine art of coping with demands for bribes, usually in the form of requests for personal contracts for such services as providing security "or, more typically, to supply the office with bottled water and office materials." In one case, a local king of an outlying town pressed for a larger personal contract that would net him five to ten thousand dollars, a sum, Hutto explained, that would fulfill the king's newly developed ambition of buying "his own big house" in Port Harcourt. The relatively modest amounts of money involved in such local micro-corruption pale to insignificance in comparison to the macro-corruption of Nigeria's central government. One American official in the country reportedly estimated that by 1999 some $50 billion of the country's oil income had "just disappeared overseas."[20]

The first oil well in Ogoniland, drilled by the Royal Dutch Shell Corporation, started producing in 1958. The capped wellhead is still there, a stone's throw from a small field planted with cassavas and melons. Many other Shell installations are found within a radius of only a few kilometers from that first well. In addition to other wellheads, these include flow-stations, where oil from several wells is collected and pumped onward toward its eventual destination, the export terminal in Bonny. These large sites, with their bewildering interweaving of huge olive green steel pipes, now sit silently within chain-link fences. The fences remain intact, even though Shell's operations in Ogoniland have been suspended since 1993.

THE OGONI UPRISING

By 1990, Ken Saro-Wiwa and other Ogoni leaders had become convinced that Shell's drive for oil threatened the Ogoni with cultural, if not physical, extinction. By then, Ogoniland was crisscrossed by aboveground oil pipes and by roads for the construction of oil facilities. The result was that fields traditionally devoted to agriculture were severely fragmented. The light cast by natural gas flares from nearly one hundred oil wells, which burned round the clock—and which in some cases had done so for more than three decades—seemed to have forever banished night from Ogoniland. Environmental damage from multiple oil spills had polluted creeks and streams and virtually eliminated the viability of fishing as a basic Ogoni industry. Then too, acid rain brought the pollution down to earth, undermining the agricultural foundation of Ogoni society as well as further polluting water sources.

While the physical damage to the environment was undeniably grim, in Ogoni eyes, the spiritual damage was even worse. Ogoni do not bury their dead in communal cemeteries, but rather in or near the fields that form part of the family homestead. Together with sacred groves and other natural holy places, these gravesites loom large in the Ogoni cosmology, for ancestors are the most immediate powers in the spiritual world with which the Ogoni must cope on a daily basis. The desecrating impact of the oil business on graves and other sacred sites has long been a matter of serious concern. "The ancestors," I was repeatedly assured during my visit to Ogoniland, "will not be as angry with the Shell people as with us; for we are the ones who have failed to protect them."[21] This outlook was simply unbelievable to Western oilmen. Long after Ken Saro-Wiwa's death, Ledum Mitee led an Ogoni delegation in negotiations over a possible resumption of Shell's operations in Ogoniland. Although some years had passed since that encounter, Mitee was still deeply offended by his Shell counterpart's attitude when we spoke in 2004. "He dismissed our explanations of the land's spiritual importance with a laugh," Mitee recalled. "Actually, he did the same for all of our environmental concerns. He thought it was all only public relations and that all we wanted was more money."[22]

Money, of course, was one, but not the sole, major concern of the Ogoni as they mobilized to challenge the Nigerian government and the Shell Corporation. In November 1990, Ogoni leaders—with the exception of those of the Eleme—issued the Ogoni Bill of Rights (OBR). The document laid out Ogoni grievances, stressing that in the course of the previous three decades, oil extracted from Ogoniland had "provided the Nigerian nation with a total revenue estimated at ... 30 billion dollars," and that "in return for [this] contribution, the Ogoni people have received NOTHING." The OBR specifically cited five areas in which the Ogoni had received no benefit from their land's oil wealth:

> ... today, the Ogoni people have:
>
> (i) No represenentation whatsoever in ALL institutions of the Federal Government of Nigeria.
> (ii) No pipe-borne water.
> (iii) No electricity
> (iv) No job opportunities ... in Federal, State, public sector or private sector companies.
> (v) No social or economic project of the Federal Government.[23]

Reaffirming the Ogonis' wish "to remain part of the Federal Republic of Nigeria," the declaration called for a new relationship between the Nigerian state and the Ogoni. Among the specific demands contained in the OBR were "political control of Ogoni affairs by Ogoni people"; "the right to control and use a fair proportion of OGONI economic resources for Ogoni development"; and, "The right to protect the OGONI environment and ecology from further degradation." Finally, the OBR stressed that its demands were not intended to deny the rights of "any other ethnic group in the Nigerian Federation."[24]

At about the same time as the OBR was issued, Ken Saro-Wiwa spearheaded the formation of the Movement for the Survival of the Ogoni People (MOSOP). MOSOP's structure reflected its founder's vision of what was needed—an organization that would simultaneously revitalize and regenerate an oppressed people and afford them a vehicle for effective political action. It was, therefore, constituted as an umbrella organization whose organizational members were required to have democratically functioning chapters in every Ogoni village and in each of the six Ogoni kingdoms. Each constituent member was represented at the decision-making level of MOSOP. A wide range of Ogoni organizations soon came under the MOSOP structure, including youth groups, professional associations, women's associations, and church groups.

Two key principles lay at the basis of MOSOP's struggle from its inception. The first was that its struggle would be nonviolent. On one level, the nonviolent option might have been seen as attractive in light of the fact that in 1990 Nigeria's armed forces totaled nearly 100,000 men, making it one of the largest in Africa.[25] On the other hand, Saro-Wiwa and his colleagues were fully aware that while their own movement might refrain from violence, their opponents would not. The conflict, in short, was expected to contain elements of violence, though not from the Ogoni side. Thus, the decision to follow a nonviolent approach was taken on the explicit assumption that "in non-violent struggle more people die than in armed struggle. . . ."[26]

The second major pillar of MOSOP's struggle was that its goal was decidedly "revolutionary," in the sense that it sought a fundamental restructuring of the Nigerian polity. Thus, MOSOP rejected from the beginning the idea of working solely for the benefit of the Ogoni. Instead, the Ogoni problem was seen a part of a broader problem, that of Nigeria's multiple minority ethnic groups. The solution to the Ogoni problem was considered inseparable from that of the problem confronting all minority groups in the Nigerian polity—the oppression entailed by internal exploitation at the hands of the country's dominant groups. Saro-Wiwa was convinced that Nigeria's prevailing structure "could not satisfy the yearnings of various ethnic groups for development and dignity."[27] In his final declaration to the tribunal that condemned him, Saro-Wiwa put it this way:

> The Ogoni call was therefore a call for the re-structuring of the federation, a devolution of power to all peoples [in Nigeria] that everyone would have access to the Nigerian commonwealth. The call is patriotic and will be seen to have been timely when the dust settles.[28]

As MOSOP's ideologist, Saro-Wiwa had an even wider underlying vision of the movement's significance. In an immediate sense, it extended not only to the various minorities of Nigeria but also to similarly oppressed peoples throughout the continent. By extension, his humanistic paradigm inevitably embraced marginalized communities "in Nigeria and elsewhere":

> ... MOSOP was intent on breaking new ground in the struggle for democracy and political, economic, social and environmental rights in Africa. We believe that mass-based, disciplined organizations can successfully re-vitalize moribund societies and that relying upon their ancient values, mores and cultures, such societies can successfully re-establish themselves as self-reliant communities and at the same time successfully and peacefully challenge tyrannical governments. ...
>
> MOSOP empowered the Ogoni people and destroyed the culture of subservience to a few men who derive their power and influence from the Nigerian government, whether military or civilian, and often use that power to denigrate the people. It is thus an innovation in Africa.[29]

By his own account, Ken Saro-Wiwa believed a mystic force had assigned him the uncomfortable role of "poet as prophet, as keeper of the conscience of society."[30] The experience leading to this conviction also convinced him that his cause would emerge victorious "in my lifetime or thereafter."[31] His account of the event is worth repeating:

> One night in late 1989, as I sat in my study working on a new book, I received a call to put myself, my abilities, my resources, so carefully nurtured over the years, at the foot of the Ogoni people and similar dispossessed, dispirited and disappearing peoples in Nigeria and elsewhere.
>
> The voice spoke to me, directing me what to do and assuring me of success in my lifetime or thereafter. I was adequately warned of the difficulties which this call to service would entail and the grave risks I would be running.
>
> Without hesitation, I put myself at the service of the Voice. I spoke to my family and intimated them fully of the cause to which I was about to dedicate my life and received their full understanding and blessing.[32]

But if Saro-Wiwa was moved at his core by mystic certainty, he was—at least initially—also a sharp and effective political strategist as he charted MOSOP's course. The strategy was to attack (nonviolently) the Nigerian government-Shell consortium simultaneously on two fronts. The first was the domestic Nigerian scene. Here, the Ogoni would be mobilized, in the process of which other exploited minorities would come to see the Ogoni cause as their own, thus giving weight to the demand for national restructuring. The second front was on the international level. MOSOP would tap into the growing international environmental and human rights movements, promoting the Ogoni cause and embarrassing and pressuring both the Shell Corporation and the Nigerian government. This partly explained why the already internationally recognized Saro-Wiwa eschewed serving as MOSOP's first president, choosing instead to be the organization's "Spokesman." This avoided offending the sensibilities of the traditional Ogoni chiefs, since it permitted one of them to assume the presidency, while at the same time allowing Saro-Wiwa full freedom to promote the Ogoni cause internationally.[33]

The first years of MOSOP's existence were devoted to laying the foundations of this approach. Saro-Wiwa and other MOSOP leaders took the organization's message to villages throughout Ogoniland, helping to resurrect a sense of common identity and as well as to mobilize cadres of followers who found purpose in the movement. Internationally, one of MOSOP's first priorities was to win acceptance by the Hague-based Unrepresented Nations and Peoples Organization (UNPO). This organization, which is dedicated to promoting the access of minority groups who are unrepresented within the UN system and facilitating their access to the world body, requires its members' commitment to a nonviolent pursuit of their objectives. Saro-Wiwa also intensified the group's international campaign by courting the diplomatic community in Lagos and establishing links to the United Nations, whose World Conference on Human Rights he was scheduled to attend in Vienna in June 1993. Although the Nigerian government prevented Saro-Wiwa from traveling to Vienna, detaining him at Lagos Airport and confiscating his passport, other Ogoni delegates went to the conference. Once there, they acquired an important ally in Anita Roddick, the socially conscious and activist founder of the internationally successful British cosmetic firm, The Body Shop. Roddick adopted the Ogonis' cause, provided MOSOP with an office in London, funded speaking tours by Ogoni activists, and helped spread MOSOP's message through her network of contacts around the world.[34]

The blocking of Saro-Wiwa's trip to the Vienna Conference in mid-1993 was a sign of the Nigerian government's growing alarm over MOSOP's nonviolent campaign. By late 1992, MOSOP's organizational network was fully in place, allowing the group to launch a series of actions that attracted considerable attention both within Nigeria and abroad. Largely because of its youth movement, the National Youth Council of Ogoni People (NYCOP), MOSOP's network now reached down to the level of village cells. Parallel with such organizational activities, considerable energy had also been devoted to the creation of an array of Ogoni symbols including a flag and anthem, along with rules of etiquette for their employment, such as standing at attention when the anthem was sung. Among the techniques that came to be used to rally the Ogoni behind MOSOP's leadership were mass rallies and night vigils. An Ogoni "Appeal Fund" was also successfully launched. Every Ogoni was asked to contribute the nominal sum of 1 Naira (approximately ten U.S. cents in 1992). Although the fund was successful, its major purpose was not so much to raise money as to provide a vehicle for the expression of personal material commitment to the cause.[35]

At the same time, the organization also made considerable headway in making its cause known internationally. Relying on his own financial resources, Saro-Wiwa established links to a variety of European human rights and environmental organizations, including Amnesty International, Green Peace, and the Rain Forest Action Group. His most important success, however, came in 1992, when MOSOP was admitted to UNPO. The UNPO connection promptly facilitated two important gains for MOSOP. The first of these was when the Ogonis' confrontation with the oil industry was highlighted in a film, *The Drilling Fields*, which aired on Britain's Channel 4 television in 1992. This was a major boost to MOSOP's hope of enlisting the support of Western public opinion. The validation of MOSOP's nonviolent credentials by UNPO also helped the organization gain its first hearing in a United Nations Forum in July 1992, when Saro-Wiwa arrived in Geneva to address the UN Working Group for Indigenous Populations.[36]

These achievements formed the basis for MOSOP's full entry into its nonviolent struggle. The campaign's opening sally was in the form of a "Notice of Demand" issued to Shell and the two relatively minor producers working in Ogoniland, Chevron and the Nigerian National Petroleum Corporation. The notice gave the oil producers thirty days to pay $10 billion in rents and royalties accumulated since 1958 or leave Ogoniland. It also called for negotiations to be held over future oil exploitation in Ogoniland[37] As expected, the message was ignored.

With their demands now publicly on record in concrete terms, MOSOP's leaders looked forward to the next major offensive of their nonviolent struggle. While meeting with the UN Working Group in Geneva, Saro-Wiwa learned that January 4, 1993, had been declared by the UN to mark the onset of the International Decade of the World's Indigenous People. Arguing that the Ogoni were now recognized by the world body as an indigenous people, he convinced his colleagues that a major peaceful protest should be held on that day. Chief among MOSOP's concerns was that the protest be kept peaceful at all costs. Saro-Wiwa saw it as a major test of the organization's discipline. Throughout the 1992 Christmas Season, recalls MOSOP's then General Secretary, Ben Naanen, "the people were gradually and meticulously worked up with a series of activities."[38]

The careful planning and preparation paid off handsomely. On January 4, 1993, some 300,000 Ogonis participated in the daylong protest march—which went off, as Saro-Wiwa would later proudly proclaim—"without a stone being thrown."[39] The march was without precedent in Nigerian politics, attracting considerable attention not only throughout the country but also internationally. Determined that the successful January march should not be merely an isolated successful event, MOSOP worked steadily over the following months to reinforce the Ogoni masses' commitment by employing the full range of tools it had refined earlier: the mass rallies, the night vigils, and repeated speeches and exhortations by its leaders.

As John Agbonifo notes, the broader Nigerian reaction to the Ogonis' campaign must be seen in light of a growing general impatience with military regimes. Nigerian civil society, including the free press, student and religious groups and much of academia saw the Ogoni struggle as a campaign "to install democracy, justice, fairness, and equity to all constituent parts of Nigeria."[40]

MOSOP's success in mobilizing the Ogoni inevitably heightened the fears of Nigerian officialdom, and possibly of the Shell Corporation, that a serious threat to Nigeria's long established way of doing things might be developing. From that perspective, the crux of the matter was succinctly articulated by the military administrator of Rivers State: "[The Ogoni] don't have the monopoly of petroleum in Nigeria and therefore cannot make demands that other [oil-producing groups] are not making."[41] The danger to the Nigerian military dictatorship was that the Ogoni struggle would provide an example that could galvanize other oil-producing minorities into making similar demands for a fundamental alteration of the country's political system. Recognizing this, the regime concluded that its own interest required that the Ogoni example must carry a completely different message: that any minority challenging the status quo faced the prospect of running headlong into complete catastrophe.

Various circumstances combined in 1993 to help the government undermine the Ogoni movement. The military dictatorship of General Ibrahim Babangida, which had long dragged its feet on fulfilling a promise to restore civilian rule, scheduled a presidential election in June. This divided MOSOP's leadership, for while key traditional leaders on the organization's Steering Committee saw the upcoming election as an opportunity for political maneuvering that might yield political as well as personal gains, Saro-Wiwa strongly felt otherwise. In his view, so long as Nigeria's Constitution remained unchanged, nothing could be gained by trading Ogoni votes for politicians' promises. An Ogoni boycott of the upcoming plebiscite would be a major nonviolent demonstration of Ogoni refusal to participate in the prevailing system. Saro-Wiwa believed the Ogoni's best move would be to influence an upcoming constitutional conference that was to form part of Nigeria's transition to democratic, civilian rule.

MOSOP's internal cohesion was also battered during 1993 as the nonviolent Ogoni movement became the target of a sustained and very violent campaign. Finally, the year ended with the June presidential election having been nullified and the presumed winner imprisoned, no constitutional conference having been held, and the outbreak of a renewed scramble for power among various military factions. The outcome at the national level was the seizure of power by General Sani Abacha, who would gain infamy as the most ruthless and oppressive of Nigeria's many military rulers.

THE END OF THE UPRISING

The year that greeted MOSOP with the heady success of the massive January protest march began to go sour in the spring. In April, a Shell contractor, the Willbros Group, began bulldozing newly planted fields as a first step toward laying a pipeline across a section of Ogoniland. The following day, the Willbros crew was met by a crowd of unarmed villagers protesting this invasion of their land. Nigerian troops guarding the workers fired into the crowd killing one villager and wounding eleven. The event touched off a storm of demonstrations across Ogoniland, during which at least one more Ogoni was killed.

It also led to the first serious clash among MOSOP's leaders. Friction was generated when MOSOP's president and vice president, both senior traditional chiefs, agreed to accept Shell's offer of compensation to the Willbros victims in return for permission to continue work on the pipeline. Saro-Wiwa, who was abroad when the accord was reached, strongly opposed it upon his return. He argued that the amount of compensation was insultingly small (a total of about $100,000 for all victims) and that work on the pipeline should be suspended pending an environmental impact study. When Saro-Wiwa's position caused MOSOP to go back on the Willbros agreement, the traditional leaders "felt belittled and insulted."[42] For its part, Shell implemented an earlier decision to suspend operations in Ogoniland.

The Willbros incident also signaled a growing rift between what Ben Naanen has called the Ogonis' "traditional gerontocracy" and the younger generation of Ogoni males. These "youths," as they are called, tended to support Saro-Wiwa's confrontational stands against what they perceived as the self-interested conservatism of the elders, but it became increasingly evident that many of them either failed to understand, or simply rejected, his equally determined insistence on nonviolence. Thus, when ten traditional leaders issued a public apology for the Willbros protest, the youths abandoned non-violence. Agbonifo has described the reaction:

> Feeling betrayed and disinherited by their supposed elders and leaders, the youths turned on the elders ... and went about burning their homes and properties. The latter fled from Ogoniland to "exile" in Port Harcourt .... From that time, the youths lost ... respect for the chiefs, regarding them as agents of Shell and the government, bent on sabotaging the Ogoni struggle.[43]

Saro-Wiwa's insistence that the Ogoni boycott the June national presidential election was the subject of an acrimonious MOSOP Steering Committee meeting that produced the organization's next major leadership crisis. When Saro-Wiwa carried the day, the traditional leaders who served as MOSOP's president and vice president resigned. Saro-Wiwa was subsequently elected the organization's president and Ledum Mitee picked to be his vice president. The more radical Ogoni youth once again helped undermine MOSOP's nonviolent position by forcefully ensuring that the boycott was not broken. MOSOP's vision of a democratic, participatory domestic base was rapidly becoming wishful thinking.

The summer of 1993 saw the introduction of a new factor, one that not only further reduced MOSOP's dwindling authority among the Ogoni but also severely challenged its concept of nonviolent struggle. In July, the first of a series of armed attacks against Ogoni targets was carried out. Most of the attacks were perpetrated by forces operating from territories controlled by tribes on Ogoniland's borders. One major attack occurred in Port Harcourt and was ostensibly the work of members of another tribe—the Okrika. In each case, the government explained the violence as a manifestation of intertribal tensions.

The attacks began along the line separating Ogoniland from the tribal territory of the Andoni, a group with which the Ogoni had no history of conflict. Between mid-July and mid-September, several Ogoni villages were attacked, and in some cases virtually destroyed. After overcoming the initial shock of the unexpected assaults, the Ogoni youth began organizing "vigilante" groups to defend their villages and, in at least one instance, conduct retaliatory raids on Adoni settlements. No definitive figures for the loss of life caused by the brief "Ogoni-Andoni conflict" are available, but it is generally agreed that a substantial number of casualities resulted on the Ogoni side.

Saro-Wiwa maintained from the start that the clashes had been triggered by the Nigerian security forces and not by some inexplicably sudden Andoni aggressive impulse. On trial for his life, Saro-Wiwa later argued that the mortars, grenades, and automatic weapons employed in the initial attacks indicated official Nigerian involvement and, possibly, Shell's involvement as well.[44]

Saro-Wiwa's charge was given limited support by the late Claude Ake, Nigeria's leading political scientist and perhaps Africa's most internationally renowned social scientist, who was briefly part of a government-sponsored Ogoni-Andoni peace commission. When that commission was disbanded, only to be replaced by another that drew up a peace accord providing for the resumption of economic activities in Ogoniland, Ake demurred. His reasoning was that the source of the conflict still remained too mysterious to permit prescriptive steps for its resolution:

> We should have looked closely into the intensity of the fighting and the military sophistication of the conflict because this did seem to suggest that what was involved was more than a community conflict. One could not help getting the impression that there were broader forces

> which might have been interested in perhaps putting the Ogonis under pressure probably to derail their agenda.[45]

In December, Ogoni residents in a Port Harcourt slum suddenly became targets of attack, this time by another tribal group, the Okrika. Over the course of two days, Ogoni people living near the city's waterfront were attacked and Ogoni buildings were selectively targeted for bombing. Extensive damage and loss of life resulted. Notwithstanding the presence of police and Nigerian military and security forces in this urban setting, the perpetrators were never brought to justice.

Four months later, in April 1994, Ogoniland was attacked by forces coming through its northern border, from the territory of yet another tribe, the Ndoki. Over the course of twelve days, a total of six villages were destroyed and several hundred Ogonis were killed.[46]

In mid-1995, Human Rights Watch, the well-known nongovernmental organization that since 1978 has monitored the observance of internationally recognized human rights around the world, published a report that upheld Ken Saro-Wiwa's claims regarding the Nigerian government's role in the armed attacks on Ogoniland, though not his suspicions regarding Shell's possible role. Meticulously and horrifyingly documented, the report was based on interviews with Ogoni victims and the families of victims as well as interviews with former Nigerian soldiers whose units participated in the clandestine campaign to destabilize Ogoniland. A key part of the report directly challenged Nigerian authorities:

> The Nigerian government has publicly claimed that the outbreaks of violence in Ogoniland were the result of ethnic clashes beween the Ogoni and neighboring ethnic groups, including the Andoni in July 1993, the Okrika in December 1993 and the Ndoki in April 1994. However, evidence now available shows that the government played an active role in fomenting such ethnic antagonism, and indeed that some attacks attributed to rural minority communities were in fact carried out by army troops in plainclothes.[47]

The months-long assault on Ogoniland not only took a toll in human lives and property. The established Ogoni social structure was severely shaken by the trauma of what amounted to a long siege. The incipient rift between the youth and traditional leaders broadened, becoming much uglier and, ultimately, deadlier. The man who at the time was MOSOP's young General Secretary has eloquently described the dynamic that was unleashed:

> The young men who fought to defend Ogoni now saw an opportunity to impose their own vision of a socially-sanitized Ogoni. They went

> about their self-imposed mission with draconian enthusiasm, spreading fear. In many communities vigilante groups held court, tried and dealt with men suspected of nefarious activities such as witchcraft. Some village chiefs perceived to be corrupt were deposed . . . . For some time Ogoni was in a state of flux as power actually passed from the traditional gerontocracy—chiefs and elders—to the young visionaries. It was a generational coup d'etat. Criminals also took advantage of this situation to terrorise people. MOSOP tried hard to control the situation with limited success.

MOSOP's "limited success" in this regard was symptomatic of the obvious, the movement's ability to determine the goals and strategy of the Ogonis' struggle had eroded almost to the vanishing point. Its ability to maintain the Ogoni masses as disciplined followers in a nonviolent struggle had long since reached that point.

Many of the traditional chiefs, united by their opposition to Saro-Wiwa, whom they blamed for having set loose the passions of the youth, now decided to establish an alternative to MOSOP, an organization that would pursue MOSOP's goals under their own stewardship. A conclave of five such men was scheduled to be held in the village of Giokoo, the center of the Ogoni Gokhana subgroup, on May 21, 1994.[48]

Giokoo is a fairly typical Ogoni village, a gathering of thatched roof huts, some boasting concrete plastering, others mud. Its inhabitants cultivate yams, cassava, and melons—and they are exceedingly proud of the melons which, they say, are much sought after even in Port Harcourt. There are two outstanding structures in Giokoo. The first is the palace of the *Gbeneneme*, the Gokhana's traditional ruler. It has been rebuilt since the events of 1994. Today, it is a nicely finished one-floor concrete-block building, painted a pleasing orange and enclosed by a small verandah. The second structure that attracts attention is the shrine to the Ogoni Spirit. This too is of concrete-block, though it is neither plastered nor painted. To American eyes, the simple building with its corrugated tin roof looks more like a small garage or toolshed than a holy place. It stands only four or five yards away from the palace's verandah.

On May 21, 1994, the five chiefs were meeting in the palace when they were assailed by a mob of young men chanting war songs. Four of the chiefs were hacked and bludgeoned to death. The fifth managed to survive the attack by escaping into the shrine. Even the frenzied emotions and blood lust generated by the ongoing murders of his colleagues were insufficient to overcome traditional Ogoni religious beliefs, which forbade the shrine's desecration. He was therefore eventually able to emerge unscathed.[49]

The immediate consequence of the Giokoo murders was the invasion of Ogoniland by the Nigerian army, ostensibly for the purpose of securing public order. In fact, the invasion was designed to terrify the Ogoni into quiescence. Brutality was the order of the day. The bulk of the Human Rights Watch report referred to above concentrates on events in Ogoniland after the Giokoo murders. It constitutes a highly documented and harrowing catalogue of a yearlong campaign of mass killings, torture, rape, and collective punishments inflicted on the Ogoni People.

The Giokoo massacre also provided the Abacha regime with a pretext for the frontal assault on MOSOP that took the form of the trumped up charges of murder against Ken Saro-Wiwa and his colleagues. Their 1995 executions, however, did not spell the end of the movement. MOSOP still survives, although its influence among the Ogoni people has been much weakened.[50]

Whatever the eventual fortunes of MOSOP may be, there is no doubt that the Ogoni nonviolent insurrection it spearheaded has heavily influenced Nigeria's political dynamics. The eclipse of Saro-Wiwa did not forestall the spread of political activism among the Niger Delta's other exploited communities. On the contrary, MOSOP's resistance to the inequities of Nigeria's political system became a beacon for other marginalized communities. This is why a decade after the hangings at Port Harcourt the Niger Delta is one of the most unstable and violent regions of the world. The Ogonis' story conveyed compelling lessons of resistance to the region's still-marginalized and oppressed minorities. The same story, however, did not entail much persuasive evidence that nonviolence should be the chosen means to overcoming their problems.[51]

The Meaning of MVICs

The Marginalized Violent Internal Conflicts in the Chiapas Highlands, Upper Egypt, and the Niger Delta reveal significant elements of the conditions and dynamics that in the modern world impel traditional groups to enter into conflict with opponents who by all objective standards enjoy an overwhelming superiority of force. By doing so, these MVICs also uncover important aspects of the nature and implications of the threat to international security embodied by the 9/11 attacks on the United States.

The very fact that the MVICs reviewed above occurred in such disparate locations and involved such culturally distinct groups strongly implies some common set of factors that, despite the obvious geographical and historical differences among them, placed Mexico's Highland Maya, Upper Egyptians, and Nigeria's Ogoni in parallel situations. Three such factors immediately stand out.

The first is the contradictory roles played by the state and its organs in all three cases. Viewed as the repository of true national values, the state itself (that is, the concept of the state) was in each case the insurgents' chief hope of salvation. On the other hand, the organs of the state (that is the government and its agencies) were perceived by each insurgent group as having violated those same true national values and were therefore considered to be the primary enemy.

The second element in the set of interrelated factors that placed the Maya, Upper Egyptians, and the Ogoni in similar situations was what goes under the broad rubric of "globalization," here understood as the processes through which economics, politics, and technology unleash forces that increasingly make the various societies of our world not only more interconnected but also susceptible to similar experiences, both good and bad.

The impact of pressures of globalization tended in each case to further alienate the insurgent groups from the state's governing organs. This, of course, was most plain in the Ogoni case, where the rape of natural resources at the least possible cost resulted from direct and long-term connivance between venal governments and predatory international conglomerates. But it was not deeply hidden in the other cases, where decision-making was not necessarily influenced by venality. Thus, the reversal of land-reform programs in Egypt and Mexico, while understandable as part of hard choices made in strategic restructurings of national economic policies, only further undermined the government's credibility in insurgent eyes.

The final element that helped place the Maya, Upper Egyptians, and Ogoni in similar positions was their commonly shared status as traditional and marginalized groups. Within the context of the state's politically organizing role, these groups had essentially been left out. The inevitable consequence was that the Mexican, Egyptian, and Nigerian governments gave an even lower priority to mitigating harmful effects of globalization-driven policies than might otherwise have been the case.

While it is accurate enough to characterize Mexico's Highland Maya, Upper Egyptians, and the Ogoni as "traditional," care must be taken in employing the label. The term is accurate if it is taken to signify that these groups cherished and found identity in beliefs, practices, and values that have historically been central to their cultures. It is totally inappropriate if taken to mean an uncompromising resistance to, or rejection of, change and the material benefits of the modern world. Thus, the Highland Maya eagerly responded to perceived economic opportunities offered by the "Chiapas Plan," Upper Egyptians just as eagerly flooded into universities and then into the stream of migrant Egyptian labor, and the Ogoni hoped that jobs and social advancement would be by-products of the oil sucked from their soil. Indeed, in each case, the frustration of such "nontraditional" expectations helped spark insurgency.

At the most superficial level, the MVICs experienced by Mexico, Egypt, and Nigeria carry the obvious—but important—lesson that there is a limit to the human capacity to accept marginalization, exploitation, and oppression, and that once crossed, this limit will not be restored just because of an awareness that the intolerable situation is backed by an objectively overwhelming superiority of force.

Looked at more closely, however, the three cases reveal much more detail about the dynamics that nurtured and shaped the conflicts. In the first place, the similarities in the structures of oppression in each case clearly help explain similarities in the course of the conflicts themselves. Thus, in all three cases the power structures of oppression were formed by a descending chain of clientalistic relationships that linked the central authority of the state to the local communities of marginalized groups. The result, of course, was that not all members of the marginalized groups were equally marginalized from the centers of state power. This, in turn, is why each insurgency involved not only conflict with the ruling powers of the state but also degrees of intra-group conflict within the marginalized communities themselves. While this was most obvious among the Ogoni, such tensions also figured in the Zapatista and *Gama'a al-Islamiyya* insurgencies.

The varying degrees of marginalization that exist in practice within marginalized groups also help explain why the numbers of active militants recruited by the insurgents always amounted to only a small minority of the marginalized groups from which they sprang. This is important and serves as a reminder that marginalized groups are not homogenous in their marginalization and that differences will not only affect group cohesion but also the strength and capacity of insurgent movements. On the other hand, the large extent of tacit support given to the insurgents in each case, shows that their cause resonated positively among a significant portion, if not the majority, of the marginalized group.

Such positive resonance and the broad tacit support it produced can only be explained as a consequence of the mobilizing ideologies that underpinned the insurgencies reviewed above. In each case, the ideology was rooted in central features of the marginalized group's traditional cosmology. Thus, while each ideology also incorporated elements of nontraditional religions, these took syncretistic forms that make them more accurately described as elements of Folk Religion.

Egyptian anthropologist El-Sayed El-Aswad's recent study of religion and folk cosmology in rural Egypt sheds light on the nature and force of the mobilizing ideologies that gave rise to the Zapatista, Upper Egyptian, and Ogoni insurgencies. As he intended, El-Aswad's work does much to show "that in rural Egypt, as in other parts of the world, the individual is part not only of the society but also of the total cosmological system."[52] By "cosmology," El-Aswad means "the assumptions concerning the structure of the universe ... extended here to include society as well as human and nonhuman beings and forces, both perceptible and imperceptible, as constituting integral parts of that universe."[53]

The central finding of El-Aswad's study is that traditional cosmology provides its adherents with an internalized, holistic vision that unifies visible and invisible realities in one understandable system. It is a system in which invisible reality takes precedence, giving meaning and purpose to the visible, or the empirical. In doing so, the cosmological vision also—and very significantly—provides meaning for the individual's life and relationships with others. It is, of course, here that the cosmological vision becomes essential to group identity and action.

Because invisible reality takes precedence over the visible, it also follows a different logic, which allows an understanding of the invisible to overcome "the limitations of common sense experience in this worldly life . . . "[54] Moreover, the invisible world's logic tends to support the notion that "justice will inevitably be attained by a higher power."[55] Thus, "anything is possible, because there is always room for the invisible to work."[56]

Here is the fundamental explanation of how and why ideologies based on traditional cosmologies attract sufficient followers to enter into conflict against objectively hopeless odds. El-Aswad's work supports the conclusions of Evon Vogt, who in studying the Maya found that cosmological knowledge was not transmitted formally, but rather imbibed as part of a daily socialization process.[57] In everyday life, El-Aswad notes, the religious, mundane, and mystical or magical "interface and are inseparably interconnected."[58]

El-Aswad's analysis of traditional Egyptian folk cosmology underscores a further feature that is shared by other traditional cosmologies; a willingness—indeed, an eagerness to accept modernization on certain terms:

> [traditional] peasants are neither withdrawn from this worldly life nor are they irrationally immersed in the other wordly life. They do not reject modernization—rather they have developed an indigenous kind of secular modernism. What is rejected, however, is the secularism or secular outlook that negates religious meanings and renders the moral-spiritual human into an ungodly and merciless creature.[59]

In short, then, the traditional cosmology allows scope for demands for change, but also insists on preserving the core values, beliefs, and practices upon which communal, and ultimately personal, identities are based.

This is a tall and complex order, and one that may well prove impossible to fill. But it lies at the heart of the clash between the traditional and the modern, and it has been neatly formulated by the mobilizing ideologies that sustained each of the MVIC's reviewed above. The essence of the syncretistic outlooks that led Maya Indians, Upper Egyptian peasants, and Ogoni tribesmen to challenge the vastly superior power of the states in which they lived lay in their simultaneous demands for socioeconomic-political change and cultural preservation.

Given the ambivalent core of the Mexican, Egyptian, and Nigerian insurgencies, it is hardly surprising that their leaderships came from the most nonmarginalized elements of the communities on whose behalf they acted. Being equally exposed to both the modern and traditional worlds, persons of such status were more likely to feel the need to synthesize demands for socioeconomic change and cultural purity. Thus, they were more likely than most to feel that demands for tangible beneficial change, such as greater attention to economic and social needs, were just as important and valid as specific demands for intangible benefits, such as respect, dignity and cultural sensitivity. It is notable that each insurgent group advanced both sets of demands.

One final residual lesson to be gleaned from the MVICs discussed here remains to be mentioned. It is extremely evident that insurgencies by marginalized groups can take any number of forms. The Zapatistas, for example, waged a conflict that employed a relatively low level of violence while making use of a very high level of public relations techniques and skills to garner political support. On the other hand, the *Gama'a al-Islamiyya* launched a bloody campaign of death and destruction that culminated in the 1997 Luxor Massacre. Finally, the Ogoni attempted to pursue a nonviolent insurrection, only to find extreme violence directed against themselves.

By 2007, none of these conflicts had been fully resolved. Upper Egypt remains tense and wary, if not expectant, of a renewal of terrorist attacks. Ogoniland, while currently crushed into passivity compared with neighboring regions of the Niger Delta, is still unstable and potentially explosive. Mexico, which pursued a policy of limited accommodation with the Zapatistas has made the most progress toward bringing its insurgents to abandon armed struggle in favor of inclusion in the national political system. Yet, the issue is still unresolved and it remains to be seen whether the Mexican government's inclusionary efforts will suffice to extinguish the marginalized hostility of its Zapatista opponents.

The final lesson seems to be that when social, political, and economic marginalization reach the extreme of generating fears for the very survival of existence as it is understood by individuals and groups, these will seek refuge in all that is left to them: the beliefs and practices that reaffirm—despite what appears to be an overload of empirical evidence to the contrary—the individual and groups' identities as entities of real value in this universe. It is hardly surprising that as the last line of existential defense, these beliefs and practices will be aggressively pursued.

It is now time to see if these lessons from the several Marginalized Violent Internal Conflicts reviewed here can be seen to have some explanatory power regarding the attacks of 9/11. The contention of this book, of course, is that they do ... up to a (very useful) point. As the following portion of this book seeks to make clear, however, beyond that point 9/11 stands as a unique event and MVICs offer no illumination of the terribly unfamiliar terrain into which history has led us all.

PART III

The Quest for International Security

CHAPTER 6

THE ARAB WORLD AS A WORLD PROBLEM

The "Arab World" is a broad and cumbersome label. If defined in terms of the regional organization known as the League of Arab States, it currently includes twenty-two nation states. Some of these, Comoros, Djibouti, Mauritania, and Somalia, who joined the League between 1973 and 1993, are often thought of as "African" rather than "Arab" states. Be this is at it may, the "Arab World" is typically considered, as it is here, to embrace those countries whose dominant language is Arabic, that stretch in a wide arc from Morocco to Iran. This definition excludes Turkey and Israel, though it includes occupied Palestine.

The Arab World constituted a global threat throughout most of the last half of the twentieth century. However, those were the Cold War years and the Arab World's menace was seen as derivative, or secondary, rather than essential, or primary. The danger was that the Arabs' quarrel with Israel might catapult the two superpowers of the day into direct confrontation. The 1973 Arab-Israeli War showed that such fears were not without foundation.[1]

The Cold War became part of the historical record, but the problems of the Arab World did not. In the first decade after the end of the Cold War, the region emerged as a threat to global security in its own right. How and why this happened must be understood if the current terrorist campaign is to be defeated.

Perhaps the most obvious problem of today's Arab World is the nature of the governments that rule over most of the area. While clear and important differences mark relations between rulers and ruled in the area's subregions, most fall short of what in the West would be considered minimally acceptable levels of responsibility for, and responsiveness to, the requirements of citizens' well-being.

Two personal experiences have long symbolized for me important limitations on the vision and consistency of purpose that mark too many of the Arab World's contemporary political elites. The first has undermined Arab leaders' understanding of the requirements of coping with the modern world. The second has sabotaged their efforts to do so.

My first symbolic encounter was in 1969 with General Abdul Rahman Aref, shortly after he was deposed as Iraq's President. Aref, who had succeeded his brother after the latter's death in a suspicious helicopter crash, ruled Iraq for just over two years before being removed from office. Atypically for that period in Iraqi politics, the erstwhile ruler was not killed but rather allowed to go into exile. Aref wound up in Istanbul, where he and his wife settled in the affluent seaside suburb of Yeşilyürt. A likeable, unassuming pair, the Aref's were quickly incorporated into the neighborhood's social life. Aref spoke passable Turkish and was universally known in the neighborhood as "Ekselans." His wife knew no Turkish but was a pleasant woman who reputedly played a mean game of canasta.

Then a graduate student in my early twenties, I was staying at the Yeşilyürt home of a Turkish friend when it was her parents' turn to host a weekly canasta game, a regular feature of social life on Ürgüplü Street. "Ekselans" and Mrs. Aref were among the guests. Before the card playing began, my host, a senior judge with a subtly wicked sense of humor, introduced me to the Arefs and urged me to practice my Turkish in conversation with "Ekselans." Aref and I chatted for only a few moments before he asked what I did for a living. I replied that I was a graduate student and hoped someday to embark on an academic career. There was a pause, during which "Ekselans" peered at me closely. "You are still a student?" he finally asked. When I confirmed my status, he could no longer contain himself. Aref erupted into gales of hearty laughter through which he just barely managed to gasp out the news in Arabic to his wife. Mrs. Aref also found it amusing that I was student, although not to the same extent as her husband. The judge rejoined us to learn the source of our jolly moment. When the still-chuckling "Ekselans" told him, the judge gave me a broad wink and smoothly changed the subject. I later asked the judge what it was that Aref had found so funny. "I don't know," he replied, "maybe he thinks you're too old to be a student."

If General Aref's laughter revealed something of the limited understanding of the modern world held by many who have come to power in the Arab World, another encounter—more than thirty years later—even more graphically illustrated the deep differences that divide the region's political elites, both among themselves and from the people they lead. It was shortly after the end of the war that liberated Kuwait from Saddam Hussein's clutches and I was in a European capital to interview the ambassador of a major Gulf state. I arrived at his residence around midday and was shown to a waiting room. Within minutes the very fit and energetic emissary joined me—munching an apple and inviting me to have one too. As we were still in the Islamic month of Ramadan, a period during which able-bodied Muslims are enjoined to fast between sunrise and sunset, I took his entry as a calculated performance designed to demonstrate from the outset that I was meeting a very "Westernized" person. But apple-munching was the least of the surprises the ambassador had for me that day.

He was overjoyed by the recent war's outcome and hopeful that it signaled the dawn of a new age in the Arab World. He regaled me for nearly two hours with his vision of a new power structure in the Middle East that would be based on a nexus between what he saw as new international and regional realities. Most Arabs would have denounced his vision in horror:

> The war shows that the United States is the only power in the world . . . and that's that. Power is power and the United States should dominate the Middle East. U.S. domination is, after all, benign. Americans pay dollars for our oil. The oil itself does us no good. With dollars, not oil, we buy videos, cars and houses.
>
> We [Arab Gulf states] are rich and the United States is rich. It is natural that the rich should lead the poor. But in the past, we were afraid to speak out. And the result is that the radicals—the Nasserists, Pan-Arabists, the PLO—brought disaster to the Arab world. After all, we are the pure Arabs, and we don't need lessons in Arabism from them. The United States must accept the responsibility of dominating so that the Arab World will at last be peaceful and productive and better.[2]

The ambassador had previously held diplomatic posts in the United States, and he assured me that he still spent as much time as possible in Washington trying to advance his views. These, of course, were not consistent with the official, public position of his government, for officially and publicly the ambassador's country steadily proclaimed itself committed to "Arab brotherhood" and generally opposed to outside interference in the Arab World's affairs. Yet, the ambassador's position must be taken to have reflected the dominant outlook, or at least a very strong current of opinion, within the government he represented.

The position articulated by the ambassador would have been politically untenable in any part of the Arab World, including his own country. His comments not only strikingly revealed the depth of differences among Arab countries regarding how the West should relate to the Arab World but also the degree to which the ambassador's own government was out of step with the predominant political values of the society it ruled. In this latter sense, our conversation underscored a major problem that has not been confined to any single Arab state. Regardless of ideological orientation, the states of the modern Arab World have all too often suffered from inordinately wide gaps between the publicly promoted values that ostensibly guide government policies and the operational values that actually do so. Such contradictions have become progressively harder to hide. This has been the single most important factor helping to undermine the domestic credibility and legitimacy of Arab governments in our day.

THE MARGINALIZATION OF THE ARAB WORLD

The Arab World has always been the center of the Islamic World. In the centuries that followed the Prophet's era, it also became the center of one of history's great civilizations. Under the patronage of Arab rulers, commerce, science, literature, and philosophy thrived from Andalusia to the borders of Persia. Arab armies, merchants, and missionaries carried Islam far beyond the Middle East, to the subcontinent, sub-Saharan Africa, and Asia. But the glories of the medieval Arab World passed and as the modern age dawned, Western Europe—largely building on knowledge preserved and gained by Arab thinkers—took the global lead. From about the fifteenth century onward, the Arab region and its inhabitants were increasingly marginalized as actors on the world stage.

In the sixteenth century most of the region comprising today's Arab World came under the Ottoman Empire's rule. As the Empire's strength failed in the nineteenth century, the imperial ambitions of European powers turned to the Arab World. Near the end of the eighteenth century, Napoleon invaded Egypt. Within a century France ruled Algeria and Tunisia, and British power held sway in Egypt and the Sudan. Italy seized Libya in 1912, while Morocco (never part of the Ottoman Empire) was divided into protectorates by France and Spain that same year. When the Ottoman's fateful decision to join the Axis Powers in World War I resulted in the Empire's end, Europe's role increased throughout the area. Egypt remained under British control. The League of Nations placed Palestine and Iraq under British mandates. Syria (including Lebanon) was handed to France under the same format. Only the Gulf region, then the most remote and underdeveloped part of the Arab World, remained free from official European control. And even there, British influence predominated. In the 1920s, Ibn Saud, whose political fortunes were massively helped by the British Government's India Office, united most of the Arabian Peninsula. In 1932 he proclaimed the establishment of the Kingdom of Saudi Arabia. In the process, Ibn Saud ousted another local potentate, the Hashemite Sherif of Mecca, Hussein Ibn Ali, who had allied himself with Britain during the war and whose forces played a significant role in driving the Turks from Arabia, Trans-Jordan, and Syria. Partly to offset the embarrassment of Hussein's fate, Britain subsequently set up one of his sons, Abdallah, as the ruler of Trans-Jordan (today's Jordan) and another, Faysal, as King of Iraq. British influence in the smaller independent sultanates and emirates of the Gulf was assured by various treaties that had been concluded with local rulers in the nineteenth century. Palestine, retained as a British Mandate, set out on the tortured course that would make it an intractable world problem.

These events rested on the earlier history of Arab nationalism. By the late nineteenth century, that movement rested on a growing and energetic body of thought whose many strands reflected the central idea that Arab societies would find the remedy to underdevelopment in greater self-rule. Some saw this as a possible solution within the context of a liberalized Ottoman imperial system. Others, more radically inclined, felt that full severance from the Empire was required. Then too, serious questions problematically beset the issue of any future communal identity. Was "Arabness" identical with Islam? Or did historical and cultural realities require a more limited regionally specific form of communal identity? Some, for example Mecca's Sherif Hussein, who hoped his alliance with the British in World War I would lead to a single Arab state ranging from Arabia to the Levant, tended toward a Pan-Arabist vision. Others, such as the Egyptian intellectual Taha Hussein, favored more localized forms of identity.

World War I settled—at least for a long time—some of these major issues. Forced to function within the framework of Europe's postwar colonial fragmentation of the region, Arab political aspirations progressively focused on individual Arab states, although Pan-Arabist visions long remained alive as ultimate goals. Nonetheless, by then Arab importance to World History had virtually disappeared as a consequence of profound and prolonged marginalization. From the fifteenth to the twentieth centuries the Arab World's economic, political, social, and cultural roles were eclipsed. The region therefore entered the twentieth century as a backwater, determined to catch up but lacking the human and material resources for the task.

Decades would pass before full sovereignty was accorded to those parts of the region—Egypt, Iraq, and Syria—that historically had contributed most to the Arab World's cultural, intellectual, and political life. In 1922, Egypt was granted a significant measure of self-rule, but Britain retained control of the Suez Canal Zone as well as determining influence over the national government's policies. It would take another thirty years before Gamal Abdul Nasser's rise to power returned the country to total Egyptian control. Iraq, still heavily influenced by London under its new Hashemite King, gained independence and membership in the League of Nations in 1932. Britain's leading role in the country's affairs would not be ended until the monarchy's bloody fall in 1958. Syria, now divided by the French into Syria and Lebanon, achieved independence in the mid-1940s. Unfortunately, independence did not fulfill the brightest hopes of those who saw sovereignty and the nation state as vehicles to revitalize and modernize their societies.

The Greek Orthodox Syrian historian Constantine Zurayk put it bluntly, arguing that everything would depend on whether Arab Nationalism

> ...becomes broad or narrow, tolerant or exclusive, progressive or reactionary—whether, in other words, it becomes the outward expression of an inner civilization or contracts upon itself and dies of suffocation.[3]

Zurayk offered this as a necessary though not sufficient basis for Arab development:

> In facing the difficulties that now stand in the way of their national progress, and to be able to tackle the serious problems that are confronting them, the Arabs are in need of two things: enlightened and capable leadership and a radical change in their attitude toward life. From them the new attitude requires searching self-examination; merciless rejection of all weakening and reactionary factors in their national life; objective appreciation and cultivation of universal values in their culture; readiness to assimilate Western techniques and, above all, the positive intellectual and spiritual tradition of the West.... Furthermore, the leaders of the revived Arab Nation must be capable and progressive. They must have a real understanding of the political and social conditions of the modern world, and must be able to adjust to the requirements of those conditions.[4]

These words echo today with a sad hollowness, as though resounding from a moldy museum of faded wishes. The ambitions of Arab Nationalists of Zurayk's caliber have long since been smashed on the rocks of Middle East political reality. The hope of "enlightened and capable leadership" has yielded to the reality of venal, authoritarian regimes whose existence depends, at best, on cowed acquiescence and, at worst, on sheer fear. Instead of a rejection of reactionary thinking, recent decades have witnessed the ascendancy of exclusivist, obscurantist interpretations of Islam among the populations of Arab states. Instead of societies with "a real understanding of the political and social conditions of the modern world," what has been created is just the opposite: societies that have in the main been left behind by the world's dominant currents of thought and social and cultural development. Instead of embarking on a "radical change in their attitude toward life," as Zurayk hoped, the Arab World saw the rise of a fearful atavism that not only turned threateningly inward but also promised to suffocate hopes that Arab societies might discover the joy of contributing positively to the human experience.

How did this happen? How did the Arab World reach such depths of collective desperation? On the one hand the answer lies in its long history of marginalization. However, in a more immediate sense the answer is largely to be found in the interplay between Arab and international politics in the modern world. To its misfortune, the Arab World—because of oil and its strategic geography—was inevitably caught up in global politics almost as soon as its Era of Independence dawned. In their determination to prevail in global rivalry, the world's leading powers, themselves caught up in the Cold War, showed little concern for conditions within the Arab World. Local regimes, so long as they could link themselves to one or another international patron, could, and did, indulge in the type of politics in which power is sought and retained for its own sake. Civil Society in Arab states remained tightly controlled or virtually nonexistent. Some Arab populations coped with this by slipping steadily more into a condition of political apathy and cynicism. Others, for various reasons, tried to break the mold through violence. In recent years, Egypt marked one extreme; Lebanon marked the other.

Thus, exactly thirty years after Zurayk penned his futile hopes, another observer of the region, Fuad Ajami could write this scathing obituary for Pan-Arabism:

> The seemingly harmless games played by the preceding generation, the hair-splitting arguments of Arab ideologues, gave way to a deeper and more terrifying breakdown. One generation had sown the wind and the other was now reaping the harvest. The stock in trade of men like Nasser, the Syrian Ba'athist theoretician Michel Aflaq, and the braggart Ahmed al-Shukairy of the Palestine Liberation Organization, was symbols and words. In the decade or so that followed the Six Day War, words were replaced with bullets, which now seemed the final arbiter. This generation, writes one observer, split into two groups: those who saw authority growing out of the barrel of a gun and those who packed up and left....[5]

The Six Day (1967) Arab-Israeli War referred to by Ajami marked, as he indicates, a turning point in Arab politics. The secularist, modernizationist first generation of Nationalists, Nasserists, and the Ba'ath, soon stood naked before their publics, having failed to modernize, failed to recover Palestine or even to defend their own lands, and—as was soon shown—failed to secularize their societies. In addition to undermining the credibility of these regimes and their modernizationist ethos, the 1967 War led to two other significant developments.

The first of these was enshrined by the Arab Summit at Khartoum shortly after the war's end, and, in effect, led to an understanding between so-called moderate (and Western-backed) oil-producing Arab states and so-called radical Arab Nationalist states. The essential elements of the exchange were clear: in return for much needed financial infusions, "radicals" legitimized postwar business-as-usual links between oil producers and their global markets as well as the existence of the oil producing regimes themselves.[6] An unintended, but very real, consequence of this accommodation was that the propagation throughout the Arab World of the more conservative Islamic outlooks prevailing in Arab Gulf States not only became more "legitimate" but also easier as Saudi Arabian and other Gulf money was put to this use.

The second major consequence of the 1967 War unfolded in the aftermath of the hostilities, Arabs discovered that what Constantine Zurayk had termed "the positive intellectual and spiritual tradition of the West" would be selectively applied—that is, that such proclaimed Western values as self-determination and the inadmissibility of territorial acquisition by force were apparently inapplicable to the Palestine problem. As the so-called Middle East Peace Process dragged on over the decades, this lesson resonated ever more loudly in the Arab World.

As if this were not enough to bolster the attraction of militant, fundamentalist Islam among the Arab public as an alternative to the vacuous, hypocritical modernizing ideologies of defeated Arab Nationalist regimes, events in the broader Islamic World strongly reinforced the message. The first such development came in early 1979 with the overthrow of Iran's Pahlavi Regime and its replacement by an Islamic state. The second began to take shape at the end of that year with the Soviet Union's invasion of Afghanistan and the ensuing U.S. decision to sponsor anti-Soviet fundamentalist *Mujahedeen* guerrillas. Both phenomena not only captured the imagination of thousands of Arabs who sought a socially significant framework in which to live out their lives but also seemed to point to a politically successful alternative.

The rise of Islamic fundamentalism as a political force did not, of course, go unnoticed by Arab regimes. Most soon sought to make use of it, in one way or another, though they remained determined to prevent it from prevailing politically. Egypt's Anwar El Sadat epitomized the trend, offering political space to Islamists as a counterbalance to Leftist trends in order to consolidate his new regime, and then abruptly curtailing them. As have most other Arab leaders, Sadat's successor, Hosni Mubarak, has allowed his regime to pursue Sadat's policy of measured, if erratic, accommodation with the Islamists. The result has been the ongoing spread of Islamic fundamentalism as a feature of contemporary Arab societies. It is a feature increasingly manifested in educational systems, in legal frameworks and, ultimately, in social mores. It has helped lead to societies that are, as Zurayk warned against so many years ago, contracting upon themselves.

Islamic fundamentalism is not in itself necessarily "militant." For many it simply provides a framework of values that points to a better society, and therefore to a better existence for all members of that society. Many who are inclined to fundamentalist perspectives find no difficulty, despite what are perhaps logical drawbacks, in also adhering to an essentially tolerant worldview. Yet, as fundamentalist views increasingly define the societal matrix, there are those who cannot accept the dissonance of illogic and will therefore balk at what is seen as the "betrayal" entailed by moderation. These may become militant and find in their version of "Islamic Purity" an ideology that has no patience with facts related to objective calculations of power relations.

It is because of this that many Arab regimes have had to confront Islamists on the battlefield over the past two decades. Egypt, Syria, Saudi Arabia, Algeria, Bahrain, and others serve as examples. Israel, of course, is a special case, but one that highlights the more general difficulty prevailing in the Middle East today. As Yasir Arafat's Palestinian Authority progressively turned into yet another typically venal and authoritarian Arab regime, the popularity of Islamist and fundamentalist militancy increased among the Palestinian rank and file. Hamas, the chief expression of this phenomenon, benefited accordingly.

By the same token, because of the increasingly fundamentalist coloration of Arab societies and the priority given by Arab regimes to remaining in power with the least effort, the ongoing crisis in Palestine fueled glaring contradictions. Thus, while the Mubarak regime remained solidly opposed to militant Islamic fundamentalism in Egypt, its officially appointed Sheikh of Al-Azhar waffled violently during the spring of 2002 over the question of whether Palestinian suicide bombers were or were not acting within the bounds of "true" Islam. Ranging from one extreme to the other, the learned Sheikh eventually concluded that suicide bombings were appropriately Islamic. In doing so, he simply reinforced the fundamentalist matrix from which militancy throughout the region arises.

More than twenty years ago, David Apter warned that the alienating impact of modern life threatened to produce the "Superfluous Man" as an embittered by-product of modernization. It is in the context of the political use to which Islamic values have been put by the self-serving regimes of the Arab World that we find at least the outlines of an answer to the question of why the September 11 attackers felt "superfluous." Confronted by unresponsive regimes, and militarily defeated by each Arab government they attempted to overthrow by force, the militants behind September 11 were indeed superfluous in determining the fates of their own societies. That they then attacked the chief international sponsor of the current Middle East status quo was only logical. Olivier Roy gives a succinct and penetrating description of those who now raise the threat of militant fundamentalist Islam:

> In effect, they exhibit a new characteristic: they are international and "deterritorialized," that is, their militants wander from jihad to jihad,

> generally on the margins of the Near East (Afghanistan, Kashmir, Bosnia) and are indifferent to their own nationalities. . . . They define themselves as internationalist Muslims and do not lend their militancy to any particular national cause. Their "centers" are in the no mans land of Afghano-Pakistani tribal zones.[7]

The Arab World had been pushed to the margins of World History long before Napoleon's 1798 invasion of Egypt inaugurated the West's modern penetration of the area. In the centuries since that event, the region has moved even farther back from the sidelines of the intellectual, cultural, political, and—save for its largely passive role as a provider of oil—economic currents that have shaped modern life. As founders of Islam and guardians of its geographic center, Arabs are part of a larger spiritual community, much of which has not only experienced similar structural domination by the West but also shared Arab bitterness over the apparent helplessness of Islam in the face of infidel forces. Those who constitute today's militant fundamentalist Islamic movements are only a tiny fraction of the more than 270 million who people the Arab World, and an even tinier minority of the world's estimated one billion Muslims.

In terms of available resources, the Arab World is far better off than the actual conditions facing most of its people would imply. However, despite having experienced overall improvement in standards of living over the past decades, Arab states generally "have been economic underachievers."[8] Oil, the region's most strikingly obvious resource, is not the limit of what it could count on for economic growth. There exist significant stores of human capital—as well as of unrepatriated financial capital—and a well developed physical infrastructure that could conceivably permit the Arab World to achieve significant gains through nontraditional exports.[9] But that has not happened.

Seen as a subsystem of the global order, it becomes clear that a great part of the Arab World's marginalization has long been manifested by the dominant powers' blatant unconcern with the hopes or needs of the region's inhabitants. In the best tradition of Realpolitik, the world's Great Powers have consistently pursued their own interests at the expense of the local counterpart. The story is the same, whether one looks at the 132-year French colonial adventure in Algeria, or French policies in the Levant during the interwar period, or Britain's multifaced Arab policies between 1882 and the late 1940s, or Washington's approach to the region throughout the Cold War. One of the more historically significant instances of this pattern is found in the U.S. handling of the Palestine problem during the crucially formative decade that produced the intractable Arab-Israeli problem—a period during which:

> Palestine-related decisions were rarely taken with reference to the issues at stake within Palestine itself. The fundamental reason for this was that American decision makers found little of interest in the question of whether Arab or Jew predominated in Palestine, or under what conditions some arrangement between the two might be possible. On the other hand, certain ramifications of the Arab-Zionist controversy were of great concern to these same men. These ramifications, secondary effects of the primordial contest over the ultimate political disposition of Palestine, formed a peculiarly American abstraction that in the halls of Washington constituted the "Palestine problem." It was, in fact, an abstraction composed of elements quite foreign to the points at issue within Palestine.[10]

It is now time to turn more directly to the issue of whether or not the cases of Marginalized Violent Internal Conflict presented in Part Two can shed light on 9/11. This will depend on the extent that the domestic conditions which impacted on the three marginalized groups—the Highland Maya of Chiapas, the masses of Upper Egypt, and the Ogoni of the Niger Delta—can be established as analogous to elements defining the broader realities of the Arab World. Several such factors were discussed earlier. Their cumulative impact catapulted marginalized social groups into virtually hopeless confrontations with more powerful opponents. It will be useful to recall that the foregoing analysis singled out the following factors as operationally key in fomenting the dynamics that culminated in instances of MVIC. Among these were contexts marked by highly stratified social structures; generalized patterns of clientalism in sociopolitical relations; marginalized groups with recent histories of exaggeratedly high hopes that were followed almost immediately by deep disillusionment; a pattern (among the marginalized) of markedly differential levels of marginalization; a pattern (also among the marginalized) characterized by the minority of militant activists receiving tacit support from much, if not most, of the marginalized community; the provision of leadership to marginalized militant groups by nonmarginalized members of the community; the holding of decidedly negative stereotypes of the marginalized community by the mainstream society, and the counterpart of this, which are the marginalized community's decidedly negative stereotypes of the mainstream society; and, finally, the militant minority's ideological worldview, which is informed by a cosmology that gives priority to the invisible world.

The ensuing discussion proceeds in the light of this framework.

While Arab social dynamics have not remained static, and while significant variations are to be found among Arab countries, it remains true that Arab society is on the whole highly and relatively rigidly stratified. Societal upheavals have occurred, as in Nasser's Egypt, and along with them tectonic rearrangements of social strata.[11] Still, for the individual Arab aspiring to personal betterment, social mobility remains elusive. Ancestry, family, and "connections" continue to be key determinants of life-chances. Religious, tribal, ethnic, and regional affiliations are in this regard usually more important than such personal characteristics as innate or acquired capacity, skill, drive, or plain hard effort. Limited economic development has helped undermine vehicles of social mobility, thus heightening societal rigidity. Education, notes the Arab Human Development Report 2003, has become "incapable of providing the poor with the tools and abilities they need for social mobility."[12]

National authority structures tend to perpetuate the social dynamics just described. In turn, those same authority structures have long been maintained—and in many cases were created—by external powers. In short, most of the Arab World's national power structures, which rely on clientalistic links to exercise authority in their own domains, are in turn dependent on clientalistic relations with non-Arab global powers. The links themselves are varied. Most directly, they can be seen in the form of overt regime-dependence. Such, for example, is Egypt's case where the ruling regime relies on some $2.25 billion of international foreign aid annually, or in the case of relatively tiny Jordan, whose budget is annually subsidized by over $500 million of foreign assistance.[13] Less visible, but equally significant, are official establishments, such as the military, that develop vested interests in external dependence, and major business concerns, whose lucrative external linkages depend on the status quo.

Perhaps no region has been more directly affected than the Arab World by the globalization of the world's economy. For more than a half-century, petro-dollars have tied the area to the global economy. Oil-rich Arab regimes put their wealth to political use, fueling self-serving domestic policies, inter-Arab rivalries, arms races, and major wars—all of which helped undermine the quality of life of the region's people. At the same time, the region, and particularly the most economically vulnerable of its population, directly experienced the uncontrollable impact of dependency on the vicissitudes of the international economy. This has been most sharply evident in the unfortunately unstable recent history of the regional migrant labor market. Periods of boom, particularly in the Gulf States and Iraq offered jobs, along with soaring hopes for long-term material benefit, to millions of Arabs who faced very limited or no opportunities in their homelands. That market, however, proved susceptible to severe downturns due to several factors, including the inelasticity of demand for major infrastructural projects, negative fluctuations in the oil market, and political events in the oil-producing states. The reduction of employment opportunities signaled the shattering of hope for massive numbers of people throughout the Arab World.[14]

On the other hand, the region's increasing incorporation into the world economy has continued to benefit the minority of Arabs who are in positions to take advantage of it. The result, seen not only in the Gulf but also in the affluent neighborhoods and suburbs of Cairo, Beirut, Amman, and other cities, is the enormous disparity of income and lifestyles that have become typical of the Arab World. Conspicuous consumption is but a small part of what this translates into in daily life. More important than the obvious differences in comfort separating those who ride in Mercedes cars from those riding in donkey-carts or swelteringly overcrowded buses, are the inevitable implications regarding life-quality and life-chances. Members of the affluent minority not only can, and do, enjoy the best of what the modern world offers in terms of luxury goods, education for themselves and their children, health care, and all the rest, but also more or less realistically count on retaining that privileged position. The rest, not only do not have access to such things, but also cannot realistically aspire to gain it in their lifetimes. This recipe for division and bitterness has prevailed for decades.

Internationalization of the militant campaign launched by Islamic militants came only after such movements failed to attain their objectives at the national state level. Defeated or cowed into quiescence in Syria, Egypt, Jordan, Iraq, Saudi Arabia, and the smaller Gulf States, the militants opted to declare war on the international system of which the Middle East is part. When it attacked the United States on September 11, 2001, this militant network revealed that it could be a formidable foe as a nonstate international actor. That reality has been reinforced in the years since by the terrorist atrocities in Kenya, Indonesia, Turkey, and Spain. Arab-led and largely Arab-staffed, al-Qaeda nonetheless receives active support from only an extremely small percentage of the Arab World's population. On the other hand, it is the focus of a considerably larger share of psychological investment: the vicarious satisfaction that some Arabs have struck back at their tormentors.[15]

The relative handful of militants comprising al-Qaeda's fighting force has not only declared war on the world's most powerful state but on the state system itself. In terms of sheer imbalance of power between the sides, there has certainly never before been such an asymmetrical conflict. While Arab governments have taken stands against al-Qaeda in the War on Terrorism, there is widespread sympathy for the movement in the Arab World. Early indications of popular jubilation over the attacks of September 11 only heralded what was to develop throughout the region—a strong undertone of approval of the militants' ongoing attacks. Opinion polls show that Osama Bin Laden is viewed favorably by significant numbers of Arabs.[16]

Evidence that al-Qaeda's anti-Western exploits excite widespread satisfaction among Arabs is not difficult to find. Egypt's quasi-legal Muslim Brotherhood, though banned from acting as a political party, is probably the country's most popular opposition group. Only five days after the Madrid bombing of March 2004, an Egyptian university student group published an interview with the Brotherhood's Supreme Guide, Mohamed Mahdy Akef.

Akef carefully distanced his organization from al-Qaeda, while simultaneously railing against foreign "occupation." In a region where "occupation" can, and does, mean anything from the current U.S. occupation of Iraq, to Israel's existence, to the U.S. presence in Saudi Arabia and the Gulf, to the very presence of Westerners in any significant numbers, the terminology left no doubt of his group's sympathies:

> Muslim Brotherhood ideologies can never lead to 9/11. Al-Qaeda is an illusion that has no tangible existence. Evil is everywhere.... Resisting occupiers with any possible means is a duty...I endorse everything against the occupation until it leaves our lands.[17]

Nor is there doubt that such views find ready acceptance. The student interviewer, an undergraduate at Cairo's American University, was visibly relieved and favorably impressed by his encounter with the leader of an Islamist organization that has frequently been demonized by the Egyptian regime's official spokesmen.[18]

Neither the known leaders of al-Qaeda nor many of its operatives who have come to public light can be classified as "marginalized" individuals. Osama Bin Laden's family, fortune, and connections to the Saudi regime afforded him a virtually unlimited range of choices. His reputed chief lieutenant, the Egyptian physician Ayman El-Zawahiri, is also not a marginalized person. The same can be said for many of the nineteen hijackers who died on September 11, 2001 and for many al-Qaeda agents who have since been apprehended.

The West's rise to global preeminence in the modern age has meant the predominance of a culturally rooted outlook that, at worst, disparages Arabs and, at best, condescends to them. Italian Prime Minister Silvio Berlusconi's claim that Western civilization is superior to Islamic culture exposed a large strand of Western bias.[19] This negative stereotype—though challenged within the West whenever it is made explicit—is nonetheless a reality that keeps emerging in multiple ways and therefore cannot be hidden. Whether through films, novels, occasional face-to-face encounters, or the unguarded remarks of politicians, Western anti-Arab prejudice continues to reveal itself.

The Arab World has its own counter-stereotype of Western societies, and it is equally negative. Many Western women who visit Cairo or other major Arab cities, for example, will leave with endless tales of unwelcome sexual advances, the inevitable result of the extremely widespread notion that the West and Westerners are morally depraved. Recently, the leader of Egypt's Muslim Brotherhood once again put this into a political context by attacking the West's leading power in terms that reinforced the popular stereotype: "American Democracy," he said, "allows corruption, alcohol drinking and homosexuality."[20]

The ideology with which the al-Qaeda network has mobilized active support is grounded in Islam. Yet, evidence indicates that it is an Islam permeated by esoteric elements that are not prominent in the "orthodox" Islam of established *ulema*. A videotape captured by U.S. forces near the end of 2001 shows this in the gloating of Bin Laden and his followers over the 9/11 attacks. Journalist James Poniewozik offered this perceptive assessment:

> ...the tape is a firsthand look at the absolute religious certainty of bin Laden and his followers. Repeatedly, he and the sheikh [who appears on the tape] talk about visions and dreams that associates had, before the attack, about planes crashing into buildings. This, perhaps, is something that Americans do not yet fully appreciate: these people live in another millennium, another mental universe. These are people who think magically, who see the world in terms of visions and fate, who honestly feel they have a divine mandate. We can say all we want, however truthfully, that September 11 does not represent true Islam. But we will never fully understand it until we understand, as this video graphically showed, that their entire world is defined by their belief in their divine sanction.[21]

In short, it seems clear that the dynamics of MVIC, as brought out by the earlier discussions of the Zapatista, Upper Egyptian, and Ogoni conflicts, shed considerable light on 9/11.

THE THREAT OF MILITANT ISLAMIC FUNDAMENTALISM

Several factors played roles in promoting the rise of militant Islam in the Arab World. Among these were: the negative stereotyping and general disparagement in the West of anything "Arab"; the prevailing poverty and unresponsive governments that plague the Arab World; the rigidly hierarchical structure that marks Arab societies; and the rise of a widespread phenomenon—the spread of fundamentalist values throughout all levels of Arab society. In the last decade of the twentieth century, the confluence of similar factors in Mexico, Egypt, and Nigeria produced violent political conflicts at the level of the national state. In the first years of the twenty-first century, the same conflation of factors in the Middle East produced a panorama of violent confrontation between Islamically oriented fundamentalist groups and the modern international political system. One can and should ask "what was this 'confluence,' how did these factors interrelate to produce militants who were prepared to engage in violent political contests that were guaranteed, or nearly guaranteed, to be suicidal?"

Descending as it does to the realm of individual psychology and motivation, this question cannot be satisfactorily answered through techniques available to social or political analysis. In all probability, various combinations of economic deprivation, political impotence, humiliation, hopelessness, and a sense of existential threat combined in diverse ways to produce the militancy of different individuals. However, in a general sense, it is possible—indeed, necessary—to conclude that the conflicts in Mexico, Egypt, and Nigeria, as well as today's international struggle against fundamentalist Islamist terrorists, tell us something useful about social dynamics. It is this: that an enduring situation of marginalization, and the attendant threats to identity and dignity entailed by that condition, will tend to produce a committed minority who will not reject violence as an option, regardless of how adverse the balance of power against them may be.

In itself, this might be a fully satisfying explanation—but only if it could be established that the militants in question were pressed by circumstances into aberration, into utter irrationality, into what lawyers could claim is insanity, temporary or otherwise. However, evidence does not support this view. "Chapo" and other Zapatista fighters in the mid-1990s, though surrounded by overwhelming numbers of Mexican troops, remained calm, rational, and purposeful—and "optimistic" only in the sense of a conviction that future generations would win the battle if they themselves fell. All accounts of Ken Saro-Wiwa and his chief lieutenants similarly highlight their rationality. Saad Eddin Ibrahim's studies of rank and file Islamic militants found equally strong signs of sanity.[22]

Obviously, something is glaringly missing from the "insanity" thesis. What is missing is precisely what makes the apparently "irrational" perfectly rational in the mental frameworks of such militants. It is what lies at the foundation of those frameworks. It is the transcendent quality of the mobilizing idea. That is, it is the ultimate and thoroughly subjective solution the individual gives to the mystery of the universe's purpose and his or her own role in it. At such levels of existential conclusion, rational critique offers no hope of distinguishing between the "aberrant" and the "sane." All that is left is for the "rational," with all the limitations that bar it from finding "certainty," to choose: will it recognize the impossibility of reconciliation with its opposite, or will it not? Will it proclaim and glory in its commitment to "uncertainty" and, in a supreme paradox, defend that stance with "certainty," or will it not? As discussed below, answers to such questions will inevitably determine how the international system will respond to today's threat. Part of that threat, indeed, lies precisely in the danger that the international system may retreat from its own commitment to rationality in formulating the answers.

To try to comprehend the dynamics of today's militant Islamist fundamentalism is neither to excuse the phenomenon nor to minimize the threat it poses. On the contrary, any real understanding of the movement can only enhance an appreciation of its menace. The nature of that threat is actually dual. There is, of course, the military threat, but there is also another, perhaps more long-term and definitely more insidious. Discussion of this second threat is reserved for later. For now, the focus will be on the military threat.

The full dangers of violence become apparent when one goes beyond simply reviewing similarities between today's Islamist challenge and MVICs in Latin America, the Arab World, and Africa to examine the differences. Among the latter, the most significant lies in the related areas of the militants' sense of identity and political objectives. It will be recalled that each of the MVIC insurgent groups examined earlier identified itself as the purveyor of the nation's "true" values. In doing so, each group identified itself with the nation as a whole. A logical extension of this stance was each group's claim that its supreme political objective was to benefit all members of the national society. A clearly implied derivative of this was that each group's use of violence would be tempered by an effort to avoid harming innocent fellow citizens.

In contrast, the militant Islamist international campaign sees no shared identity with its target. The enemy is not simply a corrupt subgroup of the national community. It is altogether an "other." At the same time, the Islamists' goals are not clear. Arguments can be made to the effect that these include any or all of the following: to end the Western presence in the Muslim Holy Lands of Saudi Arabia, or in the Arab World as a whole; to wreak vengeance for past wrongs (colonialism, Israel's creation, neocolonialism, etc.); to force an end to ongoing injustices against Arabs and Muslims (Israel's existence, restrictions on the wearing of headscarves in Western countries, etc.); or to destroy Western economic, political, and military supremacy in the world.[23]

Nonetheless, al-Qaeda's demands on the United States seem to boil down to a dual irreducible minimum that includes, first, the curtailment of the American presence in Saudi Arabia along with the American support for the House of Saud, and, second, abandonment of the U.S. policy in support of Israel. Needless to say, such unrealistic demands cannot form the basis of any conceivable compromise that Washington might enter into with the proponents of Islamic fundamentalism. The result is a zero-sum confrontation, one in which fundamentalist demands are as unacceptable to Washington as are the basic elements of U.S. Middle East policy to fundamentalists. The formula is classic for establishing scenarios that lead to war.

The misguided American intervention in Iraq has now become a focal point of the basic confrontation between the United States and Islamist forces. The heavy-handed effort to occupy and democratize Iraq was initially based on the erroneous assumption that Iraqis of all stripes would welcome the demise of Saddam Hussein's regime. It was a striking example of the Bush administration's willingness to succumb to neoconservative hubris when it mattered most. The result of this tragic exercise in nation-building was predictable: massive numbers of Iraqis and other Arabs were deeply offended by the Americans' arrogance, and many of them rushed to join the multiplying centers of resistance to the occupation. Arab nationalists, Iraqi patriots, Shia' and Sunni partisans and tribesmen whose honor had been violated by American forces joined the fray. Non-Iraqis, militant fundamentalists for the most part, arrived from various regions of the Arab World. Bin Laden could only have rejoiced at Washington's approach to Iraq.[24]

And through it all, there has remained the uneasy realization that the ideology of militant Islam does not necessarily call for restraint when violence is employed. The worldwide spate of attacks since 9/11, which have ranged across countries as diverse as Indonesia, Kenya, Turkey, Spain, and the United Kingdom, have kept alive the ultimate fear: that terrorists will not hesitate to employ weapons of mass destruction at the first opportunity.

Nothing could be more threatening in this high-tech world. A quarter of a century ago, the astronomer Paul Davies pondered the relationship between technological development and species-survival. He penned what is perhaps the most succinct description of the threat that now faces the developed world:

> There are several ways in which our technical society could collapse: global warfare, with use of nuclear, biological or chemical weapons, is an obvious one. Alternatively, over-industrialization leading to an insupportable level of pollution and geological deterioration would choke technology in its own produce. The breakdown of social order under the increasing strain of the unequal distribution of wealth and raw materials, over-population and food shortage is another way. *The problem is that a high level of technology requires an increasingly sophisticated and complex social organization to sustain it. It then becomes all the more vulnerable to instabilities and disaffection by minority groups. This has been dramatically demonstrated in recent years by the tactics of a number of terrorist groups who can wreak havoc by the simple expedient of capturing an aircraft or blowing up a vital pipeline.* If this experience is typical of technological societies, it could be that, although life is abundant throughout the galaxy, technology is rather rare. Whereas intelligence has good positive survival value, technology could actually be detrimental to survival.[25]

Paul Davies' apocalyptic speculation may be unimportant here, but his insights into the vulnerability of modern societies are keen. In the post-9/11 era, the astronomer's musings on the nature of life in the universe have, in this respect, been paralleled by daily newspapers. In 2004, the *New York Times* offered these two scenarios to its readers:

> A 10-kiloton nuclear bomb (a pipsqueak in weapons terms) is smuggled into Manhattan and explodes at Grand Central. Some 500,000 people are killed, and the U.S. suffers $1 trillion in direct economic damage.
> That scenario . . . could be a glimpse of our future. . . . [or]
> A stick of cobalt, an inch thick and a foot long, is taken from among hundreds of such sticks at a food irradiation plant. It is blown up with just 10 pounds of explosives in a "dirty bomb" at the lower tip of Manhattan, with a one-mile-per-hour breeze blowing. Some 1,000 square kilometers in three states is contaminated, and some areas of New York City become uninhabitable for decades.[26]

With such grim possibilities now in the realm of reality, and with al-Qaeda's reputed second-in-command, Ayman El-Zawahiri, recently claiming that the organization has purchased "some suitcase [nuclear] bombs" in Central Asia, the necessity of an international military response to militant Islamic fundamentalism is obvious.[27] Whatever the accuracy of al-Zawahiri's statements, the chilling element of intent cannot be overlooked.

Here, the second threat that militant Islamic fundamentalism poses to the international system becomes relevant. This threat, as noted earlier is both longer-term and more insidious than the military challenge presented by that movement. It lies in the very dynamics that the struggle against internationalized militant Islamism necessarily entails and stems from the inevitable tendency of parties in conflict to fall back on and adopt fundamentalist perspectives of their own. Locked in a battle not of its own choosing, the West is not immune from this syndrome. The danger of succumbing to fundamentalist outlooks lies not only in the possibility that distorted views—such as the notions that Islam itself is the enemy or that all militant Islamic political movements are necessarily parts of al-Qaeda,[28] or that security can be won only through military action—can lead to self-defeating measures but also in the prospect that they will prevent a full understanding of challenges facing the international system.

THE PALESTINE PROBLEM

Westerners, particularly Americans, have long been mystified by the power of the Palestine problem to generate visceral reactions throughout the Arab World. To mention "Palestine" to any Arab is almost certain to elicit an outpouring of outrage over Israel's mistreatment of Palestine's Arab community and bitter condemnation of Western support of Israeli practices. Most Westerners are unable to comprehend this reaction, pointing out that the struggle for Palestine actually began over a century ago when Theodore Herzl successfully convened the First Zionist Congress in Basle, and that Israel's creation occurred over fifty years ago.

Fifty years is a long time. It is not surprising that Westerners typically react by expressing wonder at the "Arab" capacity for bearing historical grudges. Then too, as most Westerners have become acquainted through news reports with the sad history of Palestinian relations with other Arabs, there is an understandable readiness to dismiss protestations of lofty Arab concern over the cruel fate of the Palestinians as amounting only to crocodile tears.

There is much to be said for skeptical approaches to Arab declarations of solidarity with the Palestinians' plight. To speak of Arab "public opinion" in regard to Palestine, as well as of anything else, is to misconstrue the nature of politics in the Arab World. No Arab state is either democratic or pluralistic; hence the nature and force of public opinion bear little relation to their counterparts in Western democracies. Although the degree of authoritarianism varies across the region, what is constant is the overwhelming importance of governments in shaping the content and forms of expression of public opinion. Thus, Jordanians supported King Hussein's 1968 claim that "we are all Fedayeen," as well as his onslaught against the burgeoning power of Palestinian guerrillas in Jordan less than five years later.[29] Egyptians capped decades of anti-Israel militancy by acquiescing to Anwar Sadat's peace with Israel, which they continued to respect even after Sadat was killed. Syrians allowed Hafez al-Asad to vacillate between pro-PLO stances and bloody anti-PLO campaigns, the most astounding coming in 1983, when Yasir Arafat and his PLO followers were besieged in Tripoli simultaneously by Israeli naval units and the Syrian Army. Kuwaitis and the populations of other Gulf states abruptly ended years of support for the Palestinian cause once the Palestinian Authority opted to support Saddam Hussein's invasion of Kuwait. Libya's Muamar Gaddafi periodically capped his own radical support of the Palestinian cause by expelling Palestinians from Libya.[30]

The reliance on governments to mold the contours of public opinion is symptomatic of the Arab World's political underdevelopment. It injects a large dose of unpredictability into Arab policies and limits the degree to which any given policy can be institutionalized. The eternal problem confronting analysts of the Arab World is precisely that of determining the degree of real commitment entailed by any declared policy direction. Be this as it may, there are nonetheless real grounds for the widespread Arab support of the Palestinian cause. In short, it is one thing to admit that Arab public opinion on Palestine has been manipulated by Arab governments in accordance with the latter's perceptions of "reasons of state," and quite something else to assert that Arab support of Palestinians and hostility to Israel are baseless. On the contrary, the record provides a convincing rationale for the dominant reaction among Arabs.

The common Western perception that a half-century is "a long time" and its distorted conclusion that entails bemusement at the "Arabs' capacity for bearing historical grudges," is actually a function of Western ignorance rather than evidence of Arab peculiarity. The fact is that Palestine has imposed itself on Arab consciousness with an undeniable immediacy on a daily basis at least since 1948. Wars in 1956, 1967, and 1973, together with almost daily clashes between Israeli and Arab forces, the occupation of a large slice of Lebanon between 1978 and 2000, and the ongoing Israeli occupation of the bulk of the West Bank and Syria's Golan Heights ensured that memories of the Palestine would remain fresh. The equally long history of clandestine Israeli operations, prominently including targeted assassinations of leading Palestinian militants, has had the same effect.

An additional enduring sore point was the problem of Palestinian refugees, a bitter daily reminder of what had been lost and the terrible price that had been paid. In 1948, some 750,000 to 1 million Palestinians became refugees. Again, in 1967, a new flood of refugees, estimated at approximately 300,000, was generated when Israel occupied the West Bank and Gaza. In June 2004, the United Nations agency charged with caring for the refugees reported that in its areas of operation, including the West Bank, Gaza, Jordan, Syria, Lebanon, it counted some 4 million refugees, 25 percent of whom resided in camps. With refugees residing throughout the world, estimates of the total of Palestinian refugees worldwide reached 8 million by 2004.[31]

To be sure, the Arab World played a major role in perpetuating the refugee issue. Only Jordan offered citizenship to the refugees. Apart from that, and a limited extension of citizenship by Iraq to certain Palestinians in 2000, Arab governments steadily opposed all measures that might lead to the integration of Palestinians in their national communities.[32] The public rationale was that the refugees themselves rejected any form of resettlement, preferring to wait until their full repatriation became possible. It was a supremely cynical argument that benefited only the governments who used it. The argument served the interests of Arab rulers precisely by keeping alive the general hostility to Israel. The ploy's success depended almost entirely on the Arab World's political underdevelopment. Because of this, a strong measure of responsibility for perpetuating the Palestine problem must be assigned to Arab governments, but this does not detract from the sincerity with which most Arabs reacted to the refugees' plight.

Among other factors that helped the Palestine issue retain its immediacy, three stood out. These combined recent and somewhat more distant historical experiences. The first was the colonial experience, the legacy of an era that is still well within the lifetimes of senior Arabs. For that entire generation the memory of the British Mandate and the duplicity of London's colonial policy in the Arab World is more than enough to blame perfidious Albion for the Palestine tragedy and to erect on that foundation a broad theory to the effect that Israel had been inserted by the West as part of a postcolonial plot to weaken the Arab World. This point often found its way into the boilerplate rhetoric of the Palestinian Revolution.[33]

The second factor extended somewhat farther back into Arab history, a holdover from earlier days when Jews were a minority in Muslim lands. Tolerated, and in some cases even accorded the highest administrative positions in the Ottoman Empire, Jews nonetheless shared a second-class status with other non-Muslims, that of *Dhimmi*.[34] As such, Jews were not considered the social equal of Muslims. While *Dhimmi* could rise to socially prominent positions, the limits imposed by Muslim superiority were unquestioned. Israel's establishment therefore violated the perceived natural order of things. The resentment this occasioned is still visible in much of the anti-Semitic discourse that is prompted by the Palestine issue.[35]

Finally, the consciousness of what it means to be a Palestinian in today's world is reinforced on multiple levels by the actions of Israel's leading sponsors in the international community. The United States has been a major force in promoting Arab disillusionment with the instruments of international order. As a member of the UN Security Council, Washington has set records with its use of the veto to protect Israel from condemnation by the world body. A high point was perhaps reached in 1991, when the United States initiated its diplomatic drive to force Iraq to end its illegal occupation of Kuwait. With Israel having not only occupied a large expanse of Arab land since 1967, but also progressively altering its demography by pursuing an aggressive policy of resettling Jews in the area, the Arab outcry against Washington's "double standard" was only to have been expected.

The Arab World's marginalization has been a phenomenon of historic proportions, but its cutting edge has been maintained up to the present moment by the combined force of factors intrinsic to the region as well as those contributed by non-Arab actors. In retrospect it was not surprising that Arab rage was directed at the United States on 9/11. The problem remains that of coming to terms with the lesson that 9/11 entails.

Perhaps the simplest way of beginning to do this is to return to the three Key Questions raised by the attacks of 9/11. It will be recalled that this work offered an alternative to Bush's answer to the first of these, "what did the attack mean; what did it signify?" While the President offered a morally charged explanation, these pages have tried to suggest a more useful analytical answer: "What happened on September 11, 2001, was an act of asymmetrical war." In a similar vein, the answers offered here to the two remaining Key Questions also eschew moralizing in favor of an analytical thrust. Thus, the response to the second question raised by 9/11—"Why did it happen?"—can be summarized as follows: 9/11 occurred because an ideologically committed group of militants expressed the rage and fear that was widely generalized among an entire culture, causing it to believe that its identity was mortally threatened by the sociocultural dynamics that are most clearly represented by the United States. By the same token, the response to the final Key Question—"What did the attack imply for the security of the United States?"—can also be summarized directly: the attacks will compel the United States to employ its full power—military, economic, and political—to undermine the threat to its security. Militant terrorists will be subdued by force; political and economic means will be used to remove sources of friction with the bulk of inhabitants of the Middle East and the Muslim World.

The challenge facing the United States at this point is to seize the opportunity to promote its own national security while simultaneously exerting true leadership on behalf of international security.

THE FINAL HALF OF THE SECOND G. W.BUSH ADMINISTRATION

History, as noted above, has the nasty habit of "moving on." During 2006, the historical treadmill had already produced significant changes in the pressures shaping the American war on terror. The most important of these occurred in the Middle East, where the year began with Israeli Prime Minister Ariel Sharon suffering the stroke that ended his political career. But the one constant pressure was the steadily intensifying U.S. struggle to occupy Iraq. By the beginning of 2007, U.S. troops had sustained some 25,000 casualties, of whom over 3,000 had been killed. The carnage was unrelenting. In the final month of 2006, the death toll among American troops rose to 111. During the same period, of course, vastly more Iraqis died as a direct consequence of the violence engendered by the occupation.[36] At the very end of 2006, Saddam Hussein, held in American custody ever since his apprehension three years earlier, was executed by hanging, the decision of an Iraqi court that found him guilty of crimes against humanity.

It was against this backdrop that 2006 saw a progressive disillusionment with the Bush administration's insistence that the United States must persevere in the war on terror, including both the wars in Afghanistan and Iraq. However, it was clearly Iraq that dominated the headlines and which, in consequence, became the touchstone of the shifting weight of U.S. public opinion. By November, with midterm elections for the full membership of the House and one-third of the Senate only days away, polls found that only 35 percent of American adults approved of the President's performance in office. In contrast, 61 percent of those polled disapproved of his handling of the office and, of those, fully 41 percent stated that their votes would reflect such views of the president.[37]

In effect, then, the congressional midterm elections of 2006 became a referendum on the Bush administration's security policies. The results had already been predicted: Democrats managed to reverse the existing balance of power in both the Senate and the House. In the former, where a Republican majority had prevailed since 2003, Democrats now equaled the Republicans with forty-nine seats. However, they also benefited from two independents who caucused with them. Thus the Democratic Party emerged from the elections holding an effective majority of fifty-one. In the House, which had been dominated for over a decade by Republicans, the Democratic surge led the party to a victory of 233 seats to the Republicans' 202.

As a "referendum," the elections failed to provide clear guidance to the Administration. The one indisputable signal was that Americans were dissatisfied with the war in Iraq and that a majority of them no longer believed the Administration's assurances that victory over the insurgents was only a matter of time during which a viable democracy could be erected. Apart from this, little else could be said by way of an unambiguous interpretation of the election's outcome. In itself, the range of antiwar positions espoused by Democrats precluded any single message from being cited as "the lesson" of 2006. Those positions had ranged from calls for a full and immediate withdrawal of U.S. troops from Iraq to a variety of less drastic measures. In a press conference on the day following the elections, President Bush referred to this point:

> Obviously we've got a lot of work to do with some members of Congress. I don't know how many members of Congress said, ["]get out right now ["]—I mean the candidates running for Congress in the Senate. I haven't seen that chart. Some of the comments I read where they said ["]well, look, we just need a different approach to make sure we succeed["]; well, you can find common ground there.[38]

Bush's search for common ground with Congress took on immediate meaning that same day. In a move that had been orchestrated prior to the elections, the president announced that he had accepted Donald Rumsfeld's resignation as Secretary of Defense. According to Bush, the move had been mutually agreed upon as a necessary tactic for "bringing in a fresh perspective during a critical period in this war."[39] There seemed to be no reason to doubt the President's version.

A month after the midterm election, the long-awaited report of the bipartisan Iraq Study Group was made public. The group, also known as the Baker-Hamilton Commission, had been formed by Congress in March to review policy options for Iraq. It was cochaired by the Republican ex-Secretary of State James Baker and Lee Hamilton, the Democratic ex-Representative from Indiana. It was a wide-ranging document that suffered from the Commission's desire to achieve a consensus, the result being a report that failed to offer a clear and firm policy option for the United States. It considered the possibility of suggesting a precipitate end to the U.S. intervention in Iraq, but discarded that option as all too likely to create more problems than it could resolve. The same was true for three other alternatives: "staying the course," "providing more troops for Iraq," and "devolving Iraq into three semi-autonomous regions with loose central control."[40] In the end, the Report favored an approach that involved two dimensions—a diplomatic effort to muster support for a stable, productive Iraq from its neighbors in the Middle East, and a renewed U.S. focus on promoting internal Iraqi policies that would work toward the same end.

The Commission offered some keen insights into the complexities of Middle East politics:

> Iraq cannot be addressed effectively in isolation from other major regional issues, interests and unresolved conflicts. To put it simply, all key issues in the Middle East—the Arab-Israeli conflict, Iraq, Iran, the need for political and economic reforms, and extremism and terrorism—are inextricably linked.[41]

On this basis, the Report recommended that the United States try to enlist both Syria and Iran in the effort to contain the violence in Iraq. "No country in the region," it affirmed, "wants a chaotic Iraq. Yet Iraq's neighbors are doing little to help it, and some are undercutting its stability."[42] As highly questionable as it was, the assumption that Iraq's neighbors did not want chaos in that country seemed necessary if the United States were to seek their support for an altered approach. The Commission members suggested an approach that was possibly plausible in Syria's case. Essentially, Syria might be tempted to help Washington out of its difficulties in Iraq in return for American support of Damascus' longstanding demand for an Israeli return of the Golan Heights.

The Commission had no such clearcut suggestion for approaching Iran. Here a potpourri of more or less possibly useful ideas for eliciting Iranian cooperation were advanced, including appeals to Iran's rational self-interest (Iran would not wish to see Iraq "disintegrate"), security concerns (the United States would have a "continuing role" in preventing the Taliban from coming to power in Afghanistan), economic and political benefits (U.S. Support for Iran's accession to international organizations, including the World Trade Organization; Iran would enjoy "enhanced diplomatic relations with the United States" and the "prospect of a U.S. policy that emphasizes political and economic reforms instead of . . . advocating regime change"). The final benefit to be offered in return for Iran's cooperation was a "real, complete, and secure peace to be negotiated between Israel and Syria, with U.S. involvement . . . "[43]

The second dimension of the Baker-Hamilton Report's policy recommendations dealt with Iraqi internal matters and what the United States might do to encourage the Iraqi government to reform itself. This section focused on a variety of major issues, including national reconciliation, security, military forces, criminal justice, the oil sector, and budget preparation and U.S. economic and reconstruction aid. While some elements of this portion of the report were important and carefully crafted, it was obvious that the primary recommendations came in the earlier discussion of the importance of forging politically supportive ties between the United States and Iraq's key regional neighbors.

George Bush reacted to the Baker-Hamilton Report noncommittally. He would, he said, consider it along with other studies being prepared by U.S. intelligence agencies and formulate a new approach to Iraq early in 2007. It was a wise move, for the previous year had not treated the president's plans for Iraq kindly and he did well to declare a brief time-out as his administration sought to regroup.

By giving such a central role to the Palestine issue, the Baker-Hamilton Report had in effect taken a clear position on what in the United States has been a highly controversial issue for well over five decades. American pundits have long been split by the question of the Arab-Israeli conflict's true significance to the politics of the Middle East. The debate over this point has been ongoing to the present day. In late 2006, for example, former President Jimmy Carter published his latest book, *Palestine: Peace Not Apartheid*, which charged Israel with violating agreements it had undertaken at various times, including during Carter's presidency, in order to pursue policies that further marginalized the Palestinians rather than seeking peace. Carter clearly assigned such policies the lion's share of blame for the failure of the Middle East peace process.[44]

Thus, some American analysts argued that the record of inter-Arab discord proved Arab protestations of solidarity with the Palestinian people were utterly false. However, others maintained that the evidence indicated an underlying unity of concern over the fate of Palestinians. In short, some observers claimed the Palestine issue was empty of real content, while others saw it as a centrally defining one for Arab political attitudes. By linking Iran as well as Syria to the Palestine issue, the Baker-Hamilton Report left no doubt that its authors not only adhered to the latter position but also extended it to include non-Arab Muslims. The Commission deserves much credit for its acumen.

The Palestinian issue had deteriorated steadily since Yasir Arafat's rather mysterious death near the end of 2004. When elections were held some two months later, Mahmoud Abbas (Abu Mazen), the leader of *Fatah*, succeeded Arafat as the Palestinian Authority's president. A year later, in January 2006, Palestinian parliamentary elections produced an overwhelming victory for *Hamas*, the radical Islamic movement. The outcome shocked Washington and other major members of the international community. The United States and the European Union promptly cut off funds to the Palestinian government pending *Hamas*' reversal of its enduring rejection of Israel, opposition to the PLO's agreements with the Jewish state, and its commitment to violent struggle. By the summer of 2006, tensions between Israel and the *Hamas* militia in the Gaza Strip were spiraling out of control, a phenomenon that was soon replicated by Israel's relations with *Hizballah*—the militant Lebanese *Shi'a* group.

On June 25, 2006, units of the *Hamas* militia attacked an Israeli patrol on the outskirts of Gaza, killing two of its members, wounding four, and capturing one.[45] Israel quickly retaliated by taking prisoner dozens of *Hamas* cabinet ministers and other officials. From this point on, the cascading events seemed determined to plunge the region into major war. By July 12, the still raging armed confrontations between Israel and *Hamas* inspired *Hizballah* to act.

That organization's leader, Sheikh Hassan Nasrallah, would subsequently admit that he badly miscalculated the ferocity of Israel's reaction. Be that as it may, on July 12, Nasrallah ordered his men to attack another Israeli patrol near the Lebanese border. This time, the militants killed three Israeli soldiers and captured two more.[46] With this, Israel unleashed a full-scale war against *Hizballah* in Lebanon. The fighting went on for just over a month—until August 14—and cost some 1,000 civilian dead in Lebanon and perhaps as many as fifty civilian dead in Israel.[47] Military casualties were also heavy. The Israelis lost some 120 soldiers while *Hizballah*'s death toll was estimated at anywhere between 250 to over 700.[48]

The year 2006 was a portentous period for the United States. After an agonizingly slow buildup of popular dissatisfaction with the war on terror, the results of the November congressional elections finally forced the president to acknowledge that a change of approach was needed. Yet, even while doing so, Bush refused to admit that most Americans now disagreed with his understanding of the significance of Iraq:

> I'd like our troops to come home, too, but I want them to come home with victory, and that is a country that can govern itself, sustain itself and defend itself. And I can understand Americans saying ["]come home.["] But I don't know if they said ["]come home and leave behind an Iraq that could become a safe haven for al Qaeda.["] I don't believe they said that. And so, I'm committed to victory.[49]

The year ended with no announcement of a basic change of policy toward Iraq, but with the promise that one would soon be forthcoming. On January 10, 2007, the president unveiled his new strategy for Iraq. Its most prominent and controversial feature entailed the commitment of over 20,000 additional U.S. troops to the battle for Iraq. Additionally, the Iraqi government would be encouraged to play a greater role in putting down the insurgency.[50] Bush clearly felt he had little option but to explore this route. "Failure in Iraq," he warned, "would be a disaster for the United States" and went on to recite a host of horrible consequences that could be expected to flow directly from that outcome:

> Radical Islamic extremists would grow in strength and gain recruits. They would be in a better position to topple moderate governments,

> create chaos in the region, and use oil revenues to fund their ambitions. Iran would be emboldened in its pursuit of nuclear weapons. Our enemies would have a safe haven from which to plan and launch attacks on the American people. On September 11, 2001, we saw what a refuge for extremists on the other side of the world could bring to the streets of our own cities. For the safety of our people, America must succeed in Iraq.[51]

The speech was also notable for its lack of any indication that the Administration might care to explore or develop a political approach to its rising difficulties in Iraq. Bush paid an essentially empty tribute to "the thoughtful recommendations" of the Baker-Hamilton Commission, but he did not take up the most serious of them—those related to Syria and Iran—in any form. Indeed, Syria and Iran were mentioned only as problems against which force in some degree would be employed.

The year 2006 also ended with the most of the rest of the Middle East in worse shape than had been the case a year earlier. Iran remained committed to its nuclear program, despite the application of UN sanctions. Syria continued to facilitate the insurgency in Iraq. Lebanon had suffered tremendous damage from the Summer War with Israel. As 2007 began, Palestine was wracked by almost daily clashes between the forces of *Hamas* and *Fatah* troops loyal to Palestinian Authority President Mahmoud Abbas. Iraq, of course, remained tragically in the grip of its terrible insurgency.

The horrifying truth, from a Western perspective, had already been made explicit less than a month earlier by the Baker-Hamilton Report's recognition that all of the modern Middle East's many problems were interrelated in various ways. At some point—were the United States not to be overwhelmed by the legion of Middle East problems it confronted—the region's multiple challenges would have to be faced by some administration in Washington. That, in turn, promised to entail a two-step process. The first would be the intellectual exercise of understanding the interrelationships among the area's various issues. The second would be to devise, and then act upon, a strategic approach for pursuing their resolution. Such an approach might well be multi-dimensional, but at a bare minimum it would have to rely at least as much on political persuasion as on force to gain its ends.

Given the urgency of this task in light of need to defend the United States from further attacks by al-Qaeda, an obvious starting point for considering a defensive political strategy focused on the Middle East would be one that sought, as recommended by the Baker-Hamilton Report, a definitive end to the Palestinian-Israeli conflict.

Chapter 7

Turning Point: Toward Global Security

In early 2003, I was one of two faculty members at the American University in Cairo who spoke out publicly in support of the impending war in Iraq. A few others on the faculty shared this view, but the pressures of anti-American opinion caused them to remain silent. At the time, almost daily demonstrations in support of Saddam Hussein were being held by faculty and students. The Iraqi flag waved on campus proudly and Saddam was the hero of the hour. It was not an inviting moment to champion a U.S. policy that was clearly seeking war. My colleague and I opted to hold a two-member panel discussion during which each of us would speak for fifteen minutes. The remaining half-hour would be devoted to questions and comments from our audience. Despite our minority view, the packed lecture hall gave us a respectful hearing, and the questions and comments were on the whole thoughtful. I doubt that our efforts changed anyone's mind, but at least the dissenting outlook got its proverbial day in court.

My arguments had been worked out over the months that led to the critical days of early 2003. I did not trust Saddam Hussein and considered him a blight on the Arab World. More to the point, while I kept an open mind on the issue of Iraq's pursuit of weapons of mass destruction, I was quite prepared to believe that Baghdad would seek such weapons as soon as the possibility arose. These thoughts, in turn, led to my essential reason for supporting Washington's drive toward war. Given the dynamics of the region, a confrontation between the U.S. and Saddam Hussein's regime was sooner or later almost inevitable. Logic and humanitarian considerations joined to uphold a war that would be fought as soon as possible, thus minimizing the harm that would be wrought.

At the time, I still did not believe that the U.S. goal would be to occupy Iraq and, as the neoconservatives wanted, attempt to bring democracy to that country. Shortly after hostilities commenced, I was interviewed by *The Christian Science Monitor*. I warned then that any effort to occupy and democratize Iraq "would be begging for catastrophe."[1] I was, of course, sadly mistaken as to the Bush administration's war aims. The neoconservative agenda had already been adopted by the White House.

We are paying the price of that mistake. The weight of history, of culture, and of recent experience militate against the imminent creation of a democratic Iraq. The goal itself might have been laudable, but the means were guaranteed to produce just what has occurred in that tragic country: Iraqis flocked to join the fight against the Americans and many rallied to Bin Laden's banner. George W. Bush would have done better to heed his own 2000 campaign promise to refrain from committing American troops to action on behalf of "nation-building."[2] The Iraq adventure was the absolute antithesis of that pledge, and the price—now standing at over 3000 American dead—has been an obscene waste. Democracy cannot be imposed, nor did Saddam Hussein's removal require his replacement by a Made-in-the-USA democratic system. It would have sufficed to ensure that the new Iraqi regime be relatively stable, moderately authoritarian, and committed to long-term constitutional change. This would have been much the same scenario that Washington currently faces with its closest Arab allies, such as Egypt. It would also, of course, have demanded different policies from the start. The Iraqi Army would have been kept intact and only a selective barring of Ba'athist officials would have occurred, the American role in such a postwar Iraqi setting would have been brief and limited—there would have been no need for an American proconsul such as Paul Bremmer, and even less for his role to include assigning contracts to American companies for rebuilding Iraq.

These things did not happen. The result, in a very literal sense, was that Iraq became not part of the solution, but a—large, not to say "central"—part of the problem.

THE AL-QAEDA CHALLENGE

On September 11, 2001, al-Qaeda launched an asymmetrical war on the United States. In 2004, on the eve of George Bush's resounding victory in the election that gave him a second-term presidency, Osama Bin Laden revealed part of his victory calculus. Allah and economics would doom the American Empire, just as had been true nearly a decade and a half earlier for the Soviet Empire. Al-Qaeda, fresh from savoring the fact that four stolen airplanes and a handful of suicidal operatives had imposed a great cost on the United States, could now look forward to Washington spending itself out of existence. The American proclivity to accept the self-destructive role Bin Laden assigned to it would be spurred on by the ever-present threat of weapons of mass destruction.[3] It was a double whammy, a two-pronged strategy that maximized the advantages of exploiting American weaknesses. Iraq and Afghanistan would drain America's military and economic power. Homeland Defense would become a permanent drag on America's economy. For the Americans to drop their guard even for a moment could prove fatal, permitting the threat of weapons of mass destruction to be realized. The Achilles' heel of the American Empire seemed to have been exposed.

George W. Bush misled the American public, mainly by offering a simplistic explanation of 9/11, one that flattered the victimized party by dismissing the sources of Arab anger as "only" fanaticism. The blame for 9/11 was placed squarely on the jealousy and hatred with which Bin Laden and his followers reacted to American freedom. In fact, 9/11 was a by-product of an insidious syndrome of marginalization that directly motivated a relatively small group of activists while simultaneously influencing the attitudes and opinions of a much broader stream of public sentiment in the Arab world.

The Bush administration's record has been mixed. The decision to confront al-Qaeda in Afghanistan and oust the Taliban was understandable and correct. Al-Qaeda was responsible for 9/11 and the Taliban regime must be presumed to have supported the attack in principle. Second, the clandestine war on al-Qaeda operatives—which so far is known to have spread from Europe, to the Middle East, to South Asia—has also yielded benefits.[4] Third, even the campaign to encourage democratizing change in the Arab World—with the exception of the radical military campaign in Iraq—has also seen limited success.[5] On the other hand, Iraq had no links to al-Qaeda and bore no responsibility for the attacks in New York and Washington, D.C. Saddam's cutthroat regime merited replacement on many grounds, but that was a very different matter from occupying the country and trying to impose a democratic system.

But Iraq has happened, and there is no option but to make the best of it. This implies that the political cost of the U.S. intervention in that country can be contained. America's enemies in the Arab World have gained an incalculable boost in consequence of Iraq, and this must be ended. The unenviable choice now is between terminating our occupation of Iraq or persisting in that unwise and self-destructive policy. The latter option will continue to cost American and Iraqi lives, continue to be a magnet for anti-American activities, and continue to undermine U.S. relations with the Arab World. More important, it risks a civilizational clash with the Arab World. In short, by dragging out the occupation of Iraq the United States will ultimately risk creating its own absolute truth, its own absolute cause. That tendency was already apparent in much of the neoconservative discourse that painted the American "mission" in terms of Historical Necessity and Divine Providence.

This poses a danger to the United States, one at least as menacing as al-Qaeda. For, as Bill Clinton pointed out, the struggle against al-Qaeda is at bottom a confrontation between two opposing worldviews: the obscurantist conviction that al-Qaeda's truth is absolute, versus the post-Enlightenment faith in reason and an acceptance of probabilistic truth. Were the United States to adopt a mirror-image of al-Qaeda's version of "truth," it would in effect surrender before joining the battle. That prospect must be rejected from the start.

The conclusion, then, is that the most attractive option for Washington at this juncture is the humiliating one of terminating the occupation of Iraq as quickly as it can. The downside of the choice is clear: U.S. credibility would suffer and the prestige of America's enemies in the Arab World would be bolstered. These negative consequences would not be negligible. But they would not promise the open-ended flirtation with catastrophe that clinging to the occupation will entail.

The glee of America's enemies in the region would soon enough be tempered by the relief of its friends, who could be expected to welcome the end of a policy that they find embarrassing at best, and threatening at worst. So far as credibility goes, the ending of Iraq's occupation would provide an opportunity for enhancing the credibility of Washington's war on terrorism. The freeing up of military assets currently committed to Iraq would constitute a major boon for planners worrying about other potential threats from al-Qaeda. The happy outcries of America's enemies in Baghdad will count for little once the purposeful pursuit of American victory is resumed.

The suggested reordering of Washington's policy toward Iraq should form part of an overall package to reform the American approach to the Arab World. The centerpiece of such a change must be our policy toward Israel. There is no doubt that the United States has incurred a deep and enduring commitment to the Jewish State, but it is neither absolute nor open-ended. Nearly sixty years after that state's foundation, it is time for some limits to be placed on American support. The essential purpose of Washington's initial support of Israel was to uphold the state's right to exist. That commitment broadened over the years, increasingly sounding like a mantra to some primordial obligation over which Washington had no control. Actually, such was never the case. While there was an oft-reaffirmed American pledge to support Israel's sovereignty, there has never been any commitment to support Israeli expansionism. Even less, of course, has there been any U.S. commitment to support or acquiesce in the Likud's program for the Occupied Territiories, including the construction of Israel's wall across much of the area.[6]

The always surprising politics of the Middle East offer some prospects for fruitful American diplomacy. As the sixth anniversary of the 9/11 events approached, new developments affecting both key protagonists held out some degree of hope that after so many years of frozen diplomacy the way might be found for pursuing serious peace-making. Prior to his stroke, Prime Minister Ariel Sharon had formed a new political party, Kadima. At almost the same time, Shimon Peres, then serving as Deputy Prime Minister in Israel's Likud-led coalition government, was ousted as the Labor Party's leader. By late December 2005, Peres pledged to support Sharon's new Party in the national elections, which had already been scheduled for March, 2006. The prospect was that these two titans of Israel's right- and left-wing political pillars would now back a centrist party platform to offer Palestinians a deal that Washington could more easily support as consonant with American objectives and values.[7]

However, when Sharon was felled by the major stroke that ended his public life, his deputy, Ehud Olmert, assumed the role of Israel's Acting Prime Minister and carried Kadima's banner to a resounding victory in the March 28 elections. He campaigned along lines that had already been indicated by Sharon: while Israel would seek Palestinian agreement to a two-state solution, it would, if necessary, be prepared to define the Jewish State's geographical boundaries unilaterally.

Events on the Palestinian side also proceeded swiftly. The January 2006 parliamentary elections left *Hamas* the clear winner. The corruption and nepotism that had become endemic to *Fatah*, whose members had dominated Palestinian politics since the formation of the Palestinian Authority in 1994, so alienated voters that the movement obtained only forty-three of 132 parliamentary seats.[8] But despite its victor *Hamas* remained largely isolated. The United States, Canada, the European Union, and other international donors suspended financial aid to the *Hamas*-led Palestinian Cabinet, insisting that it would not be resumed until *Hamas* accepted Israel's right to exist and renounced terrorism.

The summer of 2006 saw the Israel-*Hamas-Hizballah* war in Lebanon and Gaza, while the rest of the year was consumed with clashes both between Israeli and Palestinian forces as well as outbreaks of internecine violence among Palestinian factions.

The questions that confronted both key parties were stark: Could *Hamas* cling to its rejectionist position while remaining responsible for the consequences that would inevitably be paid by the Palestinian people? On the other hand, could an Israeli government cling to expansionist ambitions that were preventing *Hamas*' own position from becoming amenable to realistic peacemaking? Within the parameters of politically creative possibilities that attended such unknowns there appeared to lie new and hopeful realms for a reordering of the U.S. approach to the Middle East.

Part and parcel of the revised American approach to the Middle East must include reestablishing a respect for international law as a component of U.S. policy. In no area of the world have the United States and other great powers been more remiss in this respect. As Professor Jean Allain correctly observes at the outset of a recent book, *International Law in the Middle East—Closer to Power Than Justice*:

> Where international law in the Middle East is concerned it is impossible to escape the simple fact that law on the books and law in practice do not equate. Much as the underclass in a domestic legal system feels the punitive, repressive and selective nature of law so does the local population of the Middle East experience international law not as a shield but as a sword. As a result, international law in the Middle East lacks legitimacy.[9]

Increasingly, it will be important that some agreed standard serve to determine the legitimacy of actions taken in the name of sovereign states. International law should provide such a standard.

TURNING POINT

The world changed fundamentally on 9/11, and the American position vis-à-vis the rest of the world must follow suit. For the most part, the modifications in U.S. policy required in the interest of security will find roots in America's past. Thus, the changes demanded of the United States will be solidly grounded in America's historical experience. Only in terms of very recent political history will required alterations appear radical. George W. Bush tilted the balance of U.S. policymaking in foreign affairs decidedly toward an emphasis on unilateralism. When combined with the neoconservative influences of his key advisors, the upshot was an overall American approach that relied on U.S. power, far more than on any balance between power and persuasion. It is in reaction to this that a relatively radical policy shift will have to be made.

Although nothing is sure in this world, there is small chance that the Bush administration will recognize, much less heed the implications of, the "turning point" that has been reached in American foreign policy. It will almost certainly be left to a new administration to opt for the needed policy shift. The new orientation will require several elements, all of which break down into two broad categories. The first, the military, will require the war against terrorism to be prosecuted as vigorously as possible on as many levels as possible. The second, will involve a reorientation of Washington's approach to the Middle East, particularly insofar as tempering U.S. support of Israel. This will demand that Washington limit its support of Israel to that state's rights within international law, ensuring that primacy is accorded to the Jewish State's right to exist.

If the United States succeeds in revamping its approach to foreign policy in such ways, it will not only maximize the prospects for its own survival but also the possibilities of exerting a positive impact on world politics. For the hard truth of the matter is that 9/11 was far more than just a wake-up call from the Middle East. The violence that exploded on September 11, 2001, bespoke the rage of millions of marginalized people who have watched as the benefits of modern life went to others. They are found in every corner of the globe, and they are angry.

In a very real sense, then, the long-term threat raised by 9/11 marked a fundamental turning point in global international relations. The obvious paradox lies in the implication that the individual state must be weakened so the state-system itself may be strengthened. In other words, international politics must give priority to creating political and economic conditions that will allow, persuade, and even require governments to function in ways that not only sustain their own legitimacy but also that of the state-dominated international system.

It is now more than evident that the world cannot afford to allow nonstate actors to employ international war on behalf of their political ends. To permit this would unleash the Hobbesian horrors of a high-tech war of all against all. Yet, the world also cannot afford to strengthen the state in ways that will allow it to promote, rather than reduce, marginalization within its borders, for to do so will only enhance the chances of militant nonstate actors appearing on the world stage. In the interest of greater security for all, the powers of the state must therefore be directed toward reducing marginalization. By doing so, the state will legitimize the state system. True global security demands that the legitimacy of the state-system take precedence over the legitimacy of the state itself. The use of political and economic instruments by the international community to ensure this will increasingly have to be the foundation upon which global security rests.

This clearly points to the need of yet another instrument, a key matrix that must be relied upon to lend consistency, purposefulness, and predictability to what would otherwise be only provocative political and economic interventions. Such a matrix exists: international law and, particularly international human rights law. The strengthening of international law must no longer be looked at as an ideal to be deferred to the indefinite future but rather seen as a vital task whose time has come.

The instances of Marginalized Violent Internal Conflict reviewed earlier offer some hope of working toward a world in which international security will be realistically attainable within the confines of the existing state system. The lessons of Nigeria and Egypt highlight the limitations on force as a means of guaranteeing security. Egypt's consistently hard-line approach to the *Gama'a al-Islamiyya* crushed that organization into quiescence but its possible re-emergence remains an ongoing threat to a regime that continues to function as "a democracy of fangs and claws."[10] By the same token, the brutal fate of the Ogoni successfully cowed the leading activists of the uprising. Yet, a decade later, the instability and potential explosiveness of

Nigeria's West Coast make a mockery of the state's claim to have ensured the security of its oil.[11]

While the final chapter of the Zapatista Rebellion has not yet been written, there is much to commend Mexico's unique mix of force and political steps designed to reverse the marginalization that has for so long been the lot of Chiapas' Maya communities. The Mexican government's willingness to undertake limited reforms gives hope that a political solution may ultimately prevail instead of a decisive trial of strength.

The world we have created is severely unbalanced—unfair—in what it offers to those who people it. Evidence for this assertion is readily available and need not be recited here. It is enough to point out that decades of such recitals have not altered the situation. The world system's economic, political, and social dynamics grind on, confirming, maintaining, and exacerbating the same imbalances, the same unfairness. At the same time, and most ominously, the possibility that the technology of anger—the means to inflict massive damage upon developed countries—will spread appears to increase by the hour.

Al-Qaeda must, and probably will, be eliminated. But unless we are to confront a future in which successive nonstate actors opt to challenge the international system with rising levels of technological sophistication, things must change. The impact of prolonged marginalization has generated a major threat from the Arab World in the form of Islamic fundamentalism and the same dynamics can be expected to produce similar threats in other marginalized regions. Should it be required, the marginalized of this world can always find or create some suitable mobilizing ideology, religious or secular. One could, for example, not unreasonably speculate that if things do not change, Sub-Saharan Africa could become fertile ground for nonstate challenges to the international system mobilized on the basis of ideologies linked to racist values.

Some politically influential world figures grasped the far-reaching implications of this very early on. Near the end of 2001, former President Bill Clinton offered his views on the international crisis. In addition to stressing the necessity of defeating the terrorists who had attacked the United States, Clinton argued that 9/11 was, in effect, a wake-up call—forcing recognition that long-term security requirements not only require a military response but also movement toward a more equitable international economy.

More recently, British Prime Minister Tony Blair developed a parallel, though wider, theme. Blair more directly focused on the need for changes in a variety of elements in the world system, including the usually sacrosanct concept of state sovereignty. In a remarkable speech delivered in March 2004, the prime minister explained the evolution of his own thinking on international security. Even prior to 9/11, he said, he had begun to move away from the traditional philosophy of international relations "that has held sway since the Treaty of Westphalia in 1648; namely that a country's internal affairs are for it and you don't interfere. . . ."[12] However, Blair noted, September 11 had been "a revelation" for him. "What had seemed inchoate," he declared, "came together."[13]

The direction taken by Blair's thinking led to his growing conviction that self-interest in today's world requires modification of the concept of sovereignty and, therefore, of international law. He was, in short, advocating the view that international order cannot be maintained if states marginalize or oppress portions of their own populations and that the international community should therefore retain a legal option to intervene:

> It may well be that under international law as presently constituted, a regime can systematically brutalise and oppress its people and there is nothing anyone can do, when dialogue, diplomacy and even sanctions fail, unless it comes within the definition of a humanitarian catastrophe. . . .
>
> This may be the law, but should it be?[14]

Such signs of creative thinking offer hope of a more secure international environment. The nation-state remains the basic unit of global organization and will in all likelihood continue to do so. But the requirements of the twenty-first century now demand that that same unit be assigned greater, and new, responsibilities for ensuring international security—and that it be held accountable for meeting them. In short, the world cannot and should not continue to tolerate regimes whose actions or inactions further conditions that can give rise to militant nonstate actors who might launch their own "world wars."

Almost coincidentally with the dawn of the new millennium, the marginalized of our planet spoke out in a terrible outpouring of rage. The militants who threaten the civilized world must now prepare for their own destruction. However, the real challenge facing the civilized world is even more profound: will the element of justice that underlay the explosion of 9/11 be recognized, and, if so, will it elicit a response in keeping with our professed values?

NOTES

CHAPTER 1. THE MYSTIFICATION OF 9/11

1. G. W. Bush, Address to the Nation, Sept. 11, 2001. Online at http://www.frwebgate1.access.gpo.gov/cgi-bin/waisgate.cgi?WAISdocID=348798389332+3+0+0&WAIS action=retrieve

2. For example, see the excellent commentary published by the prestigious Foreign Policy Research Institute in August, 2004: Stephen Gale and Lawrence Husick, "Observations on the '9/11 Commission Report'," Foreign Policy Research Institute E-Notes, August 13, 2004, www.fpri.org/enotes/20040813. americawar.galehusick.911commission.html

3. For the earlier version, see "Bill Clinton Speaks," text of Clinton's speech of October 6, 2001 at Yale University; available online at: http://archive.salon.com/news/feature/2001/10/25/clinton/print/html

4. William Clinton, "The Struggle for the Soul of the 21st Century," available online at www.angelfire.com/indie/pearly/htmls/bill-soul.html

5. Ibid.

6. Ibid.

7. Ibid.

8. Ibid.

9. Ibid.

10. Ibid.

11. Ibid.

12. Ibid.

13. Ibid.

14. Ibid.

15. David Apter, *The Politics of Modernization* (Chicago and London: The University of Chicago Press, 1965), pp. 22–33; 236–40.

16. Paul Seabury and Angelo Codevilla, *War: Ends and Means* (New York: Basic Books, 1989), p. 162.

17. "Spheres of Influence," *The Christian Science Monitor*, available online at: http://www.csmonitor.com/specials/neocon/spheresInfluence.html

18. For a good discussion of this point, see Irving Kristol, "The Neoconservative Persuasion," *The Weekly Standard*, 8 (47) August 25, 2003, http://www.Weekly standard.com/

19. Patrick E. Tyler, "Pentagon Drops Goal of Blocking New Superpowers," *The New York Times*, May 23, 1992, at http://www.disinfopedia.org/wiki.phtml?title= Defense_Policy_Guidance_1992–1994.

20. Kristol, "The Neoconservative Persuasion," op. cit.

21. William Kristol and Robert Kagan, "Toward a Neo-Reaganite Foreign Policy," *Foreign Affairs* (July/August, 1996), at http://www.ceip.org/files/Publications/ foreignaffairs.asp?from=pubauthor

22. Ibid.

23. Ibid.

24. Ibid.

25. Ibid.

26. Ibid.

27. Ibid.

28. Ibid.

29. Project for the New American Century, "Statement of Principles," http:// www.newqamericancentury.org/

30. See http://www.csmonitor.com/specials/neocon/

31. "Netanyahu, Benjamin," MEDEA, European Institute for Research on Mediterranean and Euro-Arab Cooperation, http://www.medea.be/index.html? page=&lang=en&doc=137&highlight=netanyahu

32. Ibid.

33. Robert J. Loewenberg, "Arik Sharon's Strategy: Barak or the Linchpin of Unity Government—Part I, Institute for Advanced Strategic and Political Studies, Op. Ed., February 25, 2001, http://www.iasps.org/

34. Tom Barry, "Douglas Feith: Portrait of a Neoconservative," www.antiwar. com/orig/barry.php?articleid=3545

35. Ibid.

36. David Wurmser online biography available at http://rightweb.irc-online.org/ ind/wurmser_d/wurmser-d.php

37. "A Clean Break: A New Strategy for Securing the Realm," text available online at http://www.freerepublic.com/focus/news/860941/posts

38. Ibid.

39. Ibid.

40. The Centre for Counterintelligence and Security Studies, "Larry Franklin Case," http://www.cicentre.com/Documents/DOC_Larry_Franklin_Case.htm "Open Letter to the President, February 18, 1998," text available online at: http://www. centerforsecuritypolicy.org/index.jsp?section=papers&code=01-D_76

41. Ibid.

42. *Rebuilding America's Defenses:, Strategy, Forces and Resources, A Report of the Project for a New American Century*, September, 2000, p. 14, http://www. newamericancentury.org/RebuildingAmericasDefenses.pdf

43. Ibid., p. 10.

44. Donna E. Arzt, *From Refugees to Citizens: Palestinians and the End of the Arab-Israeli Conflict* (New York: Council on Foreign Relations Press, 1999. See also "Palestinian Refugee Return," online at http://www.arts.mcgill.ca/MEPP/PRRN/papers/artz99.html

45. See Dan Tschirgi, "Resolving the Palestinian Refugee Problem: Edward A. Norman's Unintended Contribution to Relevant Lessons in Perspectives, Values, and Consequences," in Dietrich Jung, *The Middle East and Palestine: Global Politics and Regional Conflict* (New York: Palgrave Macmillan, 2004), pp. 183–220. Reproduced with permission of Palgrave Macmillan.

46. Ibid., p. 189; http://WWW.arts.mcgill.ca/MEPP/PRRN/papers/arch-4.html., pp. l–4.

47. At http://www.arts.mcgill.ca/MEPP/PRRN/papers/arch-4.html, p. 6.; Cited in Tschirgi, *Resolving the Palestinian Refugee Problem*, op. cit., p. 190.

48. Joseph Alpher and Khalil Shikaki, "The Palestinian Refugee Problem and the Right of Return," Weatherhead Center for International Affairs, Harvard University, Program on International Conflict Analysis and Resolution, Paper No. 98–7 (1998).

49. Ibid., p. 1.

50. See Edward Said, "The Right of Return, At Last," *al Ahram Weekly Online*, February 10–16, 2000, http://www.ahram.org.eg/weekly/2000/468/opl.htm; see also Joseph Massad, "Return or Permanent Exile? Palestinian Refugees and the Ends of Oslo," *Critique* (Spring, 1999), 5–23.

51. Tschirgi, "Resolving the Palestinian Refugee Problem," op. cit.

52. Saed Okasha, "Uncharacteristic Noises, Strange Bedfellows: Hardline Iraq Goes Soft on Palestinian Refugees, Old Rivals Discuss Alliances," *Cairo Times*, May 4–10, 2000; available online at: www.cairotimes.com/content/archiv04/Iraq.html

53. In 1994, for example, British and Israeli newspapers claimed that Iraqi Deputy Prime Minister Tariq Aziz had met in Morocco with two Iraqi-born Israeli cabinet ministers, Benyamin Ben Eliezer and Moshe Shahal, for a wide-ranging round of talks on a variety of topics, including the possible resettlement in Iraq of Palestinian refugees residing in Lebanon. See Peretz Kidron, "Israel Plays the Iraqi Card," *Middle East International*, September 23, 1994.

54. See "U.S. Scheme to Resettle Palestinian Refugees in Iraq," *Mideast Mirror*, October 13, 1999, online: www.idrel.com/lb/shufme/archives/docsme/memirror991013.html.

55. Maariv, December 13, 1999, cited in "Israel Reportedly Opens Secret Negotiations With Iraq," *Middle East Intelligence Bulletin*, 1 (12), December, 1999, p. 1; online: www.meib.org/articles/9912_me4.html.

56. See, for example, "Palestinian Refugees May be Displaced to Iraq," *IANA Radionet*, May 22, 2000; online: www.ianradionet.com/E_newstext, 2000/may/5_22.html.

57. Laura Drake, "Palestinian Refugees in Lebanon: The Walls of History are Closing In," *Washington Report on Middle East* Affairs, January/February, 2000, pp. 11–12. Available online at: www.washington-report.org/backissues/0100/0002011.html

58. The idea that the transferal of Palestinian Arabs to Iraq would be beneficial to Palestinians, Iraq and Zionists was advanced in 1918 by the Oxford orientalist Edwyn Bevan. In the 1930s, it was taken up and vigorously pursued through what can only be described as secret private diplomacy by Edward A. Norman, a non-Zionist American Jewish philanthropist. See Tschirgi, "Resolving the Palestinian Refugee Problem," op. cit.

59. As the prospect of the 2003 war against Iraq loomed ominously closer, a few commentaries appeared in print warning that Israel and the US might seek to utilize the upcoming upheaval and its aftermath to effect the massive transfer of Palestinians to other parts of the Arab World, including Iraq. Thus, in early October, 2002 Will Youmans, a third-year law student at the University of California, Berkeley and a self-described "activist," warned that Palestinians were threatened by displacement en masse and noted that "observers have speculated that Western Iraq may provide a place for Israel to expel Palestinians to." Will Youmans, "Israel May 'Transfer' Palestinians During the War on Iraq," *Counterpunch*, October 9, 2002, available online at: *http://www.counterpunch.org/youmans 1009.html*. A more elaborate and carefully thought out effort to comprehend the motives that led Washington to attack Iraq in 2003 was provided by the same publication a few months later in the form of an article written by Bill Cristison, a former CIA analyst, who argued that three interrelated reasons underlay the administration's drive to war against Iraq: oil, the desire to extend "the U.S. drive for global domination," and, finally, "the desire of many dominant leaders of the Bush administration in the U.S., in partnership with the Sharon government in Israel, that a conquest of Iraq become the first stage of a 'strategic transformation' of the entire Middle East." It was, the author wrote, this "third and last reason ... that the Bush administration *really* [did not] want to publicize..." See Bill Christison, "Categories of War—The U.S. Gameplan for Iraq, *Counterpunch*, February 8, 2003, available online at: http://www.counterpunch.org/christinson02082003.html.

60. Norman Podhoretz, "World War IV: How It Started, What It Means, and Why We Have to Win," *Commentary*, Sept., 2004. Online version, p. 47. www.commentarymagazine.com/A11802017_1.pdf

61. Particularly noteworthy in this respect is Podhoretz's tendentious summary of the circumstances surrounding Israel's birth in 1948, an imaginative account that could almost have been drawn straight from Leon Uris' 1958 novel, *Exodus*. Podhoretz was either utterly unaware of, or totally uninterested in, the considerable progress toward accuracy regarding that event that historians have made in the past four decades. Ibid., p. 34.

62. Bernard Lewis, *From Babel to Dragomans: Interpreting the Middle East* (London: Weidenfeld & Nicolson, 2004), p. 2.

63. Bernard Lewis, "The Roots of Muslim Rage," in Bernard Lewis, *From Babel to Dragomans: Interpreting the Middle East* (London: Weidenfeld and Nicolson, 2004), p. 330. The article was first published in September, 1990 in the *Atlantic Monthly*.

64. Ibid.

65. Text of the letter is available online at http://encyclopedia.thefreedictionary.com/committee%20for%20peace%20and%secur....

66. Lewis, op. cit., p. 329.

CHAPTER 2. RESPONDING TO 9/11: THE IMPLICATIONS OF ACTION AND THE LIMITS OF DISCOURSE

1. George W. Bush, "Address to the Nation on the Terrorist Attacks," Weekly Compilation of Presidential Documents, from th4e 2001 Presidential Documents Online via GPO Access [frwais.access.gpo.gov], Doc. I.D.: pd17se01_txt-15

2. Dan Tschirgi, "The War on Terror: Marginalized Conflict as a Challenge to the International System," *Perceptions: Journal of International Affairs*, VII (3) (Sept.–Nov., 2002), pp. 108–23.

3. Richard A. Clarke, *Against All Enemies: Inside America's War on Terror* (New York: Free Press, 2004), pp. 1–13.

4. Jake Tapper, "Bush, Challenged," http://archive.salo.com/politics/feature/2001/09/11/bush; http://coopeerativeresearch.org, timeline, September 11, 2001, 12, noon.

5. Clarke, op. cit., p. 23.

6. George W. Bush, "Address to the Nation on the Terrorist Attacks. . . ." Sept. 11, 2001.

7. James Mann, *The Rise of the Vulcans: The History of Bush's War Cabinet*, p. 363.

8. Clarke, op. cit. p. 30.

9. Mann, op. cit. p. 363.

10. Bob Woodward, *Plan of Attack* (New York : Simon & Schuster, 2004), p. 26.

11. Bryan Burrough, Eugenia Peretz, David Rose, David Wise, "The Path to War," *Vanity Fair*, May, 2004.

12. Clarke, op. cit. pp. 265–66.

13. George W. Bush, "Graduation Speech at West Point," June 1, 2002. Available online at: http://www.whitehouse.gov/news/releases/2002/06/print/20020601-3.html

14. "President Bush Discusses Freedom in Iraq and Middle East: Remarks by the President at the 20th Anniversary of the National Endowment for Democracy," November 6, 2003, http://frwebgate1.access.gpo.gov/cgi-bin/waisgate.cgi?WAISdocID=601081331274+7+0+0&WAISaction=retrieve

15. Michael Hirsh, *At War with Ourselves: Why America is Squandering Its Chance to Build a Better World* (New York: Oxford University Press, 2003), p. 51.

16. Ibid.

17. *Los Angeles Times*, March 9, 2002. Available online at: http://www.commondreams.org/views02/0309-04.htm

18. Michael D. Intriligator, "U.S. Nuclear Weapons Policy under the Bush Administration," Nuclear Age Peace Foundation, Publication 31, 2004, available online at: http://www.wagingpeace.org/articles/2004/07/00_intriligator_us-policy-bush.htm

19. Nuclear Posture Review [Excerpts], www.globalsecurity.org/wmd/library/policy/dod/npr.htm.

20. "President Bush Discusses Freedom in Iraq and Middle East," op. cit.

21. Ibid.

22. Ibid.
23. Ibid.
24. President Holds Press Conference, January 26, 2005, http://www.whitehouse.gov/news/releases/2005/01/print/20050126-3.html.
25. Gary C. Gambil, "Jumpstarting Arab Reform: The Bush Administration's Greater Middle East Initiative," *Middle East Intelligence Bulletin*, 6 (6–7) http://www.meib.org/articles/0407_me2.htm The G-8 countries are: Canada, France, Germany, Italy, Japan, Russia,the U.K., and the U.S.
26. Ibid.
27. Marina Ottaway and Thomas Carothers, "The Greater Middle East Initiative: Off to a False Start," The Carnegie Endowment for International Peace, *Policy Brief*, No. 29, www.carnegieendowment.org/publications/index.cfm?fa=view&id=1480&prog=zgp&proj=zdrl,zme.
28. Ibid.
29. Mustapha K. El Sayyid, "The Third Wave of Democratization in the Arab World," in Dan Tschirgi (ed.), *The Arab World Today* (Boulder and London: Lynne Rienner Publishers, 1994, pp. 182–83.
30. Ottaway and Carothers, op. cit.
31. Cited in Ottaway and Carothers, op. cit.
32. Ibid.
33. "Partnership for Progress and a Common Future with the Region of the Boader Middle East and North Africa," June 9, 2004. Online at: http://www.g8.utoronto.ca/summit/2004seaisland/partnership.html
34. Ottaway and Carothers, op. cit.
35. See Tamara Cofman Wittes, "The New U.S. Proposal for a Greater Middle East Initiative: An Evaluation," *Global Politics*, The Brookings Institution Saban Center for Middle East Policy, http://www.brookings.edu/views/op-ed/fellows/wittes20040510.htm.
36. Susan Sontag, "Talk of the Town," *The New Yorker*, September 24, 2001, http://newyorker.com/talk/content/?010924ta_talk_wtc.
37. Norman Mailer, *Why We Are at War* (New York: Random House, 2003), p. 52.
38. Ibid.
39. Noam Chomsky, *9/11* (New York: /Seven Stories Press, 2001), p. 16.
40. Ibid., see pp. 16, 35, and 83.
41. Chalmers Johnson, *The Sorrows of Empire: Militarism, Secrecy, and the End of the Republic* (New York: Metropolitan Books, Henry Holt and Company, 2004), p. 227.
42. Ibid., pp. 23–24.
43. Ibid., p. 284.
44. Ibid.
45. Ibid., p. 285.
46. Ibid., p. 312.
47. Zbigniew Brzezinski, *The Choice: Global Domination or Global Leadership* (New York: Basic Books, 2004), p. 229.
48. Ibid., p. 217.
49. Ibid.
50. Ibid., p. 18.

51. Ibid., p. 35.
52. Ibid., p. 219.
53. Clarke, op. cit.
54. Ibid., p. i.
55. Ibid., p. 264.
56. Ibid., p. 267.
57. Ibid., p. 263.
58. Ibid., p. 287.
59. Anonymous, *Imperial Hubris: Why the West is Losing the War on Terror* (Dulles, VA, Brassey's, Inc., 2004).
60. Ibid., p. 262.
61. Ibid., p. 166.
62. Ibid., pp. 9–10.
63. Ibid., p. 167.
64. Ibid., p. 242.
65. Ibid., p. 158.
66. Ibid., pp. 256–57.
67. Ibid., pp. 251–52.
68. Ibid., pp. 242–42.
69. Ibid., p. 253.
70. Ibid., p. 207.
71. National Endowment for the Arts, "Reading at Risk: A Survey of Literary Reading in America," Research Division Report No. 46, p. vii. http://www.nea.gov/pub/ReadingAtRisk.pdf
72. Ibid.
73. Joan Hinde Stewart, "Letter to the Hamilton Community," *Faculty Newsletter*, available online at http://www.hamilton.edu/news/more_news/display.cfm?id=9073
74. Ibid.
75. Ibid.
76. At www.hamilton.edu/news/more_news/display.cfm?ID=9020
77. "Gov. Owens Letter Calls for Churchill to Step Down," www.thedenverchannel.com/news/4151452/detail.html.
78. Scott Smallwood, "Colorado Regents Will Investigate Professor Who Compared September 11 Victims to Nazis," *Chronicle of Higher Education*, February 4, 2005, www.kersplebedeb.com/mystuff/ s11/churchill_chronicle.html
79. Ibid.
80. Ibid.
81. Ibid.
82. By 2007 Churchill's fortunes had somewhat changed in this respect. A Web Site for members of the University of Colorado Boulder student community listed various pro-Churchill petitions students could sign. See: http://www.pirateballerina.com/index.php
83. "Letter to Hamilton Community," op. cit.
84. "Colorado Regents Will Investigate Professor" op. cit.
85. "Questions Stoke Ward Churchill's Firebrand's Past," *Denver Post*, February 13, 2005, http://www.denverpost.com/Stories/0,1413,36%257E23827%257E2709008,00.html.

86. Ward Churchill, "Some People Push Back: On the Justice of Roosting Chickens," http://www.kersplebedeb.com/mystuff/s11/churchill.html.

87. Quoted in Ibid., p. 3.

88. Ibid., p. 3.

89. Ibid., p. 4.

90. Ibid.

91. Ibid., p. 5.

92. Ibid., p.6.

93. Ibid., p. 8.

94. Ibid., p. 9.

95. Ibid., p. 10.

96. Ibid., p. 11.

97. Ibid., pp. 12–13

98. Ibid., p. 5.

99. "CU to Fire Ward Churchill," http://www.thedenverchannel.com/new.9424240/detail.html June 26, 2006.

100. New York Professor Loses Post over Churchill Controversy, *Denver Post*, February 13, 2005, http://www.denverpost.com/Stories/0,1413,36%257E11676%257E2706340,00.html.

101. See Hirsh, op. cit., pp. 74–75.

102. Patrick J. Buchanan, "Reform Party Nomination Acceptance Speech," August 12, 2000, www.buchanan.org/pa-00-0812-speechnomination.html.

103. Ibid.

104. Ibid.

105. He had, of course, already expounded them at length in his 1999 book, *A Republic, Not Empire* (Chicago: Regnery, 1999).

106. Patrick Buchanan, "To Hell with Empire," www.tcrnews2.com/Buchanan.html.

107. Ibid.

108. Paul Schroeder, "The Case Against Preemptive War," *The American Conservative*, October 21, 2002, www.amconmag.com/.

109. Ibid.

110. Jason Vest, "The Men from JINSA and CSP," *The Nation*, August 2002, www.thenation.com/doc.mhtml%3Fi=20020902&s=vest.

111. Ibid.

112. Ibid.

113. Ibid.

114. Georgie Anne Geyer, "Iraq Bait and Switch Deprives Americans of Real Answers," August 5, 2003, www.uexpress.com/georgieannegeyer/?uc_full_date=20030805.

115. Robert Novak, "Sharon's War," www.cnn.com/2002/ALLPOLITICS/12/26/column.novak.opinion.sharon/.

116. David Harrison, "Moran, War and Inevitability," *The Reston Connection*, March 5, 2003, www.connectionnewspapers.com/ article.asp?archive=true&article=16491&paper=71&cat=104.

117. Ernest F. Hollings, "Why We're in Iraq," *The State.Com*, www.thestate.com/mld/state/news/opinion/ 8609339.htm?template.

118. Eric M. Weiss and Spencer S. Hsu, "Va.'s Moran Condemned for Remarks," *Washington Post*, March 12, 2003. www.washingtonpost.com/wp-dyn/articles/A12681-2003Mar11.html.

119. Peter Hardin, "Moran Issues Second Apology," *Richmond Times-Dispatch*, March 11, 2003.

120. Remarks by Ernest F. Hollings, *Congressional Record*, May 20, 2004, Senate, p. S5924.

121. "GOP, Dems Bicker As Hollings Blames Pro-Israel Crowd for Iraq Mess," *Jewish News*, n.d., www.njjewishnews.com/njjn.com/52704/bessgop.html.

122. Dore Gold, "Wartime Witch Hunt: Blaming Israel for the Iraq War," *Jerusalem Issue Brief*, 3 (25) June 3, 2004 (Institute for Comporary Affairs), www.jcpa.org/brief/brief3-25.htm. Original emphasis.

123. Uri Avnery, "The Night After: The Easier the Victory, the Harder the Peace," *Counterpunch*, April 10, 2003. www.counterpunch.org/avnery04102003.html.

124. Ibid.

125. Ibid.

126. Patrick J. Buchanan, "Whose War?" *The American Conservative*, March 24, 2003. www.amconmag.com/03_24_03/cover.html, pp. 2, 3–4.

127. Ibid., p. 3.

128. Ibid., p. 8.

129. Ibid., p. 12.

130. Norman Podhoretz, "World War IV: How It Started, What It Means, and Why We Have to Win," *Commentary* September, 2004. www.commentarymagazine.com/podhoretz.htm.

131. Podhoretz op. cit., p. 33.

132. Ibid.

133. Ibid.

134. Mark Weber, "Iraq: A War for Israel?" www.ihr.org/leaflets/iraqwar.shtml

135. See his comment at http://www.nesa.org.uk/latest_issue/html/israel_controls_the_united_sta.htm.

136. For example, see Chapter 9 of the U.S. Department of Defense's 1997 *Annual Defense Report*, available online at http://www.defenselink.mil/execsec/adr97/chap9.html#top. See also, Julian Borger ad Ewen MacAskill, "Bin Laden is Looking for a Nuclear Weapon: How Close Has He Come?" *The Guardian*, November 7, 2001.

137. Graham Allison, *Nuclear Terrorism: The Ultimate Preventable Catastrophe* (New York: Henry Holt and Company, LLC, 2004); Stephen Flynn, *America the Vulnerable: How Our Government is Failing to Protect Us from Terrorism* (New York: Harper Collins, 2004).

138. See Anonymous, *Imperial Hubris*, op. cit., pp. 87–91.

139. "Bush to Say More Qaeda Leaders Killed, Captured," *Reuters* August 31, 2004, www.globalsecurity.org/ org/news/2004/040831.

140. "State of the Union Address," Feb. 2, 2005, http://www.whitehouse.gov/news/releases/2005/02/print/20050202-11.html.

141. "President Bush Discusses Freedom in Iraq and the Middle East," op. cit.

142. See Department of Defense, "DoD News Briefing—Secretary Rumsfeld and Gen. Myers, April 25, 2003, http://www.defenselink.mil/transcripts/2003/

tr20030424-secdef0126.html. See also "Rumsfeld Rules out Islamic Regime in Iraq," http://www.islamonline.net/English/News/2003-04/25/article02.shtml.

143. See "President Bush Discusses Freedom in Iraq and the Middle East," op. cit.

144. Brzezinski, op. cit., p. 225. Brzezinski points out that the histories of Germany and Japan had provided "social foundations on which the United States after World War II was able to construct democratic constitutions."

145. George Bush, Second Inaugural Address, http://www.whitehouse.gov/inaugural/.

146. Ibid.

CHAPTER 3. MEXICO'S ZAPATISTA REBELLION

1. For obvious reasons, this is a pseudonym.
2. Interview, Chiapas, Mexico, August 18, 1995.
3. Interviews, San Cristóbal de las Casas, Chiapas, August, 1995. See also Carlos Acosta Cordoval, "La Transformación de Zedillo Se Inicío Con La Devaluación y Culminó Con la Llegada de los Fondos del FMI," *Proceso*, February 13, 1995, p. 11.
4. Interview with Manuel Burguete, San Cristóbal de Las Casas, August 12, 1995.
5. Interview with Dr. Raymundo Sánchez Barraza, San Cristóbal de Las Casas, August 13, 1995.
6. Field Notes on the Zapatista Rebellion, Chiapas, Mexico, August 1995.
7. Samuel P. Huntington, *Political Order in Changing Societies* (New Haven: Yale University Press, 1968), *passim*.
8. J. Bowyer Bell, "Arms Transfers, Conflict, and Violence at the Substate Level," in Uri Ra'anan, Robert Pfaltzgraff, Jr., and Geoffrey Kemp (eds.), *Arms Transfers to the Third World: The Military Buildup in Less Developed Countries* (Boulderco: Westview Press, 1978), pp. 321–22.
9. Boutros Boutros-Ghali, *Building Peace and Development, 1994: Annual Report on the Work of the Organization From the Forty-Eigth to the Forty-Ninth Session of the General Assembly* (New York: United Nations, 1994), p. 279.
10. Ibid., pp. 162–257.
11. Ibid., p. 162.
12. See Dan Tschirgi, "Marginalized Violent Internal Conflict in the Age of Globalization: Mexico and Egypt," *Arab Studies Quarterly*, 21 (3) (Summer, 1999). Reprinted with permission of *Arab Studies Quarterly*. Republished in Shereen T. Ismael (ed.), *Globalization: Policies, Challenges and Responses* (Calgary: Deselig Enterprises, Ltd., 2000). See also, Dan Tschirgi, "Conflicts d'un nouveau type en Egypte et au Mexique: Des islamistes aux zapatistes, la revolte des 'marginaux de la terre,'" also published in English as "In Egypt and Mexico, A New Type of Conflict: Zapatistas and Islamists Fight the Odds," in German as "Zapatisten und Islamisten im Vergeich: Wenn die Peripherie rebelliert," and in Italian as "Dall'Egitto al Chiapas, la rivolta dei diseredati," *Le Monde Diplomatique* (January, 2000); See also, "Du Mexique a l'Egypte, la revote de marginaux," in *11 Septembre 2001: Ondes de Choc, Maniere de Voir 60* (Novembre-Decembre, 2001), pp. 59–63; See also, Dan Tschirgi, "On the War on Terrorism: from Zapatistas to Al-Qaida," *Humanitaire* (Hiver, 2001–2002), pp. 57–67; see also, Dan Tschirgi, "Od zbrojnego islamu

politycznego po zapatyzm. Zmarginalizowany gwaltowny konflikt wewnetrzny w dobie globalizacji: Egipt I Meksyk," *Rewolucja*, No. 2 (Nov., 2002), pp. 180–207. See also, Jeffrey A. Nodoroscik, Dina Younis, El Sayed Gad Mohammed and Mónica Serrano, "Lessons in Violent Internal Conflict: Egypt and Mexico," SYLFF (The Ryoichi Sasakawa Young Leaders Fellowship Fund) *Working Papers*, No. 8 (Tokyo: March, 1998).

13. I differ here with Pierre Bourdieu, who argues that neoliberalism is an "infernal machine" whose tentacles must produce structural violence wherever they reach. It seems to me that Bourdieu's view not only evades the question of how and why neoliberal policies sometimes do generate violence, but also ignores the patent fact that such policies have neither universally nor consistently provoked social violence. See Pierre Bourdieu, "Utopia of Endless Exploitation: The Essence of Neoliberalism," *Le Monde Diplomatique*, December, 1998, www.monde-diplomatique.fr/en/12/08bouirdieu.html. Translated by Jeremy L. Shapiro, p. 3.

14. Dan Tschirgi, "Introduction," in Dan Tschirgi (ed.), *Development in the Age of Liberalization: Egypt and Mexico* (Cairo: The American University in Cairo Press, 1996), p. 9. Reprinted with permission of the American University in Cairo Press.

15. David E. Apter, *Rethinking Development: Modernization, Dependency and Postmodern Politics*, (Beverly Hills, CA: Sage Publications, 1987), pp. 316–17.

16. The work, collectively known as *The Information Age*, was published in three volumes: (Volume I) *The Rise of Network Society* (Malden, MA: Blackwell Publishers, 1996; (Volume II) *The Power of Identity* (Malden, MA: Blackwell Publishers, 1997); and (Volume III) *End of Millennium* (Malden, MA: Blackwell Publishers, 1998).

17. Castells, *The Power of Identity*, op. cit. pp. 68–69.

18. Alan Riding, *Distant Neighbors: A Portrait of the Mexicans* (New York: Vintage Books, 1986), p. 306.

19. Carlos Tello Díaz, *La Rebelion de las Cañadas* (México: Cal y Arena, 1995), p. 15; Arturo de Jésus Urbina Nandayapa, *Las Razones de Chiapas: Causas, Desarrollo, Consecuencias, Personajes y Perspectivas del Alzamiento en los Altos de Chiapas*, 2nd. ed. (México, DF: Editorial PAC, 1994), p. 24.

20. Tello, p. 18.

21. Urbina, p. 8; Tello, pp. 19–20.

22. Tello, pp. 27–32; Urbina, pp. 56–70.

23. My own tour of parts of the Conflict Zone only eighteen months after the rebellion's outbreak confirmed this. I not only found both "pro" and "anti"-Zapatista villages and settlements in the same Zapatista-controlled valley but also—and not infrequently—families whose members were similarly divided.

24. Tim Goldman, "Mexican Rebels are Retreating; Issues Are Not," *New York Times*, January 4, 1994, p. 1. For an account of the role of *milicianos*, see the collection of documents related to the Zapatista Rebellion entitled *La Palabra de los Armados de Verdad y Fuego*, (México, DF: Fueteovejuna, 1994). See particularly Volume l, pp. 92–95.

25. *La Palabra de Los Armados de Verdad y Fuego*, México, DF: Editorial Fuenteovejua, 1994, Vol. 1, pp. 36–40.

26. Ibid., "Sobre el EZLN y Las Condiciones Para el Diálogo," pp. 67–68.

27. "Subcomandante Marcos," Fundación CIDOB, http://www.cidob.org/bios/castellano/lideres/m-060.htm

28. Andrés Oppenheimer, *México en la Frontera del Caos: La Crisis Mexicana de los Noventa y la Esperanza del Nuevo Milenio*, 2nd Edition (México, DF: Ediciones B México, S.A. de C.V., 2002), pp. 219–51.

29. Interview with confidential source. Chiapas, August, 1998.

30. Documentos Básicos del Frente Zapatista de Liberación Nacional, http://www.geocities.com/ccd-utopia/fzln/documentos_basicos_fzln.html?200522.

31. See "Ten Years into the Rebellion: John Ross Interviewed by Chris Arsenault," *ZNet*, November 5, 2004, http://www.zmag.org/content/showarticle.cfm?SectionID=59&ItemID=6582.

32. Susana Hayword, "Mexican Bishops Call for Chiapas Probe," *Knight Ridder Newspapers*, February 15, 2005, http://www.realcities.com/mld/krwashington/news/columnists/susana_hayward/10908253....3/18/2005.

33. Diego Cevallos, "Zapatista Guerrillas Quiet But Still Present in Chiapas," IPS, January 12, 2005, http://lists.indymedia.org/pipermail/imc-nm/2005-January/0118-fo.html.

34. "Ten Years Into the Rebellion," op. cit.

35. Andrés Aubrey, "El Movimiento Zapatista en el Continuum del la Historia de Chiapas," in Silvia Soriano Hernández (ed.), *A Proposito de la Insurgencia en Chiapas* (México, DF: Asociación Para el Desarrollo de la Investigación Cientifica y Humanistica en Chiapas, 1994), p. 50.

36. David R. Dávila Villers, "Chiapas: Democratization and the Military in Mexico." Paper presented to the Latin American Association XIX International Congress, Washington, DC, September, 1995.

37. Sergio Mota Marín, "La Estructura Economica de Chiapas," in María Luisa Armendáriz (ed.), *Chiapas, Una Radiografía* (México DF: Fondo de Cultura Económica, 1994), pp. 339–45.

38. Interviews, Chiapas, 1995, 1996, 1998, 2000.

39. Ibid.

40. "Chiapas en Cifras," *El Financiero*, August 31, 1995.

41. Calculated from Charts 3 and 4 in Daniel Villafuerte Solís and María del Carmen García Aguilar, "Los Altos de Chiapas en el Contexto del Neoliberalismo: Causas y Razones dels Conflicto indígena," in Silvia Soriano Hernández (ed.), *A Propósito de la Insurgencia en Chiapas* (México, DF: Asociación Para el Desarrollo de la Investigación Cientifica y Humanista en Chiapas, 1994), pp. 98–100.

42. Dávila, op. cit.

43. Villafuerte and García, op. cit., pp. 91–97.

44. Studies conducted in 1987 by Mexico's National Institute of Nutrition found that 57 percent of infants in the Highlands suffered from first, second, or third degree malnutrition. Cited by Villafuerte and García, op. cit., p. 96. Personal observations and various conversations with health workers in the Highland confirmed the disastrous lack of health care. A physician working in one Highland valley stressed the difficulties of "making rounds," which included occasional visits to villages in the valley's interior. Asked to describe her most difficult recent experience, she related details of a nine-hour trip, on foot and horseback, to a village that had not seen a medical worker in two years. While distances are not great in the Highlands, the

terrain's rugged nature frequently makes traveling even a few kilometers a very arduous and time-consuming affair.

45. Villafuerte and García, op. cit., p. 98.

46. See, for example, Susan Tax Freeman, "Notes from the Chiapas Project: Zinacantan, Summer, 1959," in V. R. Bricker and G. H. Gossen, *Ethnographic Encounters in Mesoamerica: Essays in Honor of Evon Zartman Vogt, Jr.* (Albany: Institute for Mesoamerican Studies, The University at Albany, State University of New York: 1989), pp. 89–100, and Gary H. Gossen, "Life, Death and Apotheosis of a Chamula Protestant Leader: Biography as Social History," Ibid., pp. 217–29.

47. Mónica Serrano, "Civil Violence in Chiapas: The Origins and the Causes of the Revolt," in Mónica Serrano (ed)., *Mexico: Assessing Neo-Liberal Reform* (London, Institute of Latin American Studies, 1997), pp. 75–93; Tello, pp. 59–61.

48. "Testimonios del Dia Primero," *La Palabra de los Armados de Verdad y Fuego*, Vol. 1, op. cit., p. 37.

49. See, for example, Evon Z. Vogt, *The Zinacantecos of Mexico: A Modern Maya Way of Life* (New York: Holt, Rinehart and Winston, 1970). See also, Andrés Fabregas Puig, "Los Pueblos de Chiapas," in María Luisa Armendariz (ed.) (México, DF: Fondo de Cultura Economica, 1994), pp. 172–97.

50. Vogt, op. cit., p. l2.

51. Technically, the Chamula seceded from the Roman Catholic Church in the 1980s, when the Bishop imposed a ban on priestly services as punishment for the murder of a protestant leader. The Chamula elders responded by breaking their ties with Rome and joining the Mexican Orthodox Church of San Pascualito. This little known organization had developed during the Revolution as a nationalized Catholicism. In the 1960s the leader of the "Orthodox" Church established his seat in a sanctuary in Tuxtla, the capital of Chiapas, proclaimed it a cathedral, and declared himself Archbishop and Patriarch. The Orthodox Patriarch offers an old-style mass in Latin and visits his flock in Chamula only a few times a year, while otherwise leaving the local church to the Maya shamans. See Ronald Wright, *Time Among the Maya: Travels in Belize, Guatemala and Mexico* (Penguin Books Canada, Markham, Ontario, 1989), pp. 287–88.

52. Vogt, op. cit., *passim*; Puig, op. cit.; Graciela Freyermuth Enciso, "La Practica Medica Indigena en los Altos de Chiapas," in Armendáriz, op. cit., pp. 252–53.

53. Vogt, op. cit., p. 67.

54. Villafuerte and García, op. cit., pp. 83–117.

55. Riding, op. cit., pp. 424–25.

56. Serrano, op. cit.

57. Ibid. See also Villafuerte and García, op. cit., p. 87.

58. Villafuerte and García, op cit., p. 89.

59. Ibid., pp. 85–86.

60. Subcomandante Marcos, "Chiapas: La Treceava Estela, Segunda Parte: Una Muerte," www.nodo50.org/pChiapas/Chiapas/ documentos/calenda/Chiapas2.htm

61. The label appears to have been born at some point in the nineteenth century, when San Cristóbal's Ladinos persisted in wearing the Coleto, a leather jerkin, long after it had gone out of fashion in other areas of Mexico

62. Interview with Manuel Burguete, San Cristóbal de las Casas, August 12, 1995.

63. *La Jornada*, May 13, 1994, cited by Tello, op. cit., p. 59.

64. "Walking with the Poor: Campesinos, Land, and Human Rights in Salto de Agua, Chiapas," Interview with Fr. Nadolny of Salto de Agua, by Lindsey Hilson of the BBC in March, 1995 (San Cristóbal de las Casas: Centro de Derechos Humanos Fray Bartolome de Las Casas, 1995), p. 6.
65. Tello, op. cit., pp. 80–130.
66. Oppenhemer, op. cit., pp. 55–56.

Chapter 4. Upper Egypt and the *Gama'a al-Islamiyya*

1. Nadia Farah Ramsis, "Historical Roots of Contemporary Economic Development in Egypt," in Dan Tschirgi (ed.), *Development in the Age of Liberalization* (Cairo: The American University in Cairo Press, 1996), p. 22.
2. Ibid., p. 23.
3. Library of Congress, *A Country Study: Egypt*, Library of Congress call number DT46E32 1991, "Towns and Cities", Web site: http://lcweb2.loc.gov/cgi-bin/query/r?frd/cstdy:@field(DOCID+eg0033) See also, *The Census of Egypt Taken in 1907* (Cairo: National Printing Department, 1909), pp. 129–30.
4. Federal Research Division, Library of Congress, *A Country Study: Egypt,* Rural Society, http://lcweb2.loc.gov/cgi-bin/query/r?frd/cstdy:@field(DOCID+eg0072).
5. Farah Ramsis, op. cit., p. 23.
6. United Nations Development Program, *Egypt Human Development Report 2002–2003,* Chapter 2, " Status of Human Development in Egypt," p. 37. http://www.undp.org.eg/publications/ENHDR_2003/P27-40.PDF. See also "The Growth of Poverty in Egypt" (Cairo: Almishkat, 1998), http://www.almishkat.org/engdoc98/rn12/rn12_in.htm.
7. The World Bank Group, "Better Measurement of Poverty Can Help Design Better Policies," http://www.worldbank.org/progress/egypt/html See also http://web.worldbank.org/WBSITE/EXTERNAL/COUNTRIES/MENAEXT/EGYPTEXTN/0,,contentMDK:20136665~pagePK:141137~piPK:217854~theSitePK:256307,00.html.
8. "Transition to Adulthood: Survey Paints Broad Picture of Egyptian Adolescents," *Population Briefs*, 5 (1) (The Population Council, April, 1999), http://www.popcouncil.org/publications/popbriefs/pb5(1)_5.html
9. Soheir A. Morsy, *Gender, Sickness, and Healing in Rural Egypt: Ethnography in Historical Context (*Boulder, CO: Westview Press, 1993), pp. 102–10 and 151–57.
10. "Better Measurement of Poverty Can Help Design Better Policies," op. cit.
11. For an excellent discussion of this point, see Reem Saad, "Hegemony in the Periphery: Community and Exclusion in an Upper Egyptian Village," in N. Hopkins and K. Westergaard (eds.). *Directions of Change in Rural Egypt* (Cairo: The American University in Cairo Press, 1998), pp. 113–129.
12. Ibid., p. 118.
13. The operative definition of status groups, including tribe, is not necessarily defined in all parts of Upper Egypt in terms of lineage, and some status groups are not defined in terms of tribe or clan but rather of occupation. See Reem Saad, op. cit.
14. Ibid.

15. Chr. Korsholm Nielsen, "Settling Disputes in Upper Egypt," *Law and Society, ISIM (International Institute for the Study of Islam in the Modern World) Newsletter 13*, December, 2003, http://www.isim.nl/files/newsl_13-12.pdf.

16. See Nazek Nosseir, "Egypt: Population, Urbanization, and Development," in Dan Tschirgi (ed.) *Development in the Age of Liberalization*, op. cit., p. 188.

17. See Saad, op. cit., p. 119.

18. Uri M. Kupferschmidt, "Reformist and Militant Islam in Urban and Rural Egypt," *Middle East Studies*, 23 (October, 1987), p. 409.

19. Library of Congress, *Country Study: Egypt*, Library of Congress card catalogue Number DT 46 E32 1991, Web site: "Emigration" http://lcweb2.loc.gov/cgi-bin/query/r?frd/cstdy:@field(DOCID+eg0068).

20. Robert Springborg, "Identity in Crisis: Egyptian Political Identity in the Face of Globalization," *Harvard International Review*, 25 (2003), http://hir.harvard.edu/articles/?id=1140.

21. Maye Kassem, *Egyptian Politics: The Dynamics of Authoritarian Rule* (Boulder, CO: Lynne Rienner Publishers, Inc., 2004), p. 134.

22. The quotation is from Kassem, op. cit., p. 137.

23. Ibid., p. 142.

24. Amina Elbendery, "The Long Revolution," *Al Ahram Weekly Online*, 18–24 July, 2002, http://weekly.ahram.org.eg/2002/595/sc2.htm.

25. Kassem, op. cit., p. 148.

26. Walid M. Abdelnasser, "Islamic Organizations in Egypt and the Iranian Revolution of 1979: The Experience of the First Few Years, " *Arab Studies Quarterly* (Spring, 1997), *passim*.

27. Kassem, op. cit., pp. 139–40.

28. Kassem, op. cit., pp. 145–47.

29. Michael Collins Dunn, "Fundamentalism in Egypt," *Middle East Policy*, 11 (3) 1993, p. 72.

30. Reem Saad, "State, Landlord, Parliament and Peasant: The Story of the 1992 Tenancy Law in Egypt," in Alan Bowman and Eugene Rogan, (eds.). *Agriculture in Egypt From Pharaonic to Modern Times, Proceedings of the British Academy*, Vol. 96 (Oxford: Oxford University Press, 1998), pp. 89, 387.

31. On Egypt's military, see: "Egypt: National Security," http://www.photius.com/countries/egypt/national_security/egypt_national_security_national_security.html. On Egypt's security forces, only part of which included the paramilitary Central Security Force (CSF), see http://www.photius.com/countries/egypt/national_security/egypt_national_security_central_security_for~8005.html.

32. Audrey Kurth Cronin, et al. "CRS Report for Congress: Foreign Terrorist Organization" (Congressional Research Service, February 4, 2004), p. 25, http://www.fas.org/irp/crs/RL32223.pdf.

33. Dunn, op. cit, p. 75.

34. Dunn, op. cit., p. 69.

35. "Upper Egypt: The Battle against the Leagues," *The Economist*, July 4, 1992, p. 38. Similar accounts of conditions in Upper Egypt continued to be published throughout the early years of the *Gama'a's* campaign. See, for example, "Egypt Loses Ground to Muslim Militants and Fear," *New York Times*, February 11, 1994, p. A-3.

36. Amnesty International, "Egypt: Human Rights Abuses by Armed Groups," December 22, 1998, http://web.amnesty.org.library/print/ENGMDE120221998, p. 1.

37. Simon Apiku, "Military Tribunal Slams Militants," *Middle East Times*, October 8, 1999, http://metimes.com/issue99-17/eg/egyptian_military_tribunal.htm; Geneive Abo, *No God But God: Egypt and the Triumph of Islam* (Oxford University Press, New York, 2000), p. 21.

38. Ibid.

39. Ibid.

40. Ibid., p. 25.

41. Amnesty International, "Egypt: Human Rights Abuses by Armed Groups," op. cit., p. 3.

42. Ibid., p. 3.

43. Ibid., p. 3.

44. Ibid., p.4.

45. Ibid., p. 4.

46. "Ex-Minister Dies," *Al-Ahram Weekly Online*, http://weekly.ahram.org.eg/2003/648/eg4.htm.

47. Details regarding these murders were provided by sources who visited the scene shortly after the attack. Some unconfirmed accounts indicate that one of the assailants was killed by his comrades and the remaining five died at the hands of Egyptian forces.

48. Reuters news report, "Egyptian Tour Guides to Get Counter-Terror Training," May 24, 1998, http://www.ict.org.il/spotlight/det.cfm?id=88.

49. See, Martin Mowforth, "Tourism, Terrorism and Climate Change," unpublished paper prepared for the NATO Advanced Research Workshop on "Climate Change and Tourism: Assessment and Coping Strategies," Warsaw, Poland, November 6–8, 2003, pp. 3–4. See also, Arthur Andersen, "Tourism and Terrorism—The Road to Recovery in Egypt," December 2000, http://www.hotel-online.com/Trends/Andersen/2001_Egypt.html

50. Jeongmin Seo, "Government Response to Radical Islamic Movements during the Mubarak Regime," unpublished M.A. thesis, The American University in Cairo, 1996.

51. Richard Engle, "Militants Condemn Luxor Bloodbath," *Middle East Times*, December 7, 1997, p. 1.

52. Jailan Halawi, "Act of Despair: DNA Tests Reveal Identity of the Al-Azhar Suicide Bomber," *Al-Ahram Weekly Online*, Apri l14–20, 2005, http://weekly.ahram.org.eg/2005/738/eg4.htm.

53. Jailan Halawi, "Bin Laden behind Luxor massacre?," *Al-Ahram Weekly Online*, May 20–26, 1999, http://weekly.ahram.org.eg/1999/430/eg21.htm

54. Kassem, op. cit., p. 159.

55. Ibid., p. 158.

56. Mamoun Fandy, "Egypt's Islamic Group: Regional Revenge" *Middle East Journal*, 48 (4) (Autumn, 1994), p. 613.

57. Saad Eddin Ibrahim, "Anatomy of Egypt's Militant Islamic Groups: Methodological Notes and Preliminary Finding," *International Journal of Middle East Studies*, 12, (1980).

58. Saad Eddin Ibrahim, "The Changing Face of Islamic Activism," in Saad Eddin Ibrahim, *Egypt, Islam and Democracy* (Cairo: The American University in Cairo Press, 1996).
59. Ibid., p. 73.
60. Fandy, op. cit, p. 612.
61. Ibid., p. 613.
62. I am indebted to Nicholas S. Hopkins, one such anthropolist, for this insight.
63. Fandy, op. cit., p. 618.
64. Fandy, Ibid., p. 613.
65. Ibid.
66. Ibid., p. 614.
67. Mamoun Fandy, "The Tensions behind the Violence in Egypt," *Middle East Policy*, 2, 1993, p. 26
68. Kassem, op. cit., p. 146.
69. Al-Hayat, No. 10870, November 13, 1992, p. 10; cited by Fandy, "Egypt's Islamic Group," op. cit., p. 609.

CHAPTER 5. THE NIGER DELTA'S OGONI UPRISING

1. Vincent Amanyie, *The Agony of the Ogoni in the Niger Delta* (Port Harcourt: Horizon Concepts, 2003), pp. 189–91.
2. "Complete Statement by Ken Saro-Wiwa to Ogoni Civil Disturbances Tribunal," http://ratical.org/corporations/KSWstmt.html, p. 21. Hereafter cited as "Complete Statement."
3. The identification of tribal or ethnic groups in Nigeria is an imprecise and rather controversial art. Thus, some estimates place the number of such divisions in the country as high as four hundred.
4. Ebiegberi Joe Alagoa and Sonpie Kpone-Tonwe, "Traditions of Origin," in Ebiegberi Joe Alagoa and Abi A. Derefaka (eds.) *The Land and People of Rivers State: Eastern Niger Delta* (Port Harcourt: Onyoma Research Publications, 2002), p. 178.
5. There is some degree of controversy over just what are the main groups into which the Ogoni fall. Vincent Amanyie (op. cit., pp. 1–2) argues that there are three, rather than four such groups. I have used the view of Mr. Bari Ala Kpalap, MOSOP Information Officer in Port Harcourt, which is far more consistent. Personal communication from Bari Ala Kpalap (via Mr. David M. Ugbe) June 10, 2005.
6. Ben Naanen, "State Movements," in Alagoa and Derefaka, op. cit., p. 350.
7. Quoted in John Agbonifo, "The 'Marginalized Violent Internal Conflict' (MVIC) Model and the Ogoni Conflict in the Niger Delta of Nigeria," Unpublished M.A. Thesis, The American University in Cairo, 2002, pp. 87–88.
8. Ibid., p. 89. See also, G.O.M. Tasie and W.O. Wotobege Weneka, "Religion," in Ebiegberi and Derefaka, op. cit., pp. 285–302, and John H. Enemugwem, M. Ediyekio, and E.C. Assoer, "Colonial Rule," in Ibid., pp. 321–31.

9. Atei Mark Okorobia and George I. J. "Social and Political Developments," in Ebiegberi and Derefaka, op. cit., pp. 303–20.

10. Agbonifo, op. cit., p. 94.

11. Interview with Ledum Mitee, Port Harcourt, July, 2004; see also Agbonifo, p. 83.

12. Mitee interview.

13. V. Isumonah, "The Making of the Ogoni Ethnic Group," *Africa Magazine*, June 22, 2004, p. 5, http://www.highbeam.com/library/doc3.asp?DOCID=1G1:132241877&num=1&ctr1Info=. The author refers to the results of the study, a field survey that he himself conducted in late 2002.

14. Ibid., p. 10.

15. Jessica Piombo, "The Import of Nigeria's April 2003 Elections," *Strategic Insights*, II (6) (June, 2003), pp. 1, 3, www.ccc.nps.navy.mil/si/june03/africa.asp.

16. Agbonifo, op. cit., p. 37. Between 1994 and 1998, 95 percent of total revenues (including those resulting from oil production) accrued to Nigeria's central government. Measures have subsequently been taken with a view to increasing to 13 percent the share of oil revenues assigned to oil-producing states. However, serious imbalances in oil-revenue distribution continue to be a serious destabilizing factor for Nigeria. See Etisham Ahmed and Raju Singh, "Political Economy of Oil-Revenue Sharing in a Developing Country: Illustrations from Nigeria," IMF Working Paper, WP/ 03/16, International Monetary Fund, January, 2003, pp. 9–14.

17. See ibid., p. 3.

18. UNDP, "Human development report, 2004, human development index," http://hdr.undp.org/statistics/data/indic/indic_4_1_1.html The countries with lower per capita GDPs than Nigeria's were: Burundi, Congo, Ethiopía, Guinea-Bissau, Madagascar, Malawi, Níger, Sierra Leone, Tanzania, and Zambia.

19. Economist Research Tools Suveys, "A Tale of Two Giants: Why Indonesia Has Beaten Nigeria Hands Down" (from *The Economist* print edition January 13, 2000). Web site: http://www.economist.com/surveys/PrinterFriendly.cfm?Story_ID=273185.

20. Norimitsu Onishi, "Deep in the Republic of Chevron," *Sunday New York Times Magazine*, July 4, 1999, http://www.globalpolicy.org/nations/chevron.htm

21. Interviews, Ogoniland, July, 2004.

22. Mitee Interview, op. cit.

23. Ogoni Bill of Rights, Article 11. Available online at: http://www.dawodu.net/ogoni1.htm.

24. Ibid., p. 2.

25. "Nigeria National Security," http://www.photius.com/countries/nigeria/national_security/nigeria_national_security_national_security.html.

26. Complete Statement, op. cit., p. 4.

27. Ibid., p. 24.

28. Ibid., p. 27.

29. Ibid., p. 4.

30. Ibid., p. 26.

31. Ibid., p. 25.

32. Ibid., pp. 25–26.

33. Agbonifo, op. cit., pp. 34–35.
34. Ken Saro-Wiwa, op. cit., pp. 130–31.
35. Ben Naanen, "Effective Non-Violent Struggle in the Niger Delta," Sephis Papers (South-South Exchange Programme for Research on the History of Development), http://www.sephis.org/pdf/ogonipeople.pdf, pp. 15–17.
36. Ibid., p. 23.
37. Agbonifo, op. cit., p. 72.
38. Naanen, op. cit., p. 14.
39. Complete Statement, op. cit., p. 2.
40. Agbonifo, op. cit., pp. 109–12.
41. Cited in Ibid., p. 69.
42. Naanen, op. cit., p.33.
43. Agbonifo, op. cit., pp. 103–04.
44. Complete Statement, op. cit., pp. 10–12.
45. Cited in Ibid., p. 110.
46. Complete Statement, p. 16.
47. Human Rights Watch, "Nigeria: The Ogoni Crisis, A Case-Study of Military Repression in Southeastern Nigeria," 7 (5) (July, 1995), p. 11, http://hrw.org/reports/1995/Nigeria.htm.
48. Naanan, op. cit., pp. 38–39.
49. Agbonifo, op. cit., p. 77.
50. This was all too apparent to me during a visit to Ogoniland in the summer of 2004. The extreme caution with which my MOSOP hosts conducted me through the area was firm proof that their writ did not extend equally throughout Ogoniland. Their willingness to facilitate my visit under such conditions only enhances my gratitude to them.
51. See Human Rights Watch, op. cit., pp. 29–33; see also, Okechukwu Ibeanu, "Oiling the Friction: Environmental Conflict Management in the Niger Delta, Nigeria," *Environmental Change & Security Project Report*, Issue 6 (Summer, 2000), www.wilsoncenter.org/topics/pubs/Report6-2.pdf, pp. 28–29.
52. El-Sayed El-Aswad, *Religion and Folk Cosmology: Scenarios of the Visible and Invisible in Rural Egypt* (Westport, CT: Praeger, 2002), p. 173.
53. Ibid., p. 2.
54. Ibid., p. 176.
55. Ibid., p. 90.
56. Ibid., p. 62.
57. See Chapter 3 above.
58. El-Aswad, op. cit., p. 110.
59. Ibid., p. 145.

CHAPTER 6. THE ARAB WORLD AS A WORLD PROBLEM

1. Dan Tschirgi, *The American Search For Mideast Peace* (New York: Praeger, 1989), pp. 79–82.
2. Confidential Interview. Although the ambassador spoke with me on a non-confidential basis, I refrain from identifying him or his country in order to avoid embarrassing both for these highly "undiplomatic" remarks that were uttered over

a decade ago, possibly in a moment of over-enthusiasm sparked by the success of the war to liberate Kuwait.

3. Constantine Zurayk, "The National and International Relations of the Arab States," in T. Cuylar Young (ed.), *Near East Culture and Society* (Princeton, NJ: Princeton University Press, 1951), p. 222.

4. Ibid., p. 223.

5. Fouad Ajami, *The Arab Predicament* (Cambridge: Cambridge University Press, 1981), p. 4.

6. Dan Tschirgi, "The United States, the Arab World and the Gulf Crisis," in Dan Tschirgi and Bassam Tibi, *Perspectives on the Gulf Crisis, Cairo Papers in Social Science*, 14 (1) (Cairo: The American University in Cairo Press, 1991), p. 16.

7. Olivier Roy, "Tragique impasse du fondamentalism sunnite," *Manier de voir 60* (Le Monde Diplomatique, Novembre-Decembre, 2001), p. 51. Author's translation.

8. Alan Richards and John Waterbury, *A Political Economy of the Middle East*, 2nd Edition (Boulderco: Westview Press, 1998), p. 398.

9. Ibid., p. 398–99.

10. Dan Tschirgi, *The Politics of Indecision: Origins and Implications of American Involvement With the Palestine Problem* (New York: Praeger Publishers, 1983), p. xvii.

11. Galal Amin, "Economic Change, Social Structure, and Religious Fanaticism," in Nicholas S. Hopkins and Saad Eddin Ibrahim, (eds.) *Arab Society* (Cairo: The American University in Cairo Press, Third Edition, 1997), pp. 575–83.

12. United Nations Development Programme, Arab Fund for Economic and Social Development, p. 142.

13. See *CIA World Factbook*, http://www.cia.gov/cia/publications/factbook/geos/eg.html#Econ and http://www.cia.gov/cia/publications/factbook/geos/jo.html#Econ

14. See Alan Richards and John Waterbury, *A Political Economy of the Middle East* (Boulderco: Westview Press, 1996), pp. 369–89.

15. In a remarkable 2004 article the eminent Syrian philosopher, Sadik Al-Azm, recalled that Islam strongly forbids *Shamateh*, "an emotion . . . of taking pleasure in the suffering of others." It is, noted Al-Azm, "forbidden when it comes to death, even the violent death of your mortal enemies." Yet, in a ruthless exercise of candor, Al-Azm went on to confront himself and his fellow Arabs:

> . . . it would be very hard these days to find an Arab, no matter how sober, cultured, and sophisticated, in whose heart there was not some room for shamateh at the suffering of Americans on September 11. I myself tried hard to contain, control, and hide it that day. And I knew intuitively that millions and millions of people throughout the Arab world and beyond experienced the same emotion.
>
> I never had any doubts, either, about who perpetrated that heinous crime; our Islamists had a deep-seated vendetta against the World Trade Center since their failed attack on it in 1993. As an Arab, I know something about the power of vengeance in our culture and its consuming force. I also knew that the United States would respond with all its force to crush the Islamist movement worldwide into oblivion. But I didn't understand my own shameful response to the slaughter of innocents. Was it the bad news from Palestine that week; the satisfaction of seeing the arrogance of power abruptly, if

> temporarily, humbled; the sight of the jihadi Frankenstein's monsters, so carefully nourished by the United States, turning suddenly on their masters; or the natural resentment of the weak and marginalized at the peripheries of empires against the center, or, in this case, against the center of the center? Does my response, and the silent shamateh of the Arab world, mean that Huntington's clash of civilizations has come true, and so quickly?

Ultimately, Al-Azm concludes that the suicidal rage that prompted 9/11 marked the essential demise of militant Islamism. Thus, he sees that event as "having signaled the last gasp of Islamism rather than the beginnings of its global challenge." Nonetheless, the wellsprings of the emotional reaction to the 9/11 attack that could bring an individual of Al-Azm's calibre vicariously, if circumspectly, to celebrate the immediate consequences of the attacks are deeply telling.

See Sadik J. Al-Azm, "Time Out of Joint: Western Dominance, Islamist Terror, and the Arab Imagination," *Boston Review: A Political and Literary Forum*, October/November, 2004, www.bostonreview.net/BR29.5/alazm.html.

16. For example, a March, 2004 poll found that Bin Laden was viewed favorably by 55 percent of respondents in Jordan and 45 percent in Morocco. http://www.Antiwar.com/?articleid=2143.

17. Hany Amber, "Supreme Director of Egyptian Muslim Brotherhood: The Autocratic Government in Egypt Is Lambasted for the Current Deteriorating Situation," *Dimensions*: The Students Journal, 1 (8) (March 16, 2004) (The American University in Cairo), p. 3.

18. The young journalist breathlessly reported his encounter as follows: "In his modest office, I met him. I was scared to death and thousands of flashing ideas backlogged on my subconscious mind. As I stepped in his room, I was greeted with a shining grin and welcoming firm voice." Ibid., p. 1.

19. Berlusconi's actual comment was as follows: ""We should be conscious of the superiority of our civilization, which consists of a value system that has given people widespread prosperity in those countries that embrace it, and guarantees respect for human rights and religion.... This respect certainly does not exist in Islamic countries." See http://www.nationalreview.com/goldberg/goldberg092801.shtml.

20. Amber, op. cit., p. 3.

21. James Poniewozik, "The Banality of bin Laden," www.time.com, December 15, 2001.

22. Fieldnotes, Chiapas, July 1995; Interview Ledum Mitee, July, 2004; Saad Eddin Ibrahim, "Egypt's Islamic Militants," in Nicholas S. Hopkins and Saad Eddin Ibrahim (eds.), *Arab Society: Social Science* (Cairo: The American University in Cairo Press, 1987), pp. 494–507. Ibrahim's work did not focus on members of the *Gama'a al-Islamiyya* but on those of another group, *al-Takfir al-Hijra*.

23. See, for example, Osama Bin Laden's interviews and commentaries over the years. For example, his interviews given to numbers of his followers and to ABC correspondent John Miller in May, 1998 (http://www.pbs.org/wgbh/pages/frontline/shows/binladen/who/interview.html) and the speech he delivered to Aljazeera in November, 2004 (http://english.aljazeera.net/NR/exres/79C6AF22-98FB-A1C-B21F-2BC36E87F61F.htm).

24. Osama Bin Laden, Full Transcript of Speech, November 1, 2004 http://english.aljazeera.net/NR/exres/79C6AF22-98FB-4A1C-B21F-2BC36E87F61F.htm.

25. Paul Davies, *The Runaway Universe* (Middlesex, New York, Victoria, Markham: Penguin Books, 1978), p. 92 (emphasis added).

26. Nicholas D. Kristof, "A Nuclear 9/11," *New York Times*, March 10, 2004.

27. The claim was made in an interview conducted by Pakistani journalist Hamid Mir for an Australian television station. http://cnn.netscape.cnn.com/news/default.jsp, March 22, 2004.

28. For example, such an assumption is frequently made regarding Hamas. However, at least up to the assassination of its founder and leader, Ahmed Yassin in March 2004; available evidence indicated that the organization's militant activities were limited to supporting extreme Palestinian nationalist claims against Israel and were not linked to al-Qaeda's campaign against the international system. I am grateful to Lt. Col. Stephen P. Lambert (USAF) for raising this point during discussions we had while this chapter was in preparation.

29. Tschirgi, *Search For Mideast Peace*, op cit., pp. 26, 71–73.

30. Since 1985, the Libyan government has issued wholesale expulsion orders to the resident Palestinian community of some 30,000 persons on at least three occasions, in 1985, 1995 and 2000. See Arab News.com, "Libya Expels Palestinians and Israel Prevents Them From Entering Gaza," http://www.arabicnews.com/ansub/Daily/Day/001110/2000111010.html; "Libya Expels Guest Workers," *Migration News*, http://migration.ucdavis.edu/mn/more.php?id=802_0_5_0 Encyclopedia of the Orient. "Libya History," www.i-cias.com/e.o/libya_5.htm.

31. Palestinian Refugee Research Net, "Palestinian Refugees: An Overview," http://www.arts.mcgill.ca/mepp/new_prrn/background/index.htm.

32. Saed Okasha, "Uncharacteristic Noises and Strange Bedfellows: Hardline Iraq Goes Soft on Palestinian Refugees, Old Rivals Discuss Alliances, *Cairo Times*, May 4–10, 2000. Online: www.cairotimes.com/content/archiv04/ iraq.html.

33. Typically, a 1970 statement on Peoples War issued by the Palestinian National Council, in 1970 argued as follows:

> The enemies of Palestinian national liberation are Zionism, the state of Israel, Imperialism and the forces tied dialectically and functionally to imperialism and colonialism.

Bichara and Naim Khader (eds.). *Texts de la Revolution Palestinienne* (Paris: Sindbad, 1975), p. 108.

34. It is regrettable that one consequence of the decades of strife between Israel and the Arab World has been the growth of anti-semitic sentiments in the latter.

35. Eastern, or Oriental, anti-Semitism differed from its Western counterpart in various ways, one of which rendered the charge of deicide inapplicable in a Muslim setting. Thus, the Muslim World did not share the centuries-long history of violent pograms against Jews. Indeed, the experience of Jews in Muslim Andalusia, the Omayed or Abbasid Empires, or the Ottoman state was marked by tolerance, tempered by the second-class status of all non-Muslim communities. It was in tacit acknowledgement of this that Jews fled Spain in 1492 and sought refuge in the Ottoman Empire.

36. In October 2006, a study conducted by the reseachers at Johns Hopkins University's Bloomberg School of Public Health concluded that a conservative estimate of Iraqis who had died since the 2003 invasion of the American-led coalition would total

"an estimated 655,000 Iraqis." The study compared mortality rates before and after the invasion from forty-seven randomly chosen areas of the country and projected its findings, drawn from a sample of 1,850 families totalling 12,800 individuals "in dozens of forty household clusters" throughout the country. President Bush and other members of his administration questioned the study's methodology and the President pronounced its conclusion, "just ... not credible." See "Huge Rise in Iraqi Death Tolls," October 11, 2006, http://news.bbc.co.uk/2/hi/middle_east/6040054.stm.

37. "Poll: Bush Approval Rating Dips to 35%," November 6, 2006, www.cnn.com/2006/POLITICS/11/06/bush.poll/index.html.

38. "Press Conference by the President," November 8, 2006, http://www.whitehouse.gov/news/releases/2006/11/20061108-2html.

39. Ibid.

40. James A. Baker, III, Lee H. Hamilton, et al., *The Iraq Study Group Report* (New York: Vintage Books, 2006), pp. 37–39.

41. Ibid., p. 44.

42. Ibid., p. 27.

43. Ibid., p. 51

44. Jimmy Carter, *Palestine: Peace Not Apartheid* (New York: Simon & Schuster, 2006).

45. Jeremy Sharp, et al., "Lebanon: The Israel-Hamas-Hizbollah Conflict" (Washington, DC: Congressional Research Service, September 15, 2006), pp. 32–33, http://www.fas.org/sgp/crs/mideast/RL33566.pdf.

46. Ibid., p. 11, citing Nasrallah's August 27, 2006. Interview with Lebanon television, in Joshua Mitnick, "Hezbollah Says Its War with Israel Was a Mistake," *Washington Times*, August 28, 2006.

47. *Israel/Lebanon:Under Fire:Hizbullah's Attacks on Northern Israel,* http://web.amnesty.org/library/index/engmde020252006, September 14, 2006, AI index:MDE 02/025/2006

48. See http://en.wikipedia.org/wiki/Casualties_of_the_2006_Israel-Lebanon_conflict#Casualties_of_involved_parties.

49. "Press Conference by the President," November 8, 2006, op. cit.

50. George W. Bush, "The New Strategy in Iraq: Primetime Address to the Nation," January 10, 2007. See: http://www.presidentialrhetoric.com/speeches/01.10.07.html.

51. Ibid.

CHAPTER 7. TURNING POINT: TOWARD GLOBAL SECURITY

1. Philip Smucker, "History Speaks as U.S. Preps for Peacekeeping," *The Christian Science Monitor*, March 21, 2003.

2. Leon Krauze, *Estados Unidos: La Casa Divida, Elecciones y Politica Mundial en la Era Bush, 2000–2008* (Mexico, DF: Editorial Planeta, 2005), p. 30.

3. In a speech aimed at the American people delivered shortly before Bush's reelection to a second term, Bin Laden boasted:

> ... we, [al-Qaeda} alongside the mujahidin, bled Russia for 10 years, until it went bankrupt and was forced to withdraw in defeat.
>
> ....

> So we are continuing this policy in bleeding America to the point of bankruptcy. Allah willing, and nothing is too great for Allah.

"Full English Transcript of Usama Bin Ladin's Speech in a Videotape Sent to Aljazeera: As Pubilished by Aljazeera, Monday, November 1, 2004," http://mprofaca.cro.net/binladen_transcript.html#references.

4. The results of the worldwide clandestine campaign that is an integral part of the American War on Terror tend to be revealed only slowly and piecemeal to the public. Thus, in early May of 2006 U.S. officials acknowledged that Mustafa Setmarian Nasar, originally a Syrian who had taken Spanish citizenship, and who was a top al-Qaeda strategist, had been captured in November, 2005, in the Pakistani city of Quetta in November, 2005. The U.S. was reported to have offered a $5 million bounty for Nasar. "U.S. Confirms Capture of Al Qaeda Strategist," *Toronto* Star, May 2, 2006. Available online at: http://www.thestar.com/NASApp/cs/ContentServer?pagename=thestar/Layout/Article_PrintFriendly&c=Article&cid=1146606638762&call_pageid=968332188492.

Reports in the spring of 2006 generally indicated that the Bush Administration was planning to expand the scope of its clandestine campaign against terrorism. See Ann Scott Tyson, "New Plans Foresee Fighting Terrorism Beyond War Zones," *The Washington Post*, April 23, 2006. Available online at: http://whttp://www.washingtonpost.com/wp-dyn/content/article/2006/04/22/AR2006042201124_pf.html ww.washingtonpost.com/wp-dyn/content/article/2006/04/22/AR2006042201124_pf.html.

5. In Egypt, for example, the prodemocracy demands of the Mubarak regime's opponents have been reinforced by the position taken by the Bush Administration. By the spring of 2006 a powerful wave of anti-Mubarak activism had become a constant feature of public life. It was notable to observers that public criticism of the regime, including the President and his immediate family, was almost unrestrained and commonplace. Even more significant was the regime's crackdown on the prestigious Judges' Club, a professional association that has so far resisted efforts to coopt its members as official spokesmen for the regime. For more than year—from the early spring of 2005 to late spring of 2006—the Mubarak regime engaged in a bitter trial of strength with the nations' judges. The struggle led to a regional conference in April, 2006, which was convened by the Egyptian Institute for Human Right at which Judges from throughout the Arab World endorsed demands for rule of law and democracy arising throughout the region, including Egypt. At the end of April, 2006, the Judges' Club issued a biting declaration demanding a full return to democratic process that proclaimed:

> There is no way of achieving security and stability in the country merely through the repression of force and the control of power. Rather, the people's hope in justice must be preserved, as well as preserving their dignity and honour, and reviving their hope in reform, and establishing a true democratic life through fair elections and real transfer of power, and lifting all exceptional laws including ending the state of emergency, and unleashing freedom of expression, and the freedom to form parties, unions, and associations, without any restrictions, so that Egypt can regain its place among nations.

This partial translation, as well as the complete Arabic text of the resolution, "Declaration of the Judges of Egypt Regarding What Is Happening," are available on the Web at http://baheyya.blogspot.com/2006/05/mubarak-fin-du-rgime.html.

6. Israel's so-called security wall was announced plans for the erection of a security barrier in 2002, under Ariel Sharon's government. By July, 2003, some 180 kilometers of the wall had been constructed. The entire barrier was planned to extend some 680 kilometers. In July 2004, the International Court of Justice issue an advisory opinion on the wall's legality under international law. The ICJ rejected Israel's argument that security concerns dictated the wall's construction to prevent attacks by suicide bombers. Instead, the court found the wall to violate international law and ordered Israel to pay compensation to Palestinians whose properties been violated, http://web.amnesty.org/library/index/ENGMDE150682002?open&of=ENG-MD.

7. Greg Myre, "Old Leftist Friend Is to Join Sharon's New Party," *New York Times*, November 30, 2005.

8. Scott Wilson, "Hamas Sweeps Palestinian Elections, Complicating Peace Efforts in Mideast," http://www.washingtonpost.com/wp-dyn/content/article/2006/01/26/AR2006012600372.html. Hamas, on the other hand, won seventy-six seats, with the remainder seats won by a collection of nationalist, leftist, and independent candidates.

9. Jean Allain, *International Law in the Middle East: Closer to Power Than Justice* (Burlington, Vt. and Aldershot, U.K.: Ashgate, 2004), p. 1.

10. Joshua Stacher, "A Democracy With Fangs and Claws and Its Effect on Egyptian Political Culture," *Arab Studies Quarterly,* 23 (3) (Summer 2001), pp. 83–99.

11. Beginning in 2004, a spate of rebellious groups began operating in Nigeria's oil-rich Delta. A major such group claimed to be fighting for the rights of the Delta's largest ethnic community, the Ijaws. Known as the Niger Delta People's Volunteer Force, this group was led by Mujahid Dokubo-Asari. By 2005 Asari had come to an agreement with the Nigerian government and disbanded the force. However, he continued to proclaim a desire for the Delta's secession from Nigeria and was arrested for treason. He remained in custody as of this writing (January 2007). By that time, another rebellious group had risen to prominence in Nigeria—the Movement for the Emancipation of the Niger Delta. MEND refrained from specifically calling for the Delta's secession, though it escalated the guerrilla war in the Delta by introducing an element of urban warfare when it placed car bombs in Port Harcourt. The continued unrest in the Delta was a significant factor in the overall increases in the price of oil during 2005 and 2006. BBC News, "Nigeria's Shadowy Oil Rebels," April 20, 2006. Available online at: http://news.bbc.co.uk/1/hi/world/africa/4732210.stm. See also, http://www.saharareporters.com/da001.php?daid=188 for information on Mujahid Dokubo-Asari.

12. Tony Blair's Speech in Sedgefield," available online at http://politics.guardian.co.uk/iraq/story/0,12956,1162991,00.html

13. Ibid.

14. Ibid.

Further Reading

Books

Abo, Geneive. *No God But God: Egypt and the Triumph of Islam*. New York: Oxford University Press, 2000.

Ajami, Fouad. *The Arab Predicament*. Cambridge: Cambridge University Press, 1981.

Alagoa, Joe and Abi A. Derefaka (eds.). *The Land and People of Rivers State: Eastern Niger Delta*. Port Harcourt, Rivers State: Onyoma Research Publications, 2002.

Allain, Jean. *International Law in the Middle East: Closer to Power Than Justice*. Burlington, VT: Ashgate, 2004.

Allison, Graham T. *Nuclear Terrorism: The Ultimate Preventable Catastrophe*. New York: Henry Holt and Company, LLC, 2004.

Amanyie, Vincent. *The Agony of the Ogoni in the Niger Delta*. Port Harcourt, Rivers State: Horizon Concepts, 2003.

Anonymous (Michael Scheuer). *Imperial Hubris: Why the West Is Losing the War on Terror*. Dulles, VA: Brassey's, Inc., 2004.

Apter, David E. *The Politics of Modernization*. Chicago: The University of Chicago Press, 1965.

———. *Rethinking Development: Modernization, Dependency and Postmodern Politics*. Beverly Hills, CA: Sage Publications, 1987.

Armendáriz, María Luisa. *Chíapas, Una Radiografía*. México D.F.: Fondo de Cultura Económica, 1994.

Arzt, Donna E. *From Refugees to Citizens: Palestinians and the End of the Arab-Israeli Conflict*. New York: Council on Foreign Relations Press, 1999.

Bowman, Alan and Eugene Rogan (eds.). *Agriculture in Egypt from Pharaonic to Modern Times, Proceedings of the British Academy*, Vol. 96. Oxford: Oxford University Press, 1998.

Bricker, V. R. and G. H. Gossen. *Ethnographic Encounters in Mesoamerica: Essays in Honor of Evon Zartman Vogt, Jr*. Albany: Institute for Mesoamerican Studies, The University at Albany, State University of New York, 1989.

Brzezinski, Zbigniew. *The Choice: Global Domination or Global Leadership*. New York: Basic Books, 2004.

Castells, Manuel. *The Information Age: The Rise of Network Society* (Vol. I); *The Power of Identity* (Vol. II); *End of Millennium* (Vol. III). Malden, MA: Blackwell Publishers, 1996, 1997, and 1998.

Chomsky, Noam. *9/11*. New York: Seven Stories Press, 2001.

Clarke, Richard A. *Against All Enemies: Inside America's War on Terror*. New York: Free Press, 2004.

El-Aswad, El-Sayed. *Religion and Folk Cosmology: Scenarios of the Visible and Invisible in Rural Egypt*. Westport, CT: Praeger, 2002.

Flynn, Stephen. *America the Vulnerable: How Our Government Is Failing to Protect Us from Terrorism*. New York: HarperCollins, 2004.

Hirsh, Michael. *At War with Ourselves: Why America Is Squandering Its Chance to Build a Better World*. New York: Oxford University Press, 2003.

Hopkins, Nicholas S. and Saad Eddin Ibrahim (eds.). *Arab Society*, 3rd ed. Cairo: The American University in Cairo Press, 1997.

Hopkins, Nicholas S. and K. Westergaard (eds.). *Directions of Change in Rural Egypt*. Cairo: The American University in Cairo Press, 1998.

Ibrahim, Saad Eddin. *Egypt, Islam and Democracy*. Cairo: The American University in Cairo Press, 1996.

Johnson, Chalmers. *The Sorrows of Empire: Militarism, Secrecy, and the End of the Republic*. New York: Metropolitan Books, Henry Holt and Company, 2004.

Jung, Dietrich (ed.). *The Middle East and Palestine: Global Politics and Regional Conflict*. New York: Palgrave Macmillan, 2004.

Kassem, Maye. *Egyptian Politics: The Dynamics of Authoritarian Rule*. Boulder, CO: Lynne Rienner Publishers, Inc., 2004.

Lesch, Ann and Dan Tschirgi. *The Origins and Development of the Arab-Israeli Conflict*. Westport, CT: Greenwood Press, 1998.

Lewis, Bernard. *From Babel to Dragomans: Interpreting the Middle East*. London: Weidenfeld & Nicolson, 2004.

Mailer, Norman. *Why We Are at War*. New York: Random House, 2003.

Mann, James. *The Rise of the Vulcans: The History of Bush's War Cabinet*. New York: Viking, 2004.

Morsy, Soheir A. *Gender, Sickness, and Healing in Rural Egypt: Ethnography in Historical Context*. Boulder, CO: Westview Press, 1993.

Oppenheimer, Andrés. *México en la Frontera del Caos: La Crisis Mexicana de los Noventa y la Esperanza del Nuevo Milenio*, 2nd ed. México, DF: Ediciones B México, S.A. de C.V., 2002.

Richards, Alan and John Waterbury. *A Political Economy of the Middle East*, 2nd ed. Boulder, CO: Westview Press, 1998.

Riding, Alan. *Distant Neighbors: A Portrait of the Mexicans*. New York: Vintage Books, 1986.

Seabury, Paul and Angelo Codevilla. *War: Ends and Means*. New York: Basic Books, 1989.

Serrano, Mónica (ed.). *Mexico: Assessing Neo-Liberal Reform*. London: Institute of Latin American Studies, 1997.

Soriano Hernández, Silvia (ed.). *A Proposito de la Insurgencia en Chíapas*. México, D.F.: Asociación Para el Desarrollo de la Investigación Cientifica y Humanistica en Chíapas, 1994.

Tello Díaz, Carlos. *La Rebelion de las Cañadas*. México: Cal y Arena, 1995.

Tschirgi, Dan. *The Politics of Indecision: Origins and Implications of American Involvement with the Palestine Problem*. New York: Praeger Publishers, 1983.

———. *The American Search for Middle East Peace*. New York: Praeger, 1989, and Cairo: AUC Press, 1991.

———. (ed). *The Arab World Today*. Boulder, CO: Lynne Rienner Publishers, 1994.

———. (ed.). *Development in the Age of Liberalization: Egypt and Mexico*. Cairo: The American University in Cairo Press, 1996.

Urbina Nandayapa, Arturo de Jésus. *Las Razones de Chíapas: Causas, Desarrollo, Consecuencias, Personajes y Perspectivas del Alzamiento en los Altos de Chíapas*, 2nd ed. México, D.F.: Editorial PAC, 1994.

Vogt, Evon Z. *The Zinacantecos of Mexico: A Modern Maya Way of Life*. New York: Holt, Rinehart and Winston, 1970.

Woodward, Bob. *Plan of Attack*. New York: Simon & Schuster, 2004.

Wright, Ronald. *Time among the Maya: Travels in Belize, Guatemala and Mexico*. Markham, Ontario: Penguin Books Canada, 1989.

Young, T. Cuylar (ed.). *Near East Culture and Society*. Princeton, NJ: Princeton University Press, 1951.

ARTICLES

Abdelnasser, Walid M. "Islamic Organizations in Egypt and the Iranian Revolution of 1979: The Experience of the First Few Years." *Arab Studies Quarterly* (Spring 1997).

Al-Azm, Sadik J. "Time Out of Joint: Western Dominance, Islamist Terror, and the Arab Imagination." *Boston Review: A Political and Literary Forum* (October/November 2004). Available online at www.bostonreview.net/BR29.5/alazm.html.

Burrough, Bryan, Eugenia Peretz, David Rose, and David Wise. "The Path to War." *Vanity Fair* (May 2004).

Christison, Bill. "Categories of War—The U.S. Gameplan for Iraq." *Counterpunch* (February 8, 2003). Available online at http://www.counterpunch.org/christinson02082003.html.

Churchill, Ward. "Some People Push Back: On the Justice of Roosting Chickens," 12 Sept. 2001. Available online at http://www.kersplebedeb.com/mystuff/s11/churchill.html.

Drake, Laura. "Palestinian Refugees in Lebanon: The Walls of History Are Closing In." *Washington Report on Middle East Affairs* (January/February 2000).

Dunn, Michael Collins. "Fundamentalism in Egypt." *Middle East Policy*, 11(3) (1993).

Fandy, Mamoun. "The Tensions Behind the Violence in Egypt." *Middle East Policy*, 2(1) (1993).

———. "Egypt's Islamic Group: Regional Revenge." *Middle East Journal*, 48(4) (1994).

Gambil, Gary C. "Jumpstarting Arab Reform: The Bush Administration's Greater Middle East Initiative." *Middle East Intelligence Bulletin*, 6(6/7). Available online at http://www.meib.org/articles/0407_me2.htm.

Ibrahim, Saad Eddin. "Anatomy of Egypt's Militant Islamic Groups: Methodological Notes and Preliminary Finding." *International Journal of Middle East Studies*, (12) (1980).

Kupferschmidt, Uri M. "Reformist and Militant Islam in Urban and Rural Egypt." *Middle East Studies*, 23 (October 1987).

Naanen, Ben. "Effective Non-Violent Struggle in the Niger Delta." Sephis Papers (South-South Exchange Programme for Research on the History of Development). Available online at http://www.sephis.org/pdf/ogonipeople.pdf.

Nodoroscik, Jeffrey A., Dina Younis, El Sayed Gad Mohammed, and Mónica Serrano. "Lessons in Violent Internal Conflict: Egypt and Mexico." SYLFF (The Ryoichi Sasakawa Young Leaders Fellowship Fund) Working Papers, No. 8 (Tokyo, March 1998).

Ottaway, Marina and Thomas Carothers. "The Greater Middle East Initiative: Off to a False Start." The Carnegie Endowment for International Peace, *Policy Brief*, No. 29. Available online at www.carnegieendowment.org/publications/index.cfm?fa=view&id=1480&prog=zgp&proj=zdrl,zme.

Podhoretz, Norman. "World War IV: How It Started, What It Means, and Why We Have to Win." *Commentary* (September 2004).

Springborg, Robert. "Identity in Crisis: Egyptian Political Identity in the Face of Globalization." *Harvard International Review*, 25 (2003).

Stacher, Joshua. "A Democracy with Fangs and Claws and Its Effect on Egyptian Political Culture." *Arab Studies Quarterly*, 23(3) (Summer 2001).

Tschirgi, Dan. "Violent Internal Conflict in the Age of Globalization: Mexico and Egypt." *Arab Studies Quarterly*, 21(3) (Summer 1999).

———. "In Egypt and Mexico, A New Type of Conflict: Zapatistas and Islamists Fight the Odds." *Le Monde Diplomatique* (January 2000).

———. "The War on Terror: Marginalized Conflict as a Challenge to the International System." *Perceptions: Journal of International Affairs*, VII(3) (September–November 2002).

———. "On the War on Terrorism: From Zapatistas to Al-Qaida." *Humanitaire* (Winter 2001–2002).

DOCUMENTS

Baker, James A. III, Lee H. Hamilton, Sandra Day O'Conner, Lawrence Eagleburger, Edwin Meese III, Alan K. Simpson, Vernon Jordan, Leon E. Panetta, William J. Perry, and Charles S. Robb. *The Iraq Study Group Report*. New York: Vintage Books, 2006.

Boutros Boutros-Ghali. *Building Peace and Development, 1994: Annual Report on the Work of the Organization from the Forty-Eighth to the Forty-Ninth Session of the General Assembly*. New York: United Nations, 1994.

Bush, George W. "Address to the Nation on the Terrorist Attacks." *Weekly Compilation of Presidential Documents, from the 2001 Presidential Documents*. 2005 Online via GPO Access [frwais.access.gpo.gov], Doc. I.D.: pd17se01_txt-15.

———. "Graduation Speech at West Point," June 1, 2002. Available online at http://www.whitehouse.gov/news/releases/2002/06/print/20020601–3.html.

———. "Remarks by the President at the 20th Anniversary of the National Endowment for Democracy," November 6, 2003. Available online at http://frwebgate1.access.gpo.gov/cgi-bin/waisgate.cgi?WAISdocID=601081331274+7+0+0&W AISaxtion=retrieve.

———. Second Inaugural Address, January 20, 2005. Available online at http://www.whitehouse.gov/inaugural/.

———. "The New Strategy in Iraq: Primetime Address to the Nation," January 10, 2007. Available online at http://www.presidentialrhetoric.com/speeches/01.10.07.html.

Human Rights Watch. "Nigeria: The Ogoni Crisis, A Case-Study of Military Repression in Southeastern Nigeria," 7 (5) (July 1995). Available online at http://hrw.org/reports/1995/Nigeria.htm.

Intriligator, Michael D. "US Nuclear Weapons Policy Under the Bush Administration," Nuclear Age Peace Foundation, Publication 31, 2004. Available online at http://www.wagingpeace.org/articles/2004/07/00_intriligator_us-policy-bush.htm.

Saro-Wiwa, Ken. "Complete Statement by Ken Saro-Wiwa to Ogoni Civil Disturbances Tribunal." Available online at http://ratical.org/corporations/KSWstmt.html.

Index

About the Author

DAN TSCHIRGI is Professor of Political Science at the American University in Cairo. He is the author of *The Politics of Indecision: Origins and Implications of American Involvement with the Palestine Problem* (Praeger, 1983), *The American Search for Mideast Peace* (Praeger, 1989), and (with Ann Lesch) *Origins and Development of the Arab-Israeli Conflict* (Greenwood, 1998).